CAMBRIDGE
Global English

Teacher's Resource

5

Annie Altamirano,
Claire Medwell and Jane Boylan

CAMBRIDGE
UNIVERSITY PRESS

CAMBRIDGE
UNIVERSITY PRESS

University Printing House, Cambridge CB2 8BS, United Kingdom

One Liberty Plaza, 20th Floor, New York, NY 10006, USA

477 Williamstown Road, Port Melbourne, VIC 3207, Australia

4843/24, 2nd Floor, Ansari Road, Daryaganj, Delhi – 110002, India

79 Anson Road, #06–04/06, Singapore 079906

Cambridge University Press is part of the University of Cambridge.

It furthers the University's mission by disseminating knowledge in the pursuit of education, learning and research at the highest international levels of excellence.

www.cambridge.org
Information on this title: education.cambridge.org

© Cambridge University Press 2016

First published 2014
20 19 18 17 16 15 14 13 12 11 10 9 8

Printed in Great Britain by CPI Group (UK) Ltd, Croydon CR0 4YY

A catalogue record for this publication is available from the British Library

ISBN 978-1-107-64612-4 Teacher's Resource
ISBN 978-1-108-40953-7 Teacher's Resource with Digital Classroom (1 year)

Additional resources for this publication at www.cambridge.org/9781107646124

Contents

Map of the Learner's Book

page	Unit	Words and expressions	Use of English	Reading/Writing
6–19	1 Talking about people	Personality: Adjectives of personality Antonyms Families and friends Favourite things and people Useful expressions for interviews	*Wh-* Questions *-ed/-ing* adjectives Dictionary definitions	Read for gist A diary page A personal profile Literature: Poems about special people Use a variety of adjectives Write a personal profile Design a webpage
20–33	2 Staying healthy	Common illnesses and symptoms Food collocations and classifiers Food groups	Quantifiers and classifiers Countable and uncount-able nouns *Should* for advice	Make predictions using visual clues An article about malaria Read a problem page in a magazine Literature: *Stone Soup* Contrast linkers Write a blog
34–35	Review 1			
36–49	3 Where we live	City, town and country Home appliances Descriptive adjectives Sequencing words	Comparatives and superlatives Subordinate clauses Past simple	Scan a text Facts about our carbon footprint Read a descriptive essay Literature: *The Lost City* Use paragraphs Write a descriptive essay Design a poster
50–63	4 Celebrations	Describe celebrations and festivals. Birthday/special day vocabulary *both, and, as well, too, also* Adjectives and antonyms	Defining relative clauses *Will* for stating future facts	Descriptive text: The Rio Carnival Informative text: Pancake day/Shrove Tuesday Visualise context Literature: *Horrid Henry* Add information Design a poster Write an article
64–65	Review 2			
66–79	5 Famous people	Professions and famous people Personal qualities Parts of a ship	Modals of speculation Question tags Conjunctions: *so, and, but, because*	Match headings to paragraphs Read biographies: Shakira; Felix Baumgartner Literature: *The Stowaway* Give reasons Use a variety of adjectives; use conjunctions Write a short biography
80–93	6 Myths and fables	Mythical creatures Prefixes *un-, ir-, dis-* Proverbs	Conjunctions: *if, and, but, where, so, when* Past simple and past continuous	Read a fable Find specific information in a text Read a story with a message Literature: *The Lambton Worm* A short story Punctuation and direct speech Write a short story
94–95	Review 3			
96–109	7 Ancient civilisations	Ancient buildings and objects Ancient Egypt and Rome Roman numerals Adjectives *whereas, too, both*	Subordinate clauses following *think, know believe, hope, say* Past simple active and passive forms Agent *by*	Use your own knowledge to understand a text Factual texts about ancient Egypt Identify Roman numerals. Literature: *There's a Pharaoh in Our Bath!* Use past tenses for telling a story Write a newspaper report
110–123	8 Weather and climate	Extreme weather Weather collocations The environment Action verbs Similes	*Should/Shouldn't* for advice Adverbs of degree Adjective order	Evaluate texts and give an opinion Factual texts: Rainforests; Rainforest animals Literature: Poems *A Visit with Mr Tree Frog* and *If I Were a Sloth* Use a variety of adjectives Write a descriptive text: A rainforest animal
124–125	Review 4			
126–139	9 Planet Earth	Animal habitats Animal characteristics Care for pets Useful expressions for giving advice	Personal pronouns *it/its* Obligation and necessity: *must, should, have to, need to*	Interpret diagrams Read about food chains; animal camouflage; a leaflet about a wildlife park Literature: Poem: *Mum Won't Let Me Keep a Rabbit* Use imperatives to write slogans Design and write a leaflet
140–141	Review 5			

Listening/Speaking	School subjects	Phonics/Word study	Critical thinking/Values
Listen for specific information Listen to, prepare, conduct and answer an interview Describe inspirational people	Maths: Calculate dates	Intonation in question forms Rhyming words	Thinking and talking about personal qualities Interpreting attitudes
Evaluate information Listen and plot points on a graph Talk about feeling unwell Do a survey Prepare and give a presentation	Maths: Graphs and charts Science: Health; malaria	Connected speech	Healthy eating – why is it important? Helping each other Completing a table Recognising symptoms Analysing ingredients
Identify opinions Describe places; talk about a story Compare living in the country or city Express opinion Use discourse markers/sequencing words Give presentations: My town and an eco school	Science: Climate change, energy efficiency	-ed endings	Looking after our environment Advantages/disadvantages of urban/rural life Reducing carbon footprint How to make cities cleaner What makes an ideal place to live?
Make connections Listen to descriptions: Celebrations Describe a festival or celebration; talk about personal celebrations Use personal information Give presentations: My coming of age celebration	Maths: 24-hour clock, quantities Comparing	-ough	Understanding and respecting different traditions Interpreting time zones Comparing cultures
Listen to descriptions of famous people Give presentations: A famous person Complete notes: Listen for information Talk about personal achievements Give presentations: A person I admire		Large numbers	Being the best of ourselves Helping others What do we admire in others? Becoming better citizens Recognising personal qualities
Listen to fables Prediction An anecdote Mythical creatures Use connectors when and as Tell an anecdote Discuss a proverb		Stressed and unstressed words	Being courageous Identifying proverbs and myths What can we learn from myths and fables
Listen for clues: Life in ancient Rome Talk about ancient civilisations Talk about discoveries Give presentations: Life in your country in ancient times	History: The Egyptians and the Romans Maths: Roman numerals	Identify tone	Being patient Comparing ancient cultures with today
Listen for important information Descriptions of extreme weather Weather reports Give presentations: Practise and present a weather report	Science: Weather	Stress important information Rhyming words	Looking after our world Why are rainforests special? Comparing extreme weather How can we protect our planet?
Listen for specific information: Note-taking Animals and their habitats Look after pets Give advice Give presentations: How to look after a pet	Geography and Science: Animal habitats; the food chain	Rhyming words Alliteration	Researching for a project. Taking care of animals Explaining the food chain Understanding camouflage

Welcome to *Cambridge Global English Stage 5*

Cambridge Global English is an eight-level English course for young learners from the beginning of primary school to the end of junior secondary (roughly ages 6–13). The course has been designed to fulfil the requirements of *Cambridge Primary English as a Second Language Curriculum Framework*. These internationally recognised standards provide a sequential framework for thorough coverage of basic English concepts and skills.

The materials reflect the following principles:

- *An international focus*. Specifically developed for young learners throughout the world, the themes, situations, and literature covered by *Cambridge Global English* strive to reflect this diversity and help learners learn about each other's lives through the medium of English. This fosters respect and interest in other cultures and leads to awareness of global citizenship.

- *An enquiry-based language-rich approach to learning*. *Cambridge Global English* engages children as active, creative thinkers. As learners participate in a wide variety of curriculum-based activities, they simultaneously acquire content knowledge, develop critical thinking skills through tasks that encourage a personal response and practise English language and literacy. The materials incorporate a 'learn to learn' approach, helping children acquire skills and strategies that will help them approach new learning situations with confidence and success.

- *English for educational success.* To meet the challenges of the future, children need to develop facility with both conversational and more formal English. From the earliest level, *Cambridge Global English* addresses both these competencies. *Cambridge Global English* presents authentic listening and reading texts, writing tasks, and culminating unit projects similar to those students might encounter in a first language school situation. Emphasis is placed on developing the listening, speaking, reading, and writing skills students will need to be successful in using authentic English-language classroom materials. At Stage 5, basic learning strategies and tips for study skills are practised. This continues to lay the foundations for developing effective study skills for future use.

- *Rich vocabulary development*. Building a large and robust vocabulary is a cornerstone to success in both conversational and academic English. *Cambridge Global English* exposes learners to a wide range of vocabulary through the text types and activities present in the materials. Many opportunities for revising these words and using them in personalised, meaningful ways are woven into the activities and lesson plans.

- *Individualised learning.* We approach learning in an individual way by both acknowledging the individual nature of the knowledge and background of each child and encouraging their specific input. We also provide for differentiated learning in the classroom by offering a range of activities of varying difficulty and extra challenges. Unit by unit support for this is provided in the unit notes in this book.

- *Integrated assessment.* Throughout the course, teachers informally assess their students' understanding of language and concepts. The Teacher's Resource provides suggestions for extending or re-teaching language skills based on learners' demonstrated proficiency. At the end of each unit, learners apply the skills and knowledge they have acquired as they work in groups to create and present a project of their choice. This provides teachers with an excellent performance assessment opportunity. An end-of-unit quiz in the Activity Book provides another evaluation measure: a quick progress check on learners' understanding of key ESL and early literacy skills.

Cambridge Global English can be used as a stand-alone ESL curriculum or it can be used as part of an innovative suite of materials created by Cambridge University Press for young learners at international primary schools:

- *Cambridge Primary Science*
- *Cambridge Primary Mathematics*
- *Cambridge Primary English (L1)*
- *Cambridge Global English*.

We encourage you to learn more about these complementary courses through the Cambridge University Press website: education.cambridge.org

We very much hope that you and your students will enjoy using these materials as much as we enjoyed developing them for you.

The *Cambridge Global English* team

A Components

Cambridge Global English offers the following components:

- The **Learner's Book** provides the core input of the course. It consists of nine thematic units of study. Each unit contains six lessons developed around a unifying theme that is also linked to a main question at the beginning of the *Reflect on your learning* section of the main units. The materials feature skills-building tasks, including listening, reading, writing, speaking, as well as language focus, catering for the needs of learners studying in a primary context. In addition, we have included a strong vocabulary building element. We also specifically explore ways of introducing basic learning skills and strategies, so that the children become aware of the act of learning and how it works through such features as:
  - Overt objectives at the beginning of each unit
  - Language and Writing tips
  - Listening and Reading strategies
  - *Use of English*
  - *Reflect on your learning*
  - *Look what I can do!*

  We try to aim our materials at the whole child with all the experiences that they bring to the classroom. We encourage the learners to see the moral and social values that exist in many of our texts and find opportunities for reflecting on these. We feel that the learner needs to be exposed to many different forms of text topics and styles in order to develop the skills of assessing, interpreting and responding appropriately. This means that the learners will see factual texts, imaginary text, dialogues, poetry, etc. on a range of different topics at the appropriate level.
- The **Audio CDs** include all the listening material needed for the Learner's Book and Activity Book. The listening material supports the Learner's Book with listening and pronunciation activities, as well as read-along stories. We recommend that learners use the Audio CDs at home to practise the stories and to show their parents what they know.
- The **Activity Book** provides additional practice activities, deepening learners' understanding of the language skills and content material introduced in the Learner's Book.

- The **Teacher's Resource** provides valuable guidance and support for using *Cambridge Global English* in your classroom. We understand that within each class there are children of different ability, particularly when children come from different pre-primary backgrounds. We think it is very important to support differentiated work in the classroom and we aim to do this through suggestions in the unit notes, with additional differentiation 'challenge' activities in the Activity Book. In addition, the production required in the project work can be graded in terms of ability.

  At the end of this book, we provide photocopiable activities for additional work. These are referred to in the unit notes. We also provide a selection of lesson-by-lesson spelling words which you can photocopy, cut out and give to the children to learn.

B Learner's Book structure

Cambridge Global English consists of nine thematic units of study roughly set out to cover three units per term in most systems. The Stage 5 Learner's Book is organised as follows:

- **Main units:** Nine thematic units provide a year's curriculum.
- **Review pages:** Every two units we provide two review pages to revise and consolidate learning.

C Unit structure

Each unit is divided up into six lessons. The length of lessons will vary from school to school, so we have not prescribed a strict time limit for each lesson. The lessons are organised as follows:

- **Lesson 1 Opening:** This lesson introduces the main topic, and prepares for the Big question which you will find at the beginning of the *Reflect on your learning* section. We also set out the unit objectives for the teacher to share with the learners. This overt teaching of objectives is part of the learning to learn strategy. The main lesson begins with a 'Talk about it' activity in which the children are expected to react to information, ideas or visuals. There is a contextualised listening or speaking text which leads to exploitation of vocabulary and grammar. A free speaking activity usually ends the lesson.

- **Lessons 2–4 Skills:** In these lessons we explore the topic in various ways using a variety of short listening and reading texts which do include cross-curricular topics. The lessons focus on the mechanics of reading, including spelling or pronunciation and use of English and integrate the four skills. Guided writing activities are included in these lessons.
- **Lesson 5 Literacy:** This literacy lesson involves reading authentic extracts, stories, poems, and factual texts of longer length. It allows the learner to explore a variety of text types with the class and develop comprehension and writing skills through related activities. The literacy lessons can include some word focus and strategies for approaching new text types and usually include value-related activities.
- **Lesson 6 Choose a project:** This is the consolidation and production section of the unit in which the learners produce language related to some element in the unit. This lesson begins with the learners taking an active role in choosing a project, carrying it out and presenting it to the class. Then they reflect on their learning and do a short self-assessment activity: *Look what I can do!*

D Activity Book

Each lesson in the Learner's Book is supported by two Activity Book pages which reinforce and extend the material introduced in the Learner's Book. It also provides opportunities for personalisation and creative work, as well as challenge activities to support differentiated classroom situations. In these activities, more confident learners can do additional work at a higher level. The last lesson of each unit offers additional assessment/self-assessment opportunities.

E Customising your lessons

We provide support for planning each lesson in the unit pages of this book. We also clearly set out the teaching objectives. Please bear in mind the following:

- These are ideas and guidelines only and you should adapt them to your situation and the needs of your learner. Do not be afraid to change things and bring in additional elements.
- Monitor your learners. If they need additional support for some elements, tailor the material to their needs.
- Bring as much 'real' material into the classroom as possible in order to create more interest for the lessons.
- Be creative in developing extension activities and role plays. We offer some suggestions, however there is much more that can be done.
- Encourage learning/teaching/showing between classes, even of different age groups.

- Don't forget to draw on parent support where possible.

When using the book, the following guidelines might be useful:

Before using the Learner's Book
- Warm up activities (songs, TPR, vocabulary games, alphabet chant, etc.).
- Pre-teach and practise key language that learners will encounter in the Learner's Book and Audio CDs. (Try to make learning experiences concrete, interactive, motivating.)

While using the Learner's Book
- Keep learners engaged in an active way.
- Use the illustrations as a conversation starter – ask learners to name everything they see; play *I Spy*, etc.
- Vary the group dynamics in the lesson: move from whole group response to individual response to pairwork, etc.
- Provide opportunities for learners to ask questions, as well as to answer them.
- Encourage learners to act out the language in the lessons.
- Encourage learners to use language structures and vocabulary to talk about their own ideas, opinions and experiences.
- In class discussions, write the learners' ideas on class charts. You can refer back to these charts in later lessons.
- Adjust your reading and writing expectations and instructions to suit the literacy level of your learners.

Using the Activity Book and further suggestions
- Use the Activity Book pages related to the Learner's Book pages.
- Depending on the ability of the learners, use the 'Additional support and practice' activities and/or 'Extend and challenge' activities suggested in the Teacher's Resource at the end of every lesson.
- Do a Wrap up activity or game at the end of every lesson.

We would strongly recommend that you supplement this core material with the following:

- An extended reading programme to provide the children with lots of practice of different types of books leading to reading independence. It is recommended that you regularly set aside time for the children to read books of their choice in class and that they are encouraged to read at home.

- Exposure to additional audiovisual material, such as television programmes, songs, film excerpts, so that the learners begin to feel confident in their ability to decode and understand a range of resources.
- Supplementary handwriting and phonics material to really help build on those skills at this crucial time.

F Setting up the primary classroom

We know that there is not always a lot of flexibility in this, but, if possible, it would be useful to set up the classroom in this way:

- Have some open space where learners can do role plays, etc.
- Have a flexible seating arrangement, so that you can mix up the groups and pairs, and the learners become flexible about working in different ways.
- Make sure that you have display areas where you and the learners can bring in pictures and items linked to the themes you're working on. Also display examples of good work and creative work. Make small cards and display important words for the learners to remember.
- Change displays regularly to keep the learners interested and engaged.

G Assessment

We recommend that you take the time and opportunity to observe and monitor the progress and development of your learners. We provide many opportunities for informal assessment through the projects, as well as self-assessment *(Look what I can do!)* in the main units of the Learner's Book. The Activity Book contains revision material at the end of each unit.

At the beginning of the year, create individual portfolio folders to keep work that shows how the children have been meeting the curriculum objectives. Use the portfolio to look over with the learners and create a feeling of progress and pride in what they have achieved. Keep this portfolio for parent–teacher meetings and send it home to show the parents/carers either at the end of each term or the end of the year. You might want to include a letter to parents/carers outlining what they have achieved.

If you would like further learner assessment opportunities, a table of how the Cambridge English Language Assessment exams for primary stages fits in with the *Cambridge Global English* levels is set out below.

Cambridge English Language Assessment exam for primary stages

Stage	Assessment	CEFR level
6		
5	Cambridge English: Key	A2
4	(KET)	
3	for Schools	
	Cambridge English: Flyers	
2	(YLE Flyers)	A1
	Cambridge English:	
1	Movers	
	(YLE movers)	
	Cambridge English:	
	Starters	
	(YLE starters)	

H Home–school relationship

Support and encouragement at home is extremely important at this age. Encourage parents to become as involved as possible in their child's learning process by asking them what they have learned after every lesson, allowing children to 'teach' them what they have learned, taking an interest in what they bring home or want to perform for them and supporting any work the learners might try to do at home.

I Icons

The following icons have been used to clearly signpost areas of special interest or as shorthand for specific instructions:

Audio and track number reference. These appear in the Learner's Book, the Activity Book and the Teacher's Resource.

Speaking opportunity/activity recommended for pairwork. These appear in the Learner's Book, the Activity Book and Teacher's Resource.

Cross-curricular maths and science topics. These appear in the Learner's Book, the Activity Book and the Teacher's Resource.

Links directly to Activity Book activity and references it. These appear in the Learner's Book and the Teacher's Resource.

Activity to be written in the learner's notebook. These appear in the Learner's Book and the Activity Book.

Activity to be done out of the book, in a more active classroom setting. These appear in the Teacher's Resource.

Framework correlations

Learning objectives from the Cambridge Primary English as a Second Language Curriculum Framework:

Stage 5 correlated with *Cambridge Global English*, Stage 5

Below you will find a table setting out specifically where to find coverage of the framework objectives for Stage 5.

Cambridge Primary English as a Second Language Framework: Stage 5	CGE Unit 1	CGE Unit 2	CGE Unit 3	CGE Unit 4	CGE Unit 5	CGE Unit 6	CGE Unit 7	CGE Unit 8	CGE Unit 9
Reading									
R1 Recognise, identify and sound, with little or no support, a wide range of language at text level	✓	✓	✓	✓	✓	✓	✓	✓	✓
R2 Read and follow, with little or no support, familiar instructions for classroom activities	✓	✓	✓	✓	✓	✓	✓	✓	✓
R3 Read, with little or no support, a range of short simple fiction and non-fiction texts with confidence and enjoyment	✓	✓	✓	✓	✓	✓	✓	✓	✓
R4 Understand the main points of a range of short simple texts on general, curricular topics by using contextual clues	✓	✓	✓	✓	✓	✓	✓	✓	✓
R5 Understand, with little or no support, specific information and detail in short, simple texts on a range of general and curricular topics	✓	✓	✓	✓	✓	✓	✓	✓	✓
R6 Recognise the difference between fact and opinion in short, simple texts on a range of general and curricular topics	✓		✓	✓		✓	✓	✓	

Cambridge Primary English as a Second Language Framework: Stage 5	CGE Unit 1	CGE Unit 2	CGE Unit 3	CGE Unit 4	CGE Unit 5	CGE Unit 6	CGE Unit 7	CGE Unit 8	CGE Unit 9
R7 Recognise the attitude or opinion of the writer in short, simple texts on a range of general and curricular topics	✓	✓		✓	✓			✓	✓
R8 Use, with little or no support, familiar paper and digital reference resources to check meaning and extend understanding	✓	✓	✓	✓	✓	✓	✓	✓	✓
Writing									
W1 Plan, write, edit and proofread work at text level with support on an increasing range of general and curricular topics	✓	✓	✓	✓	✓	✓	✓	✓	✓
W2 Write, with support, about factual and imaginary past events, activities and experiences in a paragraph on a limited range of general and curricular topics	✓	✓	✓		✓	✓	✓	✓	
W3 Write with support factual and imaginative descriptions at text level which describe people, places and objects	✓		✓	✓	✓	✓	✓	✓	✓
W4 Use joined-up handwriting in a wide range of written work across the curriculum with growing speed and fluency	✓	✓	✓	✓	✓	✓	✓	✓	✓

Cambridge Primary English as a Second Language Framework: Stage 5	CGE Unit 1	CGE Unit 2	CGE Unit 3	CGE Unit 4	CGE Unit 5	CGE Unit 6	CGE Unit 7	CGE Unit 8	CGE Unit 9
W5 Link, with little or no support, sentences into a coherent paragraph using a variety of basic connectors on a growing range of general and curricular topics		✓	✓	✓	✓	✓	✓	✓	✓
W6 Use, with little or no support, appropriate layout at text level for a limited range of written genres on familiar general and curricular topics	✓	✓	✓	✓	✓	✓	✓	✓	✓
W7 Spell most high-frequency words accurately for a growing range of familiar general and curricular topics when writing independently	✓	✓	✓	✓	✓	✓	✓	✓	✓
W8 Punctuate written work at text level on an increasing range of general and curricular topics with some accuracy when writing independently	✓	✓	✓	✓	✓	✓	✓	✓	✓

Cambridge Primary English as a Second Language Framework: Stage 5	CGE Unit 1	CGE Unit 2	CGE Unit 3	CGE Unit 4	CGE Unit 5	CGE Unit 6	CGE Unit 7	CGE Unit 8	CGE Unit 9
Use of English									
UE1 Begin to use basic abstract nouns and compound nouns; use a growing range of noun phrases describing times and location on a growing range of general and curricular topics		✓	✓	✓				✓	✓
UE2 Use quantifiers including *more, little, few, less, fewer not as many, not as much* on a growing range of general and curricular topics		✓							
UE3 Use common participles as adjectives and order adjectives correctly in front of nouns on a growing range of general and curricular topics	✓	✓	✓	✓	✓		✓		
UE4 Use a growing range of determiners including *all, other* on a growing range of general and curricular topics	✓	✓			✓		✓	✓	
UE5 Use questions including questions with *whose, how often, how long;* use a growing range of tag questions; on a growing range of general and curricular topics	✓	✓	✓	✓	✓	✓	✓	✓	✓

Cambridge Primary English as a Second Language Framework: Stage 5	CGE Unit 1	CGE Unit 2	CGE Unit 3	CGE Unit 4	CGE Unit 5	CGE Unit 6	CGE Unit 7	CGE Unit 8	CGE Unit 9
UE6 Use a growing range of personal, demonstrative and quantitative pronouns including *someone, somebody, everybody, no-one* on a growing range of general and curricular topics		✓	✓		✓				✓
UE7 Use simple perfect forms to express what has happened [indefinite and unfinished past with *for* and *since*] on a growing range of general and curricular topics			✓		✓		✓		
UE8 Use future *will* and *shall* to make offers, promises, predictions, on a growing range of general and curricular topics				✓				✓	✓
UE9 Use a growing range of present and past simple active and some passive forms on a growing range of general and curricular topics		✓	✓	✓	✓	✓	✓	✓	✓
UE10 Use present continuous forms with present and future meaning and past continuous forms for background and interrupted past actions on a growing range of general and curricular topics		✓		✓	✓	✓		✓	

Cambridge Primary English as a Second Language Framework: Stage 5	CGE Unit 1	CGE Unit 2	CGE Unit 3	CGE Unit 4	CGE Unit 5	CGE Unit 6	CGE Unit 7	CGE Unit 8	CGE Unit 9
UE11 Use common impersonal structures with *it, there* on a growing range of general and curricular topics				✓				✓	✓
UE12 Use a growing range of adverbs, including adverbs of degree *too, not enough, quite, rather*; use pre-verbal, post-verbal and end-position adverbs; on a growing range of general and curricular topics		✓	✓	✓		✓	✓	✓	✓
UE13 Use modal forms including *mustn't* (prohibition), *need* (necessity), *should* (for advice) on a growing range of general and curricular topics		✓	✓	✓	✓			✓	✓
UE14 Use a growing range of prepositions of time, location and direction; use *by* and *with* to denote agent and instrument; use prepositions preceding nouns and adjectives in common prepositional phrases; on a growing range of general and curricular topics	✓		✓	✓	✓		✓	✓	

Cambridge Primary English as a Second Language Framework: Stage 5	CGE Unit 1	CGE Unit 2	CGE Unit 3	CGE Unit 4	CGE Unit 5	CGE Unit 6	CGE Unit 7	CGE Unit 8	CGE Unit 9
UE15 Use common verbs followed by infinitive verb/verb + *ing* patterns; use infinitive of purpose	✓	✓			✓		✓	✓	✓
UE16 Use conjunctions *if, when, where, so, and, or, but, because, before, after* to link parts of sentences in short texts on a growing range of general and curricular topics	✓	✓		✓	✓	✓	✓		
UE17 Use subordinate clauses following *think, know, believe, hope, say, tell*; use subordinate clauses following *sure, certain*; use a growing range of defining relative clauses with *which, who, that, where*; on a growing range of general and curricular topics	✓	✓	✓	✓	✓		✓		✓

Cambridge Primary English as a Second Language Framework: Stage 5	CGE Unit 1	CGE Unit 2	CGE Unit 3	CGE Unit 4	CGE Unit 5	CGE Unit 6	CGE Unit 7	CGE Unit 8	CGE Unit 9
Listening									
L1 Understand longer sequences of supported classroom instructions	✓	✓	✓	✓	✓	✓	✓	✓	✓
L2 Understand more complex supported questions which ask for personal information	✓	✓	✓					✓	
L3 Understand more complex supported questions on a growing range of general and curricular topics	✓	✓	✓	✓	✓	✓	✓	✓	✓
L4 Understand, with limited support, the main points of extended talk on a range of general and curricular topics		✓	✓	✓		✓	✓	✓	✓
L5 Understand most specific information and detail of supported, extended talk on a range of general and curricular topics	✓	✓	✓	✓	✓	✓	✓	✓	✓
L6 Deduce meaning from context in supported extended talk on a range of general and curricular topics	✓	✓	✓		✓	✓	✓		✓
L7 Recognise the opinion of the speaker(s) in supported extended talk on a range of general and curricular topics		✓	✓	✓				✓	

Cambridge Primary English as a Second Language Framework: Stage 5	CGE Unit 1	CGE Unit 2	CGE Unit 3	CGE Unit 4	CGE Unit 5	CGE Unit 6	CGE Unit 7	CGE Unit 8	CGE Unit 9
L8 Understand supported narratives, including some extended talk, on a range of general and curricular topics	✓		✓	✓		✓	✓		
L9 Identify rhymes, repetition and alliteration	✓					✓		✓	✓
Speaking									
S1 Provide basic information about themselves and others at discourse level on a range of general topics	✓	✓	✓	✓	✓	✓	✓	✓	✓
S2 Ask questions to find out general information on a range of general and curricular topics	✓	✓	✓	✓	✓	✓	✓	✓	✓
S3 Give an opinion at discourse level on an increasing range of general and curricular topics	✓	✓	✓	✓	✓	✓	✓	✓	✓
S4 Respond, with limited flexibility, at both sentence and discourse level to unexpected comments on a range of general and curricular topics	✓	✓	✓			✓	✓	✓	✓
S5 Organise talk at discourse level using appropriate connectors on a range of general and curricular topics		✓	✓	✓	✓	✓	✓	✓	✓
S6 Communicate meaning clearly at sentence and discourse level during pair, group and whole class exchanges	✓	✓	✓	✓	✓	✓	✓	✓	✓

Cambridge Primary English as a Second Language Framework: Stage 5	CGE Unit 1	CGE Unit 2	CGE Unit 3	CGE Unit 4	CGE Unit 5	CGE Unit 6	CGE Unit 7	CGE Unit 8	CGE Unit 9
S7 Keep interaction going in longer exchanges on a range of general and curricular topics	✓	✓	✓			✓		✓	
S8 Relate some extended stories and events on a limited range of general and curricular topics		✓			✓	✓		✓	✓

Common European Framework of Reference (CEFR) guidelines

The Cambridge Primary English as a Second Language Curriculum Framework is mapped to the Council of Europe's Common European Framework of Reference for Languages (CEFR). For more information about the CEFR framework, please visit its website. The framework correlation to the *Cambridge Global English* stages (or levels) is set out in the table below. However, since the course material has been written for an ESL context (which has less rigid conceptions about language level) it can move more fluidly between CEFR levels.

Comparative CEFR levels for CGE stages

Cambridge Global English stage						
	1	2	3	4	5	6
Reading CEFR level	Working towards A1	Low A1	High A1	Low A2	Mid A2	High A2
Writing CEFR level	Working towards A1	Low A1	High A1	Low A2	Mid A2	High A2
Use of English CEFR level	Low A1	High A1	Low A2	Mid A2	High A2	Low B1
Listening CEFR level	Low A1	High A1	Low A2	Mid A2	High A2	Low B1
Speaking CEFR level	Low A1	High A1	Low A2	Mid A2	High A2	Low B1

1 Talking about people

Big question What are you like?

Unit overview

In this unit learners will:
- talk about their personalities
- do a personality quiz
- interview their partners about their lives
- write a *My Page* profile
- read poems about special people.

Learners will build communication and literacy skills as they read and listen to poems and interviews; read and write diary entries; do a personality quiz; develop vocabulary study skills; and speak about their favourite people and things.

At the end of the unit, they will apply and personalise what they have learned by working in small groups to complete a project of their choice: writing about their favourite person or about the day they were born.

Language focus

-ed and *-ing* adjectives

Wh- questions

Vocabulary topics: adjectives to describe personality.

Critical thinking
- Analysing what makes a poem
- Predicting
- Memorising.

Self-assessment
- I can talk about my life and what I am like.
- I can interview my partner about their life.
- I can write a profile page.
- I can understand a poem.
- I can recognise rhyming words.

Teaching tip

Ask learners to start a Vocabulary journal in their notebooks. They write the words they find the most difficult to remember and add a sentence to contextualise them.

Review the learners' work, noting areas where they demonstrate strength and areas where they need additional instruction and practice. Use this information to customise your teaching as you continue to **Unit 2**.

Lesson 1: Talking about people

Learner's Book pages: 6–7

Activity Book pages: 4–5

Lesson objectives

Listening: Listen for information, listen and match.
Speaking: Practise theme vocabulary, talk about yourself.
Reading: Read for gist, read a diary entry.
Critical thinking: Discuss personality, awareness of self.

Vocabulary: Adjectives to describe personality, opposites: *confident, lazy, generous, cheerful, bad-tempered, selfish, tidy, nervous, shy, untidy, hardworking, outgoing*

Materials: A few pictures of people in different situations, dictionaries.

Learner's Book

Warm up

- Show some pictures of people and ask learners to describe them. Ask: *What is she/he like?*
- Encourage learners to speculate about the personality of the people in the photos. Remind learners that we cannot always judge someone's personality from the way they look.
- Work with the class to come up with a list of adjectives and write it on the board.

1 💬 Talk about it

- Ask: *What are you like?* Encourage learners to reflect on this and give honest answers. Ask them to give examples to support what they say, e.g. *I think I'm … because …*
- Add to the list of adjectives on the board.
- **Critical thinking:** Encourage learners to focus on positive aspects of their personalities. Help them by asking questions, e.g. *What would you do if a friend needs help?*

> **Answers**
> Learners' own answers.

2 Vocabulary

- Ask learners to work in pairs or small groups and look at the picture. Ask them to describe what the children are doing.
- Focus on the adjectives in the box and ask learners to find children in the picture who match the adjectives. Encourage them to explain their choices.

> **Answers**
> Learners' own answers.

3 Listen

- Tell learners they are going to listen to some people speaking about the children in the picture. They listen and pay attention to the adjectives the speakers use to describe the children.
- Play the audio at least twice. Then pause after each speaker and ask learners which child is being described.
- Ask them what adjective they would use to describe the child. Encourage them to explain their choices.

> **Audioscript:** Track 2
>
> **Speaker 1:** What always surprises me about my granddaughter is the way in which she loves to take centre stage. She doesn't get nervous at all and seems quite at home speaking to lots of people.
>
> **Speaker 2:** I just don't understand why he gets so angry. If we don't pass him the ball all the time he just stops playing and walks off the football field.
>
> **Speaker 3:** I really admire my friend Aisha. She's so studious! She loves learning about new things and always has her head in a book. Needless to say she always gets top marks in class.
>
> **Speaker 4:** Camila is my best friend. She's such a kind, generous person. We share everything: our pencils, our pens, our secrets and our sweets and chocolates – of course!
>
> **Speaker 5:** Come on Natasha! Why are you hiding? It's my friend, she's just saying hello to you.
>
> **Speaker 6:** Cheng is a very tidy person. He always tidies up his bedroom and puts his food wrappers and empty bottles in the bin in the park.

> **Answers**
> Speaker 1 – confident 1; speaker 2 – bad tempered; speaker 3 – hardworking; speaker 4 – generous; speaker 5 – shy; speaker 6 – tidy.

[AB] **For further practice, see Activities 1 and 2 in the Activity Book.**

4 Word study

- Write two antonyms on the board, e.g. *hot/cold*. Tell learners that these two words are *antonyms*. Ask them what they think this word means (antonyms are words with opposite meanings). Elicit some ideas.
- Ask learners to work individually. They look at the adjectives and match them to their opposites.
- Tell them to use their dictionaries to help them.
- When they have finished, ask them to check their answers with a partner.
- Then, you may check the answers as a class.
- **Study skills:** Ask learners to write down in their notebooks the meanings of those words that are new or they have found the most difficult to understand. They can add a sentence to contextualise the word.

Answers

1 d 2 c 3 b 4 e 5 f 6 a

 For further practice, see Activity 3 in the Activity Book.

Reading strategy

- Focus on the **Reading strategy**. Read the explanation with learners. Ask them why this reading strategy is so useful when approaching a text.
- How do they think it helps them understand the text? e.g. predicting the topic, activating background knowledge, predicting the vocabulary they will encounter, understanding the attitude of the writer.

 For further practice, see Strategy check! in the Activity Book.

5 Read

- Ask learners to read the text quickly and determine the type of text it is (e.g is it a poem, a newspaper article, a story?)
- Elicit answers from the class and ask them to explain what helped them decide. Focus on features such as use of the first person and the date.
- Ask learners if they keep diaries. What sort of things do they write in their diaries?
- Ask learners what the tone and attitude of the writer is (he's angry). How do they know?
- **Study skills:** Remind learners to use the context to work out the meaning of new words. If they still have doubts, they can use their dictionary. Then they can make an entry in their Vocabulary journal or in their notebooks.

Answers
Learners' own answers.

 For further practice, see Activities 4 and 5 in the Activity Book.

6 Talk

- In pairs, learners discuss the questions. Tell them to use adjectives from **Activity 4**.
- Ask them to reflect on the last question and give honest answers.
- **Informal assessment opportunity:** Circulate, listening to learners' interactions and noting strong points and mistakes for remedial work.

Answers
Learners' own answers.

↪ Wrap up

- Discuss as a class what learners do to help around the house. What adjectives would they use to describe their attitude at home?

Activity Book

1 Adjectives

- Learners work independently. They read the adjectives and find them in the wordsearch.
- Then, they can compare their answers in pairs or small groups.
- Check the answers as a class.

Answers

N	V	Y	H	B	O	P	D	A	B	I	V	C
E	L	P	A	L	M	U	T	I	D	Y	O	S
R	G	R	R	N	C	C	T	J	X	N	R	C
V	E	E	D	N	O	H	P	G	F	L	R	U
O	N	A	W	U	N	E	G	I	O	Z	D	H
U	E	Q	O	C	F	E	D	L	C	I	S	N
S	R	O	R	E	I	R	G	U	F	I	N	Y
M	O	A	K	O	D	F	O	K	F	A	Z	G
N	U	Y	I	T	E	U	Y	L	M	A	Z	X
K	S	G	N	M	N	L	E	U	L	B	J	V
C	D	Q	G	U	T	S	O	O	S	H	Y	Z

2 Adjectives

- Learners complete the sentences with an adjective from **Activity 1**.
- Then, they can compare their answers in pairs or small groups.
- Check the answers as a class.

Answers
1 nervous
2 hardworking
3 lazy
4 cheerful
5 outgoing
6 tidy

3 Antonyms

- Learners find and match the adjectives to their opposite meaning.
- Then, they can compare their answers in pairs or small groups.
- Check the answers as a class.

Answers
bad-tempered – cheerful
tidy – untidy
lazy – hardworking
shy – outgoing
confident – nervous
selfish – generous

Strategy check!

- Tell learners to read and tick the strategies that will help them to read a text for gist.
- Tell them they should use these strategies before they read the text.

Answers
Look at pictures. ✓
Read the text quickly to find out what the topic is or the writer's feelings. ✓
Read the text quickly for the general meaning. ✓

4 Read

- Learners read the school report and choose the picture of the boy described in the report.
- Ask them if they think Juan's parents are going to be happy with his report.
- Check the answers as a class.

Answers
Picture b.
Learners' own answers.

5 Read

- Learners decide which adjectives in **Activity 3** describe Juan's personality.
- Check the answers as a class. Encourage learners to explain their answers.

Answers
cheerful, outgoing, lazy, tidy, nervous

Differentiated instruction

Additional support and practice

- Play a guessing game as a class. Describe people using **Activity 3** in the Learner's Book as a model. Learners choose an adjective from the box on page 5 to describe the person.

Extend and challenge

- Ask learners to work independently and write a short diary entry about the chores they do around the house.

Lesson 2: Our profiles

Learner's Book pages: 8–9
Activity Book pages: 6–7

Lesson objectives

Listening: Listen for specific information.

Speaking: Talk about oneself.

Reading: Read a personality quiz.

Writing: Complete a profile, complete questions.

Critical thinking: Awareness of self, being critical about one's own behaviour.

Language focus: Question words

Materials: Pictures of people in different situations, a sample profile of a real or imaginary person, a copy of **Photocopiable activity 1** for each learner.

Learner's Book

Warm up

- Show learners pictures of people and ask learners to describe them using one adjective they have learned.
- Show the class a sample profile and write the word *profile* on the board.
- Ask learners what they think a profile is (e.g. information about a person, it focuses on important or interesting things about that person).
- What information would learners expect to find in a profile? Encourage them to look at the sample, e.g. age, name, personal characteristics.

1 Talk about it

- **Critical thinking:** Focus on the positive aspects of the learners' personalities. Pay special attention and be sensitive to those learners who may have a negative self-image and encourage them to identify and talk about their strengths.
- Ask learners to reflect on what they are like and discuss the questions.

Answers
Learners' own answers.

2 Read

- Ask learners if they know what a personality quiz is. Have they ever done one? What questions do they expect to find in a quiz? Elicit some answers.
- Focus on the four questions. Ask learners to match them to the correct options in **Activity 3**.

Answers
1 B   2 D   3 A   4 C

3 Read

- Ask learners to read the questions and to choose the correct answer for them.
- When they have finished, they work out their scores and read the Results box at the end of the quiz.
- Discuss what their score is. Are they happy with it? Can they think of ways to improve their behaviour?

Answers
Learners' own answers.

 For further practice, see Activity 1 in the Activity Book.

Listening strategy

- Focus on the strategy. Ask learners how this strategy can help them, e.g. they don't need to understand everything they hear so they can concentrate on what they need to know. Make sure learners use this knowledge to help fill in the missing words in **Activity 4**.

4 Listen

- Ask learners to look carefully at the type of information they need to complete the profile.
- Tell them to listen and complete Santiago's profile. Play the audio a few times.
- When learners have finished, discuss how similar they are to Santiago.

Audioscript: Track 3

Hi, my name's Santiago. I'm from Argentina. I'm 11 years old and I live with my family: my mum, my dad and my little brother in Buenos Aires. I've got two pets, a hamster and a dog, and I play football and basketball for the school team. I've got two best friends, Pedro who is in my class at school and my cousin Luca who I've known all my life.

What do people like about me? Mmm, well ... I suppose I'm quite outgoing and cheerful most of the time, so people think I'm fun to be with.

What do I like about me? Well ... I'm quite a tidy person. I hate it if my bedroom gets messy. I'm also a patient person especially with my little brother!

What could I improve about me? Well, my family would say that I am very bad-tempered when I get up in the morning. It's something I really need to change.

> **Answers**
> **Name:** Santiago
> **Age:** 11
> **Country:** Argentina
> **Family:** mum, dad, little brother
> **Pets:** two – a hamster and a dog
> **Hobbies:** football and basketball
> **Best friends:** Pedro and Luca (cousin)
> **What people like about me:** outgoing, cheerful, fun to be with
> **What I like about myself:** tidy, patient
> **What could I improve about myself:** bad-tempered in the morning

5 Use of English

- Review the question words in the **Use of English** box. Ask learners to give some examples of questions.
- Focus on the activity and ask learners to complete questions 1–7 with the question words in the box.
- When they have finished, check the answers as a class.
- Then, learners answer the questions about Santiago in their notebook.

> **Answers**
> 1 **What** is his name? His name is Santiago.
> 2 **Where** is he from? He is from Argentina/Buenos Aires.
> 3 **Who** are the people in his family? His mum, his dad and his little brother.
> 4 **What** pets has he got? He's got a rabbit and a dog.
> 5 **What** are his hobbies? He plays football and basketball.
> 6 **Who** are his best friends? His best friends are Pedro and Luca, his cousin.
> 7 **What** do people like about him? He is outgoing, cheerful and fun to be with.

 For further practice, see Activity 2 in the Activity Book.

6 Talk

- In pairs, learners ask and answer the questions about each other and make notes.

> **Answers**
> Learners' own answers.

7 Write

- Tell learners to write a profile about their partner using the notes they made in **Activity 6**.

> **Answers**
> Learners' own answers.

For further practice, see Activities 3 and 4 in the Activity Book.

Wrap up

- Once learners have finished writing their partner's profile, ask them to share it with the class.
- **Portfolio opportunity:** Learners write their name and date on the profiles. Collect the profiles and keep them in their portfolios.
- **Home–school opportunity:** Learners take it in turns to take the profile home and show it to their family.

Activity Book

1 Read

- Learners read the profiles and match them to the correct summary.
- They work with a partner and compare their answers.
- Check the answers as a class. Encourage learners to explain their choices.

> **Answers**
> Profile 1: Lucia – 3
> Profile 2: Tasanee – 1
> Profile 3: Sam – 2

2 Use of English

- Learners make questions and answer them with information from the profile texts in **Activity 1**.
- Check the answers as a class.

> **Answers**
> 1 What pets has Lucia got?
>   She got a dog called Bruno and a cat called Silke.
> 2 What is Lucia like?
>   She's a very confident, outgoing and active person.
> 3 Where is Tasanee from?
>   She's from Thailand.
> 4 Who are the people in Tasanee's family?
>   Her mum, her dad and her brother and sister.
> 5 How old is Sam?
>   He's twelve years old.
> 6 What are Sam's hobbies?
>   Football and training his parrot.

3 Write

- Learners complete their own profile.
- They read it to the class.

> **Answers**
> Learners' own answers.

4 Challenge

- Learners interview their partner using the questions in **Activity 2** as a guide.
- They take notes in their notebook and then write sentences about their partner's life.

> **Answers**
> Learners' own answers.

Differentiated instruction

Additional support and practice

- Give each learner a copy of **Photocopiable activity 1**. They work independently and complete the questions and answer them.
- They compare their work with a partner.

Extend and challenge

- Learners use the questions in **Activity 5** of the Learner's Book to make a profile of a family member and add a picture to it.

Lesson 3: An interview

Learner's Book pages: 10–11
Activity Book pages: 8–9

Lesson objectives

Listening: Listen and choose *true* or *false*, listen and write questions, listen and mark the intonation.

Speaking: Talk about interviews, prepare an interview.

Writing: Prepare questions for an interview.

Critical thinking: Reflect on the differences between speaking in one's mother tongue and in English.

Language focus: Useful expressions *I really like ..., It makes me (angry), Sorry, could you repeat that?, What I meant was ..., I'm not very keen on ..., I don't think ..., We both like ..., I'm not sure if ...*

Learner's Book

Warm up

- Ask learners who their favourite famous person is.
- If they had the chance to interview this person, what questions would they ask? Would they ask the questions in their mother tongue or in English?

1 Talk about it

- Ask learners if they have ever had an interview either in their own language or in a foreign language. Ask them how they felt and what they talked about.
- If nobody has ever had an interview, you may invite learners to imagine how they would feel.
- **Critical thinking:** Discuss with learners what would be easier to do – to have an interview in their own language or in another language, for example in English. What difficulties might they have? How would they overcome these difficulties? Encourage them to give reasons for their answers.

> **Answers**
> Learners' own answers.

AB For further practice, see Strategy Check! in the Activity Book.

2 Listen 4

- Tell learners that they are going to listen to Ben being interviewed by his new English teacher.
- Tell learners to listen to the interview and order the topics Ben talks about.
- Play the audio at least twice. Check the answers as a class.

> **Audioscript:** Track 4
> **English teacher:** Hello Ben, How are you today?
> **Ben:** I'm fine thank you.
> **English teacher:** Tell me about your family. Have you got any brothers or sisters?
> **Ben:** Yes, Max a younger brother who is a bit of a pain!
> **English teacher:** Where were you born?
> **Ben:** I'm from ... Sorry, what I meant to say was I was born in a small town called Flintown in the USA.
> **English teacher:** Tell me about yourself. What are you like?
> **Ben:** Sorry, could you repeat that, please?
> **English teacher:** Yes, of course. What are you like?
> **Ben:** Well, I'm quite a confident person and I like to do things properly, although I'm not sure if my mum would agree with my last point. I'm quite popular at school too, I suppose.

English teacher: Who are your best friends?

Ben: Well, my best friend is Micky, he's really good fun. We've been friends for as long as I can remember. I think we met when we were babies.

English teacher: What are you good at at school?

Ben: I don't think I'm good at many things to be honest. Well, Mrs. Jones would say I'm good at singing, but I don't agree with her at all. I'm good at drawing and I'm quite good at sewing too, but don't tell anyone about that last one!

English teacher: Do you have a favourite sport?

Ben: No, I don't excel at any sport. Once Dad thought I was going to be a great rugby player, so he made me join the local team, but he was wrong, of course!

English teacher: What are your favourite things?

Ben: Well that has to be my mega collection of video games. I absolutely love playing them. Micky and I play quite a lot together. Then there's my collection of comics. I remember when Micky and I wrote our own comic strip, *Zippy Racer.*

> **Answers**
> 1 family
> 2 town
> 3 personality
> 4 friends
> 5 school
> 6 sport
> 7 favourite things

3 Listen

- Tell learners they are going to listen to the interview with Ben again and they are going to decide if the sentences are true or false.
- Allow some time for them to read the sentences before doing the task.
- Play the recording a few times. Then, check the answers as a class.

> **Answers**
> 1 false
> 2 true
> 3 true
> 4 true
> 5 true
> 6 false
> 7 true

4 Match the questions

- Ask learners to read the questions and match them to the answers. Tell them these are some of the questions they heard in the interview with Ben.
- Check the answers as a class.

> **Answers**
> 1 d   2 a   3 b   4 e   5 c

(AB) **For further practice, see Activities 1 and 2 in the Activity Book.**

5 Pronunciation

- Explain that questions in English have a special intonation depending on whether they are *wh-* questions or *yes/no* questions.
- Focus on the examples and on the arrows. What do learners think they mean?
- Tell them that they are going to listen to some questions and mark the intonation.
- Play the recording a few times and allow time for learners to mark the intonation.
- When they have finished, play the recording again. Pause after each question for learners to repeat.

> **Audioscript:** Track 5
> **1** Where were you born?
> **2** What are you like?
> **3** Who are your best friends?
> **4** What are you good at at school?
> **5** Do you have a favourite sport?
> **6** What are your favourite things?

> **Answers**
> Learners' own answers.

(AB) **For further practice, see Activity 4 in the Activity Book.**

Speaking tip

- Focus on the expressions in the box. Tell learners that these are useful expressions they can use to talk about themselves.
- Give some examples of completed sentences and ask learners to give their own.
- You could play the audio of the interview with Ben (Track 3) again and ask learners to spot the expressions.

6 Vocabulary

- Ask learners to look at the categories and at the expressions in the **Speaking tip** box. They match the expressions to the correct category.
- Check the answers as a class.

> **Answers**
> a 3   b 4   c 1 and 5   d 7   e 2 and 8

(AB) **For further practice, see Activity 3 in the Activity Book.**

7 Write

- Learners prepare a list of questions to ask their partner using the prompts provided. They write the full questions in their notebooks.

> **Answers**
> Learners' own answers.

An interview

- Tell learners to prepare their interview. They make notes under the headings and use the useful expressions in the box to describe what they like and don't like.
- In pairs, learners interview each other. Tell them to make notes about their partner's answers.
- **Informal assessment opportunity:** Circulate, listening to learners and making notes about their performance. You may wish to set up some remedial work on the most common mistakes you have observed.

Answers
Learners' own answers.

[AB] For further practice, see Activity 5 in the Activity Book.

Wrap up

- When learners have finished their interview, invite them to report back to the class about their partner's answers.

Activity Book

Strategy check!

- Tell learners to read and tick the strategies that will help them to listen for specific information.
- Then, they use these strategies before they listen to the text.

Answers
Read the text first and think about the type of words that are missing. ✓
When you listen again focus on the answers you have written. ✓
Read the completed text to check it makes sense. ✓

1 Listen 56 [CD2 Track 25]

- Learners listen and complete the dialogue between the two children.
- Check the answers as a class.

Audioscript: Track 56

Hiro: Hello, my name's Hiro. What's yours?

Ben: Hi, I'm Ben. Where are you from?

Hiro: I'm from Tokyo. And you?

Ben: I'm from New York. Have you got any brothers or sisters?

Hiro: Yes, I've got an older brother. And you?

Ben: I'm an only child.

Hiro: Sorry, could you repeat that?

Ben: Yes, there's just me. I haven't got any brothers or sisters.

Hiro: Do you have a favourite sport?

Ben: Yes, I really like playing baseball and table tennis.

Hiro: Me too! Well, I'm not so keen on baseball, but I love playing table tennis!

Ben: What are you like?

Hiro: Well, I think I'm quite hardworking and cheerful, but my mum doesn't think so. She thinks I'm a bit lazy. Not true, of course!

Ben: Ha, ha! Just like my mum! I'm quite hardworking, but mum says I spend too much time playing computer games!

Hiro: Well we both like playing computer games then. Which one is your favourite?

Answers
1 Tokyo
2 brothers and sisters
3 only child
4 baseball and table tennis
5 like
6 hardworking

2 Find an expression

- Learners find an expression highlighted in the dialogue to complete the definitions.
- Check the answers as a class.
- You may ask learners to work in pairs and roleplay the dialogue for intonation practice.

Answers
1 Sorry, could you repeat that?
2 I really like…
3 I'm not so keen on…
4 we both like…
5 I think…

3 Write

- Learners complete these sentences about themselves.
- Then, they read them to the class.

Answers
Learners' own answers.

4 Pronunciation 57 [CD2 Track 26]

- Learners read the pronunciation guide.
- Then, they listen to the audio and practise saying the questions.
- Circulate, checking for correct pronunciation and intonation.

Audioscript: Track 57
1 What are you like?
2 Where are you from?
3 Do you like playing computer games?
4 Are you outgoing?

Answers
Learners' own answers.

5 📝 Challenge

- Learners work in groups of four and ask questions from **Activity 1** to members of the group.
- They make notes. Explain that they don't need to write full sentences at this stage. It is enough to note a few words that reflect the most important information.
- Using the notes, learners compare the information and find the classmate who is most similar to themselves.
- They present their findings to the class. Tell them to use expressions from **Activity 3**.

> **Answers**
> Learners' own answers.

Differentiated instruction

Additional support and practice

- Ask learners to use their notes to write the dialogue between them and their partner. They can use the dialogue in **Activity 1** in the Activity Book as a model.

Extend and challenge

- Ask learners to look back at their partner's answers and write down a summary of the interview.

Lesson 4: Favourite things

Learner's Book pages: 12–13
Activity book pages: 10–11

Lesson objectives

Speaking: Speak about yourself.

Reading: Read for information.

Writing: Write your own *My Page*.

Language focus: *-ed* and *-ing* adjectives: *bored/boring, amazed/amazing, frightened/frightening, depressed/depressing, excited/exciting, interested/interesting*

Vocabulary: *surfer, tiger shark, attack, bite off, blood, board, major film, world-class, hiking, rollerblading, download, apps, exhilarating*

Materials: Each learner brings in a photograph of themselves, copies of **Photocopiable activity 2**.

Learner's Book

↪ Warm up

- Ask learners about their favourite activities, what they like doing in their free time and what sports they like to do or watch.

1 🗨 Talk about it

- Ask learners to look at the photos and describe them. Do they know the girl in one of them? Encourage them to say what they know about her.

- Ask learners to read the text and say what they think about Bethany. What adjectives would they use to describe her?

> **Answers**
> Learners' own answers.

2 Read

- Ask learners to read Bethany's *My Page*. Ask learners if they think they have anything in common with her.
- Ask them to look at Bethany's favourite things. Does she like the same things as the learners? What differences do they find between her and them?

> **Answers**
> Learners' own answers.

📖 For further practice, see Activity 1 in the Activity Book.

3 🗨 Talk

- Ask learners to ask and answer questions about their favourite things. Tell them to use the questions to find out.
- Encourage them to extend the questions to other aspects of their lives, e.g. favourite book, sport, film.
- Ask them to make notes of their partner's answers.

> **Answers**
> Learners' own answers.

4 📝 Read

- Ask learners to read the text again and find adjectives that describe the words in the box.
- They complete the **Use of English** box and write the rules in their notebooks.

> **Answers**
> the beach – relaxed, happy; apps – amazing; my birthday – excited; the sea – exhilarating

📖 For further practice, see Activities 2 and 3 in the Activity Book.

5 🗨 Use of English

- Tell learners to choose the correct form of the adjectives and complete the sentences.
- Then, they talk about the statements with their partner.
- Check the answers as a class.

> **Answers**
> 1 amazed
> 2 frightened
> 3 boring
> 4 exciting
> 5 depressed

📖 For further practice, see Activities 4 in the Activity Book.

Write: *My Page*

- Learners write their own *My Page*. Read through the instructions with the class and make sure they understand what is expected from them.
- Tell them to use Bethany's page as a model if necessary.
- **Writing tip:** Focus on the writing tip and ask learners to find examples in the texts that reflect this. Also, encourage them to provide their own examples.

 For further practice, see Activity 5 in the Activity Book.

Wrap up

- Learners show their *My Page* to the class and read what they have written.
- **Portfolio opportunity:** Collect the pages and file them in the learners' portfolios.
- **Home–school opportunity:** Learners take their page home and share it with the family.

Activity Book

1 Read

- Learners read and match the headings to Natalie du Toit's *My Page*.
- They compare their answers with a partner and discuss any differences.
- Check as a class and encourage learners to justify their choices.

> Answers
> 1 City/country
> 2 Family
> 3 Personality
> 4 Best feeling
> 5 Favourite place
> 6 A dream come true
> 7 Advice to others

2 Use of English

- Learners circle the adjective that best describes how Natalie feels about some things from her profile.
- They compare their answers with a partner and discuss any differences.
- Check the answers as a class.

> Answers
> 1 exhilarating
> 2 amazing
> 3 exciting

3 Write

- Learners choose the correct form of the adjectives to complete the sentences.
- Check the answers as a class.

> Answers
> 1 boring
> 2 frightened
> 3 excited
> 4 interesting
> 5 bored

4 Write

- Learners complete the sentences for themselves.
- They use -*ing*/-*ed* adjectives.
- Check the answers as a class.

> Answers
> Learners' own answers.

5 Challenge

- Learners write a *My Page* for their favourite famous person.
- Learners find out information about this person on the Internet or in a magazine. They make a selection of the most important information to use.
- They cut out photos from magazines to add to the page.
- They show their page to the class and explain what they have found.

> Answers
> Learners' own answers.

> **Differentiated instruction**
>
> **Additional support and practice**
> - Learners do **Photocopiable activity 2** for extra practice and personalisation of -*ed*/-*ing* adjectives.
>
> **Extend and challenge**
> - Learners make a *My Page* for a family member.

Lesson 5: My favourite people

Learner's Book pages: 14–17
Activity Book pages: 12–13

> **Lesson objectives**
>
> **Listening:** Listen to a poem.
>
> **Speaking:** Speak about people who inspire us.
>
> **Reading:** Read a poem.
>
> **Writing:** Write about an inspirational person.
>
> **Critical thinking:** Predicting, learning ways to find the meaning of words.

> **Vocabulary:** *superlatively, dozen, hoist, enormous, bulge, ripple, to and fro, juggle, airborne, somersault, champion, dozen, masterful, wrestle, comb, impressive, carry, expert*
>
> **Materials:** Dictionaries.

Learner's Book

 Warm up

- Ask learners if they remember a poem they have learned. Encourage them to recite it.
- Ask learners if there are any famous people they admire. Elicit some names.

1 🗨 Talk about it

- Ask learners to talk in pairs about people who inspire them and why.
- **Informal assessment opportunity:** Circulate, listening to learners' interactions and note down mistakes for future remedial work.

> **Answers**
> Learners' own answers.

2 Listen 🔆6

- Tell learners they are going to listen to two poems by Kenn Nesbit and Jack Prelutsky.
- Ask them if they have ever read anything by Kenn Nesbit. You may wish to give learners some information about him (see below).
- Play the audio at least twice.
- Then learners match a title with each poem.
- Check the answers as a class.

> **Audioscript:** Track 6
> See Learner's Book page 14.

> **Answers**
> Poem A: I am Super Samson Simpson
> Poem B: Our teacher's multi-talented

About the author

- Kenn Nesbit is a children's poet. He has written many collections of children's poetry and was Children's Poet Laureate from 2013 to 2015. He writes books of humorous poetry for children, such as *My Hippo Has the Hiccups* and *Revenge of the Lunch Ladies*. His work also appears in anthologies of humorous children's poetry. Nesbitt's poems usually make fun of school life. For more information visit http://www.poetry4kids.com/

3 Listen

- Ask learners to look at the illustrations and match them with lines from the poems.
- Check answers as a class and ask learners what helped them decide.
- **Critical thinking:** Ask learners if matching the pictures to the lines has helped them to understand

the poems better. What other ways are there to understand the meaning of new words?
- **Study skills:** Encourage learners to look for more new words and try to work out the meaning using the context.

> **Answers**
> **1** Poem A, line 2
> **2** Poem B, line 14
> **3** Poem A, line 3
> **4** Poem B, line 17
> **5** Poem B, line 8
> **6** Poem A, line 16
> **7** Poem B, line 3
> **8** Poem B, line 15
> **9** Poem B, line 18

4 Write

- Ask learners to write the sentences in their notebooks.
- Then, they read the sentences and re-read the poems on page 14 and decide if the sentences are true or false.
- Ask them to justify their decisions.

> **Answers**
> **1** true   **2** true   **3** false   **4** true   **5** false

[AB] **For further practice, see Activities 1 and 2 in the Activity Book.**

5 Word study

- Ask learners to look at the definitions and match them to the highlighted words in the poem.
- Tell learners to write the words and the definitions in their Vocabulary journal.

> **Answers**
> **1** a dozen
> **2** enormous
> **3** champion
> **4** to wrestle
> **5** hoist
> **6** superlatively

6 Read

- Tell learners to read Poem B again. They find and write the phrases in their notebook that mean *to be good at something.*
- Check the answers as a class.
- Ask learners to think of people who are good at something. They say what these people are good at using the phrases from the poem.
- Ask learners to write these sentences in their notebooks.

> **Answers**
> like an expert, quite a ..., something of a ..., a champion at ..., great at ..., masterful at ..., good at ...

7 Use of English

- Ask learners to write the words in their notebooks and find the definitions in a dictionary. Then they write the definitions.
- You may also ask learners to make sentences using the words.

Answers
1 something you admire or respect because it is special or important
2 to tidy your hair using a comb
3 to throw objects in the air and catch them
4 to hold something in your hands
5 to stick out in a round shape
6 a person with a high level of knowledge or skill about something

 For further practice, see Activities 3 and 4 in the Activity Book.

8 Talk

- In pairs, learners take turns to read a definition from **Activity 7** and guess the right word.
- **Informal assessment opportunity:** Circulate, listening to learners' interactions. Check for correct pronunciation.

Answers
Learners' own answers.

9 Write

- Ask learners to think about somebody who inspires them. Tell them to reflect on what makes this person so special.
- Then ask them to complete the sentences about them.
- Circulate, helping with additional vocabulary if necessary.
- When they have finished, ask a few learners to share their writing with the class.

Answers
Learners' own answers.

 For further practice, see Activity 5 in the Activity Book.

10 Rhyming words

- Tell learners to read the words and match those that rhyme.
- When they have finished, tell them they are going to listen to the recording and check if their answers are correct.
- Play the audio at least twice.

Audioscript: Track 7

air	spare
rings	sings
me	family
long	strong
possess	chess
cars	stars

Answers
air – spare, rings – sings, me – family, long – strong, possess – chess, cars – stars

11 Rhyming words

- Focus on the unfinished sentences and the words in the box.
- Ask learners to complete the poem with words from the box or with their own ideas.

Answers
Suggested answers:
She speaks more than **three languages**,
She's good at playing **the guitar**,
She likes to …
She's masterful at **archery**,
And not bad at **driving cars**.

 For further practice, see Activity 6 in the Activity Book.

Wrap up

- Learners read the poems they have written. You may ask them to write the poems on separate sheets of paper and display them in the classroom.
- **Portfolio opportunity:** Collect the poems and file them in the learners' portfolios.
- **Home–school opportunity:** Learners take their poems home and share them with the family.

Activity Book

1 📝 Read

- Learners read the poems *Super Samson Simpson* and *Our teacher's multi-talented* again (see Learner's Book page 14).
- They decide if the sentences are true or false.
- They correct the false sentences.
- Check the answers as a class.

Answers
1 false. He carries elephants all day long.
2 true
3 false. He can lift half a dozen elephants.
4 false. His grandma is the strongest.
5 true
6 true
7 true
8 false. We wish he'd learn how to comb his hair.

2 Vocabulary

- Learners work independently and complete the sentences with a word from the box.
- Check the answers as a class.

> **Answers**
> Suggested answers:
> **1** dozen
> **2** hoists
> **3** enormous
> **4** champion
> **5** wrestles
> **6** impressive

3 Vocabulary

- Learners find the noun in the text for the adjective *strong*.
- Check the answer as a class.

> **Answer**
> strength

4 Vocabulary

- Learners match the adjectives to the correct noun.
- Check the answers as a class.

> **Answers**
> **1** c　　**2** a　　**3** b

5 Vocabulary

- Learners complete Machine Man's profile using information from **Activity 2**.
- This could be done as a pair activity, if preferred.
- Check the answers as a class.

> **Answers**
> **Physical qualities:** enormous muscles, bionic legs
> **Talents:** he can pick up a dozen cars, he's a champion swimmer, he wrestles with tigers, he paints impressive pictures.

6 Write

- Learners write a poem about Machine Man using the information from his profile in **Activity 2**.
- Check the answers as a class.

> **Answers**
> Suggested answer:
> **Machine Man**
> His muscles **are enormous**
> His legs **are bionic** too,
> He's a champion **skiier**.
> And he **paints impressive pictures** too.

Differentiated instruction

Additional support and practice

- 🗩 Learners work in pairs and choose five words they have learned in this lesson. They write the words and the definitions on separate file cards.
- With a partner, they play a game. They put their cards on the table, face down. Then, they take turns to pick one card. If the card is a definition, they have to say the word it defines; if it is the word, they have to give a definition.

Extend and challenge

- Bring poems or books of poems by Kenn Nesbit or other poets who write for children. Ask learners to read the poems and choose the ones they like.
- They can copy a poem in their notebook and illustrate it. Then they read it to the class.
- Ask learners to explain why they have chosen a particular poem. What do they like about it? Encourage the class to give their opinion.
- If learners show interest in reading more, you may help them to search the Internet for more poems by this and other poets.

Lesson 6: Choose a project

Learner's Book pages: 18–19
Activity Book pages: 14–15

Lesson objectives

Listening: Listen to class presentations.
Speaking: Present your project to the class.
Reading: Read questions, instructions.
Writing: Write a profile or a report.

Language focus: Unit 1 Review

Materials

1 **My favourite famous person:** writing/drawing supplies, A4 sheets of paper, photographs, Internet access.
2 **The day I was born:** file cards, writing supplies, Internet access.

Learner's Book

🖙 Warm up

- Ask learners what they have enjoyed most in the unit.
- What new information have they learned? Which is their favourite new word?

Choose a project

- Learners choose an end-of-unit project to work on. Help them choose. Provide materials.

1 My favourite famous person

- Tell learners to read the questions and use them to organise their project.
- Tell them to use the Internet or reference books to find the information they need.
- Encourage them to introduce any interesting additional information they may find.

2 [1+2] The day I was born

- Tell learners to read the questions and answer them following the order in which they appear. This will help them organise their project.
- They ask parents or tutors for information or they can look it up on the Internet.

📨 Wrap up

- Learners present their work to the class.
- **Portfolio opportunity:** If possible, leave the student projects on display for a short while, then consider filing the projects, photos or scans of the work, in students' portfolios. Write the date on the work.

🗨 Reflect on your learning

- Learners think about what they have studied in the unit and answer the revision questions 1–7. Learners consider the Big question for the unit: *What personal qualities do we like to see in other people?*
- **Informal assessment opportunity:** Circulate as learners work. Informally assess their receptive and productive language skills. Ask questions. You may want to take notes on their responses.

Answers
Learners' own answers.

Look what I can do!

- **Aim:** to check that learners can do all the things from **Unit 1**.
- Review the *I can …* statements.
- Learners reflect on what aspects of the unit they have found most difficult and why.
- Do they have any ideas about how to overcome these difficulties? Encourage learners to think of strategies that may help them improve.
- Elicit what they liked most about this unit and encourage them to explain why.

Answers
Learners' own answers.

Unit 1 Revision

- Learners do the multiple-choice activity that revises the language covered in **Unit 1**.

Answers
1 c	7 c
2 b	8 b
3 b	9 c
4 b	10 b
5 c	11 b
6 a	

My global progress

- Tell learners to read the questions and think about what they have studied in this unit.
- Ask them to answer the questions. Encourage them to take time to reflect on their learning and give honest answers.
- **Portfolio opportunity:** If you have been filing learners' work all the way through this unit, you may find it useful to put all the work of this unit together. You may ask learners to make a cover for their unit work, decorating it with an image that represents what they have learned.

Photocopiable activity 1

Answers
1 What is her name? Her name is Evie.
2 Where is she from? She is from Liverpool.
3 Where does she live? She lives in the suburbs.
4 What is her pet's name? It is Night.
5 What is it? He is a black collie.
6 When does she go to school? Not too early.
7 Who is her best friend? Her best friend is Ryan.
8 What do they like doing? They like acting and reading theatre plays.
9 What is she planning to do when she finished school? She is planning to attend Drama School with Ryan

Photocopiable activity 2

Answers
interested; exciting; boring; depressed; frightened; disgusting

2 Staying healthy

Big question Why is it important to keep healthy?

Unit overview

In this unit learners will:

- talk about common illnesses and their symptoms
- read an article about malaria
- learn about healthy eating
- write a blog entry
- read and understand a world folktale.

Learners will build communication and literacy skills as they read and listen to texts about illnesses and healthy eating; listen to a story and an interview; read and write surveys and make charts to reflect the results; develop vocabulary study skills; speak about common illnesses and their symptoms; request and give advice; and write a blog entry.

At the end of the unit, they will apply and personalise what they have learned by working in small groups to complete a project of their choice: writing about a common illness or carrying out a health and food survey.

Language focus

Quantifiers

Countable and uncountable nouns

Should / shouldn't

Contrast linkers

Of to talk about collections of items

Vocabulary topics: collocations, illnesses and infections, food groups, classifying expressions

Critical thinking

- Healthy eating
- Helping each other
- Completing a table.

Self-assessment

- I can talk about common illnesses and their symptoms.
- I can understand an article about malaria.
- I can give advice on healthy eating.
- I can write a blog page entry.
- I can understand a world folktale.

Teaching tip

Some of the listening activities involve listening to lots of information and lower-level learners may find them rather difficult. So it will be useful to revise strategies for overcoming these difficulties. Before listening, discuss ideas with learners to help them make predictions about what they will hear. Ask them to predict the kind of information or words they expect to hear. Write some of the new or key vocabulary on the board and encourage learners to work out the meaning.

Review the learners' work, noting areas where they demonstrate strength and areas where they need additional instruction and practice. Use this information to customise your teaching as you continue to **Unit 3**.

Lesson 1: Staying healthy

Learner's Book pages: 20–21

Activity Book pages: 16–17

Lesson objectives

Listening: Listen for information.

Speaking: Practise theme vocabulary, talk about common illnesses and their symptoms.

Reading: Read for information, make predictions.

Language focus: *I feel/she feels …, I've got/She's got …, What's the matter?, What's the matter with (her)?*

Vocabulary: Collocations, common illnesses and symptoms: *sore throat, cold, cough, earache, fever, headache, stomach ache, energy, voice, sick, itchy, shivering, runny nose, tummy, hurt, sweating, chesty cough, blocked nose, dizzy*

Materials: Dictionaries, copies of **Photocopiable activity 3.**

Learner's Book

Warm up

- Ask learners how they are feeling, e.g. *energetic, tired, sleepy*. Have they slept well? If someone hasn't, ask what they did to solve the problem.
- Ask learners if they ever get ill. What illnesses have they had? Elicit some names of illnesses, e.g. *flu, a cold*.

1 ▢ Talk about it

- In pairs, learners talk about illnesses. They ask each other about the last time they were ill, the symptoms they had and when they get ill more frequently.
- Circulate, helping with extra vocabulary as needed. You may write the new words on the board for future use.

> **Answers**
> Learners' own answers.

2 Word study

- Ask learners to look at the words in the box and say which illnesses they have had. How did they feel? Elicit some answers from the class.
- Encourage learners to look up the words they don't know in the dictionary.
- **Study skills:** Elicit the definitions from learners and ask them to write the words and the meanings in their Vocabulary journal. They may write a sentence to contextualise the word.

3 Word study

- Focus on the pictures. Ask learners to match the words in **Activity 2** to the pictures.
- What illnesses can't they find? (earache)
- Check the answers as a class.

> **Answers**
> a a cough
> b a cold
> c a fever
> d sore throat
> e headache
> f stomach ache

> **Answers**
> Learners' own answers.

 For further practice, see Activity 1 in the Activity Book.

4 Listen ⑧

- Tell learners they are going to listen to the conversations between a doctor and some patients. They decide what illness the patients are suffering from.
- Play the audio at least twice. Ask learners to write down words that help them decide.
- Play the audio again and pause after each speaker. Ask learners what illness is being described.

> **Audioscript:** Track 8
>
> **1**
>
> **Doctor:** Hello, Maria. What's the matter?
>
> **Maria:** Well, I've got stomach ache and I feel sick.
>
> **Doctor:** How long has it been hurting you?
>
> **Maria:** Since yesterday afternoon when I came back from my friend's party.
>
> **Doctor:** What did you eat?
>
> **Maria:** I ate a few sandwiches, some crisps and two large slices of chocolate cake.
>
> **Doctor:** Hmm, well it sounds to me like you ate too much chocolate cake. You need to drink lots of water today and no chocolate!
>
> **2**
>
> **Doctor:** Hello Abdul. What seems to be the matter?
>
> **Abdul:** I've got a sore throat and I've lost my voice.
>
> **Doctor:** Yes, I can hear. Let's have a look at your throat. Say, *arrr …* Yes, it's very red. Does it hurt when you swallow?
>
> **Abdul:** Yes it does.
>
> **Doctor:** Well, you need to drink a lot of liquids and take this medicine twice a day.
>
> **3**
>
> **Doctor:** Hello Maya, What's the matter?
>
> **Maya:** I feel very cold and I keep shivering. My head hurts too.
>
> **Doctor:** Have you been sweating at night?
>
> **Maya:** Yes, a lot.

Doctor: Well I think you have a cold and a fever. Let me take your temperature. Open your mouth and put the thermometer under your tongue.

...

Oh yes, 38.5. You'll need to take this medicine every four hours and drink lots of water and fruit juices.

4

Doctor: Hello Jess. What's wrong?

Jess: Well, I keep sneezing all the time and I've got earache too.

Doctor: Have you been coughing?

Jess: No, I haven't, but I feel dizzy and I've got a very blocked nose.

Doctor: OK, you are dizzy because of the earache and you've got a cold. You need to keep warm, rest and drink lots of water. I'll give you some medicine for the earache.

Answers
1 stomach ache
2 sore throat
3 a cold and a fever
4 earache and a cold

5 Listen

- Focus on the list of symptoms in the box. With learners, explain or mime what they mean.
- Then, ask learners to listen again to the audio (Track 8) and point to the symptoms they hear.
- Play the audio once again and ask learners to help you make a list of symptoms on the board.

Answers
1 tummy hurts, feel sick
2 lost voice
3 shivering, sweating, head hurts
4 blocked nose

6 Word study

- Focus on the words in the box and ask learners to match them with the phrases *I feel / (s)he feels ...* and *I've / (s)he's got ...*
- When they have finished, play the audio again (Track 8) and learners check their answers. Write the lists on the board with the learners' answers.
- Working together as a class, elicit more words from **Activities 3** and **5** that can be added.

Answers
I feel / (s)he feels cold, sick, dizzy.
I've got / (s)he's got a cold, a headache, a sore throat, a stomach ache, a blocked nose.

(AB) **For further practice, see Activity 2 in the Activity Book.**

7 Word study

- Focus on the sentences. Tell learners that they refer to the children in the pictures in **Activity 3**.
- Ask learners to complete the sentences using *He / She feels* or *He's / She's got*.
- Check the answers as a class.

Answers
1 **He's got** a headache.
2 **She's got** a sore throat.
3 **He's got** a cough.
4 **She's** got a cold.
5 She **feels** cold.
6 He **feels** sick.

(AB) **For further practice, see Activity 3 in the Activity Book.**

8 Talk

- In pairs, learners ask and answer questions about the children in the pictures following the model question.
- **Informal assessment opportunity:** Circulate, listening to learners' interactions and noting strong points and mistakes for remedial work.

Answers
Learners' own answers.

(AB) **For further practice, see Activity 4 in the ActivityBook.**

9 Talk

- In pairs, learners mime the illnesses and then ask and answer questions to guess what illness it is.
- Tell learners to use the model questions and answers to help them.

Answers
Learners' own answers.

Wrap up

- Turn **Activity 9** into a class competition. Divide the class into two teams. Teams take it in turns to mime the illness and guess.

Activity Book

1 Vocabulary

- Learners work in pairs and categorise the words. They write the symptoms next to the correct illness.
- Check the answers as a class.

Answers

Illness	Symptoms
a sore throat	lost voice
stomach ache	tummy hurts, feel sick
a cold	blocked nose, runny nose
a fever	shivering, no energy, sweating
a headache	head hurts
a cough	chesty cough

2 Collocations

- Learners read the sick notes and circle the correct words.
- Check the answers as a class.

Answers
1 got
2 feels
3 hasn't got
4 has got
5 feels
6 has got
7 is

3 Dialogues

- Learners work in pairs. They complete the dialogues using the words from the boxes.
- Then they match them to the correct picture.
- Check the answers as a class. Ask learners what helped them decide.

Answers
1 (picture A)	1 headache 2 sick 3 head hurts	
2 (picture B)	1 hot 2 fever 3 sweating	
3 (picture C)	1 headache 2 sore throat 3 voice	

4 Challenge

- Learners write their own dialogue using the prompts.
- They compare their dialogue with a partner.
- In pairs, learners act out their dialogues.

Answers
Learners' own answers.

Differentiated instruction

Additional support and practice

- In pairs, learners take it in turns to say a symptom and guess what the illness is.

Extend and challenge

- Ask learners to do **Photocopiable activity 3**. When they have solved it, check the answers as a class.
- You may ask learners to work in pairs to do the first part of the activity.
- For the second part, each learner makes a wordsearch. Then, they exchange it with a partner. They see how many words they can find.
- They challenge each other to make sentences with the words.

Photocopiable activity 3

Answers

S	T	O	M	A	C	H	A	C	H	E
O	C	O	L	D	F	E	E	Y	E	S
R	L	V	O	I	T	C	H	Y	A	W
E	O	I	C	Z	N	O	S	E	D	E
T	A	S	C	Y	X	I	L	L	A	A
H	F	E	E	L	V	S	S	I	C	K
R	U	N	N	Y	C	O	U	G	H	S
O	E	Y	E	A	C	F	E	V	E	R
A	S	H	I	V	E	R	I	N	G	S
T	U	M	M	Y	H	U	R	T	S	A

Across: stomach ache, cold, eyes, itchy, nose, feel, ill, sick, runny, cough, fever, shivering, tummy hurts
Down: sore throat, headache

Lesson 2: Fever

Learner's Book pages: 22–23
Activity Book pages: 18–19

Lesson objectives

Listening: Listen for specific information.

Speaking: Talk about being ill, talk about charities.

Reading: Read an information text.

Writing: Complete questions.

Critical thinking: Work with graphs.

Study skills: Using visual clues to predict the content of a text.

Language focus: Quantifiers

Vocabulary: *fever, temperature, infection, disease, infect, tropical, mosquito, parasite, vaccine, net*

Learner's Book

☞ Warm up

- Remind learners of the new words they learnt in **Lesson 1**.
- Play a guessing game to review illnesses and symptoms.
- Ask learners if there are any illnesses that are common in their country.

1 Talk about it

- Ask learners to read the explanation of what a fever is. Explain what °C means if necessary.
- Encourage them to work out the meaning of new words using the illustration.
- Discuss the questions as a class and supply additional vocabulary if necessary.

> **Answers**
> Learners' own answers.

Reading strategy

- Very often, texts are accompanied by pictures. Ask learners what the purpose of the pictures is (they show what the text is about). What other things can help them find out what a text is about? (titles)

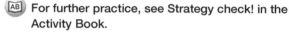 For further practice, see Strategy check! in the Activity Book.

2 🗩 Talk

- Ask learners to look at the photos and discuss what they think the text in **Activity 3** is about. Encourage them to explain their answers.
- You may wish to have an open class discussion afterwards.

> **Answers**
> Learners' own answers.

3 🖼 Read

- Ask learners to read the text. Encourage them to work out the meaning of new words from the context.
- When they have finished, they read the sentences and decide if they are true or false.
- Encourage learners to give reasons for their answers and to indicate the parts in the text where they found the information.
- **Study skills:** Ask learners to look up the new words in the dictionary. Then, they copy the words that they find most difficult in their Vocabulary journal along with the definitions.

> **Answers**
> 1 false
> 2 true
> 3 true
> 4 true
> 5 false
> 6 true

[AB] For further practice, see Activities 1 and 2 in the Activity Book.

4 Read

- Go through the explanation in the **Use of English** box with the class. Give examples of quantifiers and ask learners to supply their own.
- Ask learners to re-read the text about malaria and put the highlighted words in the correct column. With a partner, they check their answers.
- Check the answers as a class.

> **Answers**
>
> | Countable | Uncountable | Both |
> |-----------|-------------|------|
> | a few | much | some |
> | 1 many | any | no |
> | | 2 little | 4 a lot of |
> | | 3 all | 5 plenty of |

[AB] For further practice, see Activities 3 and 4 in the Activity Book.

5 🗩 Talk

- In pairs, learners discuss the questions.
- You may ask them to make notes of their ideas and have a class discussion afterwards focusing on the topic of charities.
- Elicit names of charities and ask learners to explain what they do. Do they think charity work is useful for the community? Why?

> **Answers**
> Learners' own answers.

6 Listen 9

- **Critical thinking:** Focus on the graph and ask learners what it is used for. Encourage them to think about how it works. What other information can they show on a graph like this? e.g. how much things cost over time, how far a car can go depending on the speed.
- Tell learners to listen to the audio recording and to copy and complete the graph.
- Play the audio at least twice.
- Check the answers as a class. You may copy the graph on the board and ask learners to come up and draw the answers.

> **Audioscript:** Track 9
>
> **Kodjo:** I started to feel ill in the evening. I had a headache and I felt a bit sick. Mum took my temperature, but it was normal – 37° centigrade. I started to feel much worse during the night and when mum took my temperature at 7 am it had risen to 37.5°C. By 8 am it was 38°C. I felt terrible and was sick a few times. Between 8 am and 11 am my temperature rose to 39.5°C.
>
> At 11 am Mum called the doctor. She said I should drink a lot of water, get some rest and have some medicine. She also said I should have plenty of fresh air in my room to keep me cool. Between 11 am and 2 pm my temperature dropped to 37.5°C and then I started to feel a bit better.

Answers

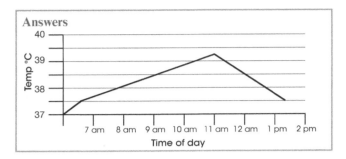

 For further practice, see Activity 5 in the Activity Book.

Wrap up

- As a class, ask learners to share their answers to **Activity 5** in the Activity Book. How similar or different are they?
- **Home–school opportunity:** Learners tell their family about malaria and the charity 'Malaria No More'. They may ask parents about other similar charities in their country and then share this information with the class.

Activity Book

Strategy check!

- Learners work individually and tick the strategies that will help them to make predictions.
- Then, they use the strategies before they read the text in **Activity 1**.

> **Answers**
> Look at pictures. ✓
> Look at the type of text (magazine article, leaflet …) ✓

1 Read

- Learners read and choose the best title for the article.
- Encourage them to justify their choice.
- Discuss as a class.

> **Answer**
> The flu

2 Read

- Tell learners to read the text again and underline items in the text with the colours indicated.
- Check the answers as a class.
- **Study skills:** Explain that using different colours to identify specific information will help them remember this information better. This technique is especially useful for those learners who are 'visual', that is, who learn better by 'seeing' things.

> **Answers**
> 1 Three illnesses (blue): flu, cold, fever
> 2 Four symptoms (red): runny nose, sneezing, coughing, headaches
> 3 Advice (green): get a lot of rest, drink plenty of liquids, take some medicine.

3 Use of English

- Tell learners to circle the correct answer. They can refer back to the information in the table in **Activity 4** of the Learner's Book for help.

> **Answers**
> 1 much
> 2 a little
> 3 plenty
> 4 some
> 5 many
> 6 some

4 Use of English

- Tell learners to use the five quantifiers highlighted in the text in **Activity 1** to complete the sentences.
- Check the answers as a class.

> **Answers**
> 1 a lot of
> 2 much, plenty of
> 3 many
> 4 some

5 Challenge

- Learners complete these sentences about themselves.
- They then write two examples of their own. Tell them to use quantifiers.
- Ask them to read their answer to the class.

> **Answers**
> Learners' own answers.

> **Differentiated instruction**
>
> **Additional support and practice**
> - Ask learners to find out about a serious illness that might be common in their country or in neighbouring countries, e.g. Chagas disease, sleeping sickness, dengue fever.
> - Tell them to make a few notes about the symptoms and the cause of these illnesses.
> - They then write a few sentences using this information.
>
> **Extend and challenge**
> - Learners work in pairs and look for information about charities in their country or region. They prepare a short presentation and make a poster.

Lesson 3: Food and health

Learner's Book pages: 24–25

Activity Book pages: 20–21

Lesson objectives

Listening: Listen and evaluate information.

Speaking Talk about healthy eating and food, make a presentation.

Writing Make notes for a presentation.

Critical thinking: Classify information, evaluate information.

Language focus *should/shouldn't*

Vocabulary: Food groups: *dairy, meat and fish, fruit and vegetables, bad fats and sweets, good fats and oils, grains and cereals*

Materials Copies of **Photocopiable activity 4**.

Learner's Book

Warm up

- Ask learners what the most popular food is among people of their own age. What do they like eating? Is there anything they don't like eating? Is there anything they never eat?
- Make a list of food words on the board.

1 🗨 Talk about it

- Ask learners to discuss if they think they eat a healthy diet. Encourage them to give reasons for their answers.
- Ask them to make a list of the kind of food they think is healthy and unhealthy.
- Have an open class conversation and ask learners to share their ideas.

Answers

Learners' own answers.

2 🖼 Word study

- Focus on the pictures and elicit the names of the food. Write the words on the board.
- Then, ask learners to look at the food groups and match the food to the correct category.
- Check the answers as a class. Are there any words that might go in more than one category?
- **Critical thinking:** Draw a table on the board with the food groups as column headings. Ask learners to classify food they know the words for.

Answers

1 fruit and vegetables
2 good fats and oils
3 grains and cereals
4 dairy
5 bad fats and sweets
6 meat and fish

3 Listen 🔟

- Ask learners to listen to the audio recording of Kaya's presentation on healthy eating.
- They listen and decide if she eats healthily or not. Play the audio at least twice.
- **Critical thinking:** learners listen and evaluate the information they hear in order to answer the question. Ask them to think about the balance of food. Does Kaya eat enough different types of food? Ask them to justify their answer. What information helped them decide?

Audioscript: Track 10

Kaya: Good morning everyone. My name's Kaya and I'm from class 5B. Today I'm going to talk about why it is important to eat healthily. Our bodies need to eat a balanced diet in order to grow strong and to fight infection and disease – if we don't eat well then we can get sick.

Fruit and vegetables

We should eat fruit and vegetables every day because they give us vitamins and minerals which our body needs to work properly. We should eat fruit as a snack instead of chocolate, sweets and cakes.

Grains and cereals

We should also include grains and cereals such as pasta, rice and bread in our diet. These foods provide our bodies with carbohydrates, which give us energy to do all the things we have to do every day.

Calcium

It is also important that we eat food that has a lot of calcium as this makes our bones and teeth strong. You can get calcium from dairy products such as milk, yogurt and cheese. In some countries people don't eat dairy foods but many vegetables like broccoli, carrots, soya beans and wasabi are very high in calcium.

Protein

Foods that have protein are meat, fish and eggs. Some people are vegetarian and so they eat more vegetables, grains and nuts, which all have protein in them and are important for our growth.

Finally, we can eat sweets, chocolates and cakes but you shouldn't eat them every day as they have a lot of fat and sugar, which can harm our teeth and bodies.

My typical lunch is a healthy balanced meal. I have vegetable soup to start, with a slice of bread. Then I have either fish or meat with vegetables and rice or potatoes. And for dessert I have a yogurt and a piece of fruit.

Answer

Yes

4 Listen

- Ask learners to listen to Kaya's presentation again and make notes. They copy the sentences and complete the notes in their notebooks.
- Play the audio again at least twice. Check the answers as a class.
- **Critical thinking:** You may wish to draw a table on the board and ask learners to fill in the information in table format. In this way they can transfer the information from one format in their notebooks to another.

Answers
1 minerals
2 pasta
3 rice
4 bread
5 bones
6 teeth
7 vegetables, grains and nuts
8 teeth
9 bodies

 For further practice, see Activities 1 and 2 in the Activity Book.

Listening strategy

- Read the strategy with learners and highlight the importance of deciding what they think about the information they hear and giving reasons for their opinion.

5 Talk

- In pairs, learners discuss the information that Kaya gives. What do they think about it? Ask them to justify their answers.
- Focus on the **Use of English** box and give some more examples. Ask learners to give their own examples.
- Explain the word *nutritious,* e.g. *nutritious food contains substances that your body needs to stay healthy: a nutritious meal* (from *Cambridge English Dictionary online*)
- Encourage learners to give their opinions using *should/shouldn't.*

Answers
Learners' own answers.

 For further practice, see Activity 3 in the Activity Book.

6 Listen

- Tell learners to look at the sentences and listen to the recording once again. They decide if the sentences are true or false.
- Play the audio again and check the answers as a class.

Answers
1 true
2 false
3 true
4 false
5 false
6 true

 For further practice, see Activity 4 in the Activity Book.

Speaking tip

- Learners often read their notes instead of using them as a guide. Read the **Speaking tip** with the class and model how to speak without looking directly at the notes. Explain that they can always glance at their notes if they feel at a loss.

7 Choose a topic

- Tell learners to prepare their presentation. They choose one of the topics and then make notes of what they want to say.
- They can prepare the steps of their presentation and add to it by using the ideas in the **Present it!** box.
- **Critical thinking:** Explain that it is very useful to highlight important aspect of their notes by using arrows or colours. This will help learners find what they are looking for in their notes more easily.
- **Informal assessment opportunity:** Circulate, listening to learners and asking them questions while they are preparing the presentation. Make notes of their performance while they are making their presentation. You may wish to set up some remedial work on the most common mistakes you have observed.

Answers
Learners' own answers.

Wrap up

- When learners have finished, ask the class if they agree with the ideas given in each presentation and vote for the best presentation.
- **Home–school opportunity:** Learners discuss with the family how healthily they eat. Should they make any changes? Learners write a few sentences about their family's diet and make some recommendations for improvement.

Activity Book

1 Read

- Tell learners to work in pairs and do the food quiz.
- Check the answers as a class. Discuss any differences in the answers.

Answers
1 a   2 c   3 b   4 b   5 c   6 b

2 Read

- Learners read the words and categorise the food. Then they compare their answers with a partner.
- You may ask them to add more words to the categories.
- Check the answers as a class.

Answers

Proteins	Carbohydrates
eggs	rice
fish	bread
nuts	pasta
cheese	
chicken	
milk	

Vitamins and minerals	Fats and sugars
lettuce	oil
carrots	chocolate
apples	
bananas	
oranges	
green beans	
onion	

3 Use of English

- Learners complete the sentences with *should* or *shouldn't* and a verb from the box.
- Check the answers as a class.

Answers
1 should eat
2 should try
3 shouldn't put
4 should exercise
5 shouldn't drink
6 shouldn't spend

4 Challenge

- Learners write sentences in their notebook about the food they eat in a typical day.
- Then they read their sentences to the class.

Answers
Learners' own answers.

Differentiated instruction

Additional support and practice

- Ask learners to do **Photocopiable activity 4**. Ask them to describe the dish and explain why the sections are in different sizes (we have to eat different amounts of each type of food to have a balanced diet).
- Then they work independently to classify the food.
- They write a lunch menu trying to make it as healthy as possible. Then they compare their menu with a partner.

Extend and challenge

- Ask learners to work in small groups and choose one food group. They search the Internet for information about the benefits of the food group of their choice and write a short summary.
- They collect all the summaries and make a *Healthy eating* poster.

Lesson 4: Health blogs

Learner's book pages: 26–27
Activity book pages: 22–23

Lesson objectives

Speaking: Speak about why people go to the doctor, talk about likes and dislikes.

Reading: Read for information, read a health blog.

Writing: Write a blog entry.

Language focus: Contrast linkers: *although, however, in spite of, despite; Have you ever had a …? Yes, I have / No, I haven't*

Vocabulary: *vaccination, appointment, eyesight test, hearing test, prescription, blood test, ear infection, allergic reaction, skin rash, chest infection, sore throat, cough, homemade, itchy, intolerance, sensitive*

Learner's Book

Warm up

- Ask learners about what they ate the previous day. How healthy was the food? Did they drink any water?

1 Talk about it

- In pairs, learners discuss why people go to the doctor's. Encourage them to reflect on how often they go to the doctor's, when they went the last time and why.
- **Informal assessment opportunity:** Circulate, listening to learners and asking them questions. Make notes of their performance. You may wish to set up some remedial work on the most common mistakes you have noticed.

Answers
Learners' own answers.

2 Word study

- Ask learners to look at the pictures. Do they know the words for any of them?
- Ask them to look at the words in the box and match them to the correct picture.
- Check the answers as a class.

Answers
1 a prescription
2 an eyesight test
3 a hearing test
4 a blood test
5 a vaccination
6 an appointment

3 Word study

- Ask learners to read the sentences and choose the correct answer.
- Check the answers as a class.
- Ask learners if they have ever had one of the tests or a vaccination. When was the last time they had one?

Answers
1 b   2 b   3 c   4 b

4 Talk

- Ask learners to read the words in the box. Ask them to help you mime the meanings.
- Tell learners that they can use their dictionaries to help them.
- In pairs, learners take it in turns to ask and answer questions.

Answers
Learners' own answers.

[AB] **For further practice, see Activities 1 and 2 in the Activity Book.**

5 Read

- Tell learners to look at the text and decide what kind of text it is. Ask them to look at the layout to help them.
- Tell them to read the text and decide who the writers are and give reasons for their answer.
- Discuss as a class.

Answers
Blog text.
Learners' own answers.

Writing tip

- Focus on the **Writing tip** box and ask learners to find examples of contrast linkers in the blog text. Discuss the meaning with the class.
- Ask learners what they think these words are used for. Are there any similar words in their own language?
- Expand the explanation. You may wish to copy the examples on the board and ask learners to help you complete the sentences.
- Elicit more examples from learners.
  Although is followed by a subject and a verb. When it starts a sentence, it is followed by a comma at the end of the clause: *Although you can eat eggs, you may …*
  However starts a sentence and is followed by a comma: *However, after an hour …*
  In spite of and *despite* are followed by a gerund (*-ing* form) or by a noun: *Despite tomatoes being …*

 For further practice, see Activities 3 and 4 in the Activity Book.

6 Talk

- In pairs, learners talk about the writer's symptoms and the suggestions he is given.
- Then, they talk about food they like and dislike using contrast linkers.
- Model the dialogue with a learner first.
- **Informal assessment opportunity:** Circulate, listening to learners. Pay special attention to the use of linkers. Make notes of their performance. You may wish to set up some remedial work afterwards.

Answers
Learners' own answers.

Write

- Tell learners that they are going to write a blog entry about one of the illnesses in the unit.
- Go through the notes with the class and explain the steps they need to follow.
- Learners write their blog entry on a sheet of paper and pass it to a partner.
- The partner writes the diagnosis and advice.

Answers
Learners' own answers.

Wrap up

- Learners read their blog entry, the diagnosis and the advice to the class. The class decides if the diagnosis and advice are correct.
- **Portfolio opportunity:** Collect the pages and file them in the learners' portfolios.
- **Home–school opportunity:** Learners take their blog page home and share it with the family.

Activity Book

1 Vocabulary

- Learners work in pairs. They read the clues and do the health crossword.
- Check the answers as a class.

> **Answers**
> **Down**
> 1 eyesight test
> 2 vaccination
> 3 skin rash
> 4 hearing test
> 5 prescription
> **Across**
> 6 ear infection
> 7 cough

2 Read

- Learners read and match the descriptions to the health problem.
- Check the answers as a class.

> **Answers**
> 1 a sore throat
> 2 a chest infection
> 3 an allergic reaction

3 Writing tip

- Learners complete the sentences with words from the box.
- Tell the class that some words can be used more than once.
- Check the answers as a class.
- You may ask learners to write some more examples in their notebooks.

> **Answers**
> 1 despite
> 2 despite/in spite of
> 3 Although
> 4 Despite/In spite of

4 Challenge

- Ask learners to imagine they are a doctor.
- They have to write advice for one of the children with a health problem in **Activity 2**.
- Remind them to use *should* and *shouldn't* to give advice.
- Check the answers as a class.

> **Answers**
> Learners' own answers.

Differentiated instruction

Additional support and practice

- Learners write sentences in their vocabulary journal using the new words in Learner's Book **Activity 4**.
- For extra practice of linkers, write a few sentences, photocopy them and cut each sentence up into two halves, e.g. (first half) *I like dairy products a lot.* (second half) *However, I have a rash each time I have a yogurt.* Then, learners match the sentence halves.

Extend and challenge

- 🗨 Learners work in pairs and write a 'fill in the blanks' activity to practise linkers. They write at least five sentences with blanks for the linkers. Then, they exchange their activity with another pair and complete the sentences.

Lesson 5: Stone Soup

Learner's Book pages: 28–31
Activity Book pages: 24–25

Lesson objectives

Listening: Listen to a story.

Speaking: Speak about helping each other.

Reading: Read a story, read and answer questions.

Writing: Answer questions.

Critical thinking: Giving opinions.

Values: Helping each other.

Language focus: *of*

Vocabulary: *onions, chunk, cabbage, sack, potatoes, smooth, mushrooms, herbs, salt and pepper, beans, carrots*

Materials: Dictionaries.

Learner's Book

🖙 Warm up

- Ask learners if they like soup. What kind of soup do they like? What do they put in it?
- **Critical thinking:** Ask learners to look at the pictures. What do they think the text they are going to read is about. Ask them to give reasons for their answers.

1 🗨 Talk about it

- Ask learners to look at the ingredients for a soup and decide which one is odd. Accept answers but don't reveal the right one (the stone).
- Ask learners if they like the ingredients they see.
- What else would they put in the soup?

> **Answers**
> Learners' own answers.

2 Listen

- Tell learners they are going to listen to a story about soup. Tell them to read and listen and see if their answer to the question in **Activity 1** is correct.
- Play the audio at least twice. Talk about the answer as a class. Were they right?

Audioscript: Track 11
See Learner's Book pages 28–30.

3 Read

- Ask learners to read the text again and answer the questions.
- Tell them to refer to the **Glossary** box for the most difficult words.
- When they have answered, discuss as a class. Elicit opinions from learners.
- **Critical thinking:** Most of the questions require learners to reflect on the text and give their opinions.

Answers
Suggested answers:
1 Because he was so sad about the lack of food in the village. (Or perhaps because he was hungry himself and was tricking the villagers into feeding him?)
2 He gave him a large pot of water and a stirring spoon.
3 They gave him a head of cabbage, a bag of onions, a chunk of meat, a bunch of carrots, a sack of potatoes, a pinch of salt and pepper, and a bowl of beans.
4 He told them the soup would be better with more ingredients.
5 Learners' own answers.
6 Learners' own answers.
7 To help each other.

 For further practice, see Activities 1 and 2 in the Activity Book.

4 Read

- Focus on the **Word study** box. Ask learners to look at the examples and the explanation.
- Provide some more examples. Write them on the board and ask learners to copy them in their notebooks.
- Tell learners to read the story again and find classifiers for the items listed.
- Check the answers as a class.

Answers
a head of cabbage, a sack of potatoes, a pinch of salt and pepper, a chunk of meat, a bowl of beans, a bunch of carrots, a bag of onions

 For further practice, see Activity 3 in the Activity Book.

5 Listen

- Focus on the **Pronunciation** box. Read the explanation of what connected speech is and provide examples.
- Ask learners to listen and repeat the phrases from the story with connected speech.

- Do this at least twice and ask learners what happens to *of*. Ask them if they have noticed any difference in the pronunciation.

Audioscript: Track 12
a sack of potatoes
a pot of water
a bunch of carrots
a pinch of salt and pepper
a bowl of beans

 For further practice, see Activity 4 in the Activity Book.

6 Values

- Ask learners to think about the answers they gave to the questions in **Activity 3**. What value did the young man teach the villagers?
- As a class, discuss the questions. Ask learners about ways in which they can help at home.
- Focus on the illustrations and discuss question 2 with learners. Encourage them to think if they can do the same in their community.

Answers
Learners' own answers.

 For further practice, see Activities 5 and 6 in the Activity Book.

7 Resolutions

- Ask learners what they think a resolution is. Ask them when people are likely to make resolutions and of what kind, e.g. New Year, start a diet or go to the gym on Monday, study more next time.

Answers
Learners' own answers.

Wrap up

- Ask learners to write their resolution on a file card and read it to the class. Collect the cards and display them.
- Tell the class that they are going to read the resolutions again in a month and see how many have done what they promised.

Activity book

1 Read

- Learners read the story again and order the sentences that summarise it.
- Tell them to compare their answers with a partner.
- Check the answers as a class. Ask learners what helped them decide.

Answers
1 i   2 a   3 d   4 c   5 e   6 g
7 f   8 k   9 h   10 b   11 j

2 Read

- Learners read and circle the correct words.
- If they need help, they can re-read the text in the Learner's Book.
- Check the answers as a class.

> **Answers**
> 1 a   2 b   3 b   4 a   5 b

3 Vocabulary

- Learners label the food pictures with the correct expression.
- Check the answers as a class.

> **Answers**
> a a sack of potatoes
> b a pinch of salt / pepper
> c a bag of onions
> d a bowl of beans
> e a bunch of carrots
> f a head of cabbage

4 Pronunciation 58 [CD2 Track 27]

- Tell learners that you are going to play an audio recording.
- They listen and repeat the mini-dialogues.
- Then they identify words which are not pronounced clearly.
- Check the answers as a class.

> **Audioscript:** Track 58
> **1 Speaker 1:** What fruit did you buy?
>
> **Speaker 2:** I bought a bunch of grapes and a bag of oranges.
>
> **2 Speaker 1:** What would you like for lunch?
>
> **Speaker 2:** A bowl of soup please and some bread and butter.
>
> **3 Speaker 1:** Should I add some salt and pepper to the soup?
>
> **Speaker 2:** Yes, please, but not too much salt.

> **Answers**
> **1 Speaker 1:** did you; **Speaker 2:** of / of
> **2 Speaker 1:** for; **Speaker 2:** of / and
> **3 Speaker 1:** and

5 Values

- Learners read and circle the correct option for them.
- Discuss as a class.

> **Answers**
> Learners' own answers.

6 Challenge

- Learners write more examples of how they help others at home, at school or in their community.
- Share answers as a class.

> **Answers**
> Learners' own answers.

Differentiated instruction

Additional support and practice

- In small groups, learners make a poster about things they can do to help in their community.

Extend and challenge

- In pairs or small groups, learners look for a recipe for a soup or another dish that is popular in their country or region. They make it into a small poster.
- In small groups, learners choose one part in the story, e.g the young man at the door of the pretty-looking house. They write the dialogue, and then act it out.

Lesson 6: Choose a project

Learner's Book pages: 32–33
Activity Book pages: 26–27

> **Lesson objectives**
>
> **Listening:** Listen to survey questions.
> **Speaking:** Present your project to the class.
> **Reading:** Read questions, instructions.
> **Writing:** Write a survey.

> **Language focus: Unit 2** Review

> **Materials**
> 1 **A common illness:** writing / drawing supplies, A3 sheets of paper or large sheets of paper for the poster, Internet access.
> 2 **A health and food survey:** writing supplies, A3 sheet of paper for the chart.

Learner's Book

Warm up

- Ask learners what they have enjoyed most in the unit. What new information have they learned?
- Ask them what part of the story in **Lesson 5** they liked most.

Choose a project

- Learners choose an end-of-unit project to work on. Help them choose. Provide materials.

1 A common illness

- Tell learners to search the Internet or use the local library and find names of common illnesses. They can also choose one of common illnesses they learnt about in this unit.
- They choose an illness to write their project about. They read the questions and use them to organise their project.

- Encourage them to introduce any interesting additional information they may find.
- When they have finished, they prepare a poster or a PowerPoint presentation.

2 [image] A health and food survey

- Tell learners to follow the steps outlined in the Learner's Book. This will help them organise their project.
- They prepare the survey sheet. Tell them to use the questions in the book and add their own questions. They can use the questions in the book as a model.
- Learners circulate, asking the class their questions
- When they have finished, they collect the results and prepare a bar chart to reflect the results.
- They make a poster with the results.

[image] Wrap up

- Learners present their work to the class.
- **Portfolio opportunity:** If possible, leave the learner projects on display for a short while, then consider filing the projects, photos or scans of the work, in learners' portfolios. Write the date on the work.

[image] Reflect on your learning

- Learners think about what they have studied in the unit and answer the questions individually. Learners consider the Big question for the unit: *Why is it important to keep healthy?*
- **Informal assessment opportunity**: Circulate as learners work. Informally assess their receptive and productive language skills. Ask questions. You may want to take notes on their responses.

> **Answers**
> Learners' own answers.

Look what I can do!

- **Aim:** to check that learners can do all the things from **Unit 2**.
- Review the *I can …* statements. Learners reflect on what aspects of the unit they have found most difficult and why.
- Do they have any ideas about how to overcome these difficulties? Encourage learners to think of strategies that may help them improve.
- Ask learners what new things they have learned about health and food. Elicit what they found most interesting about this unit and encourage them to explain why.

Activity Book

Unit 2 Revision

1 Vocabulary

- Learners read and match the sentence halves.

> **Answers**
> 1 d   2 h   3 a   4 f   5 b   6 g   7 e   8 c

2 Use of English

- Learners read and circle the correct answer.

> **Answers**
> 1 should
> 2 little
> 3 a lot
> 4 some
> 5 shouldn't
> 6 much
> 7 plenty

3 Over to you

- Learners complete sentences about their diet.

> **Answers**
> Learners' own answers.

4 [image] Write

- Learners write sentences about the food they should and shouldn't eat in their diet and why.

> **Answers**
> Learners' own answers.

My global progress

- Tell learners to read the questions and think about what they have studied in this unit.
- Ask them to answer the questions. Encourage them to take time to reflect on their learning and give honest answers.
- **Portfolio opportunity:** If you have been filing learners' work all through this unit, you may find it useful to put all the work of this unit together. You may ask learners to make a cover for their work, decorating it with an image that represents what they have learnt.

Photocopiable activity 4

> **Answers**
> a fruits and vegetables; b protein; c grains;
> d not healthy lunch; e protein, f protein

Review 1

Learner's Book pages: 34–35

1 Listen [13]

- Learners listen to the interviews and complete the table.

> **Audioscript:** Track 13
>
> 1
>
> **Interviewer:** What's your name?
>
> **Peng:** I'm Peng and this is my sister Chang.
>
> **Interviewer:** How old are you?
>
> **Peng:** I'm 11 years old.
>
> **Interviewer:** What are your hobbies?
>
> **Peng:** Well, I quite like skating, but I prefer playing the violin. I'm really shy though, so I don't play for other people very often. My sister plays the violin too, but she's more confident than I am.

2

Interviewer: Hi, what's your name?

Maria: I'm Maria and this is my sister Ana.

Interviewer: How old are you?

Maria: I'm 12 years old.

Interviewer: Where are you from?

Maria: I'm from Mexico.

Interviewer: What are your hobbies?

Maria: I love playing basketball in the local park. I usually go with my sister, but she's a bit lazy and prefers reading her magazine on the park bench most of the time.

Interviewer: What are you like?

Maria: Well, I suppose I'm quite a generous, outgoing person, really.

3

Interviewer: Hello there! What's your name?

Brad: My name's Brad.

Interviewer: How old are you Brad?

Brad: I'm 11 years old.

Interviewer: Have you got any brothers or sisters?

Brad: Yes, here he is, my little brother Tom. He's eight.

Interviewer: What are your hobbies?

Brad: I'm crazy about surfing and because I live by the beach I can go every day. I'm really good at it!

Interviewer: What do your friends like about you Brad?

Brad: I suppose they think I'm cheerful and a sociable person.

> **Answers**
> 1 11
> 2 sister, Chang
> 3 skating, violin
> 4 shy
> 5 Maria
> 6 12
> 7 sister, Ana
> 8 basketball
> 9 Brad
> 10 11
> 11 brother, Tom
> 12 cheerful, sociable

2 Talk

- Learners interview their partner. They use the prompts to help them.

> **Answers**
> Learners' own answers.

3 Vocabulary

- Tell learners to read the clues and guess the words.

> **Answers**
> 1 hardworking
> 2 bad-tempered
> 3 headache
> 4 fever
> 5 appointment
> 6 excited
> 7 fruit and vegetables
> 8 dairy

4 Use of English

- Tell learners to choose the correct word to complete the sentences.

> **Answers**
> 1 a few
> 2 dizzy
> 3 I've got
> 4 feel
> 5 a lot of
> 6 appointment
> 7 have got
> 8 fever
> 9 prescription
> 10 a few
> 11 plenty of

5 Read

- Ask learners to read the health blog in **Activity 4** again and find examples of: an illness, symptoms and a recommendation.

> **Answers**
> **illness:** a cold, fever, ear infection
> **symptoms:** headache, dizzy, cough, feel hot and cold, shiver
> **recommendation:** go to the doctor's, eat fruit and vegetables, get plenty of rest

6 Write

- Tell learners to write a diagnosis and make recommendations for a person with the symptoms indicated using *should* to give advice.

> **Answers**
> Learners' own answers.

7 Talk

- Tell learners to describe a person who is an inspiration to them. Ask them to describe the personality of the person and the things they are good at.

> **Answers**
> Learners' own answers.

3 Where we live

Unit overview

In this unit learners will:
- compare the city and the country
- read and learn about our carbon footprint
- listen to a presentation about a city
- talk about the past
- write a descriptive essay
- read a story.

Learners will build communication and literacy skills as they read and listen to texts about country life and city life; discuss advantages and disadvantages of living in the city and the country; learn about the carbon footprint and how life has changed over time; develop vocabulary and study skills; make presentations; discuss fictional places; write a descriptive essay; and read a story.

At the end of the unit, they will apply and personalise what they have learned by working in small groups to complete a project of their choice: designing a poster about the environment or making a presentation.

Language focus

Comparatives and superlatives

Subordinate clauses

Giving opinions: *I believe ..., I know ..., I hope ..., I think ...*

Past simple

Vocabulary topics: describing places, home appliances, descriptive adjectives

Critical thinking
- Looking after our environment.

Self-assessment
- I can compare the city and the country.
- I can understand an article about our carbon footprint.
- I can create a presentation about the town where I live.
- I can talk about the town where I live and what it was like in the past.
- I can write a descriptive essay.
- I can understand and talk about the story *The Lost City.*

Teaching tip

Some of the reading activities involve reading a substantial amount of information and lower-level learners may find them rather difficult. So it will be useful to revise strategies for overcoming these difficulties. Before reading, ask learners to predict the kind of information or words they will find. Write some of the new or key vocabulary on the board and encourage them to work out the meaning. Ask learners to use titles and illustrations to help them.

Review learners' work, noting areas where they demonstrate strength and areas where they need additional instruction and practice. Use this information to customise your teaching as you continue to **Unit 4.**

Lesson 1: Where we live

Learner's Book pages: 36–37

Activity Book pages: 28–29

Lesson objectives

Listening: Listen to descriptions of places.

Speaking: Practise theme vocabulary, compare and contrast places.

Reading: Read for information, read descriptions.

Write: Describe a location.

Critical thinking: Compare and contrast, find advantages and disadvantages, give opinions.

Language focus: Comparatives and superlatives

Vocabulary: *road, office buildings, village, vehicle, path, pavement, lake, forest, mountains, field;* Adjectives: *beautiful, crowded, clean, peaceful, spectacular, noisy, pretty, popular, fresh, small, modern, ancient*

Materials: Dictionaries, map of the world, map of Ireland, photos of cities and countryside, copies of **Photocopiable activity 5**.

Learner's Book

👉 Warm up

• Ask learners to close their eyes and imagine what the ideal place to live would be like. Ask them to think about the things they would have in that place and what they could do.

• Allow them a little time to visualise the place. Then ask them to open their eyes and describe the place.

• Help them with additional vocabulary if necessary.

1 🗨 Talk about it

• Show the class picture of cities and of country scenes. Which do they prefer?

• Ask learners what they can find in a city. Elicit names of buildings and features of a city, e.g. *parks, tall buildings, cinemas.* What about the countryside?

• In pairs, learners talk about where they live, the country or the city. They say what they like about it.

• Circulate, helping with extra vocabulary as needed. You may write the new words on the board for future use.

• **Critical thinking:** Encourage learners to compare and contrast both places. They give opinions and justify them.

> **Answers**
> Learners' own answers.

2 🗨 Talk

• Ask learners to look at the photos and describe what they see.

• Tell them to discuss the advantages and disadvantages of living in each place.

• Ask them to make notes of their ideas.

> **Answers**
> Learners' own answers.

3 🗨 Word study

• Ask learners to look at the photos again and find the words in the box. Tell them to use the model for their conversations.

• Encourage them to look up the words they don't know in the dictionary.

• **Study skills:** Elicit the definitions from learners and ask them to write the words and the meanings in their Vocabulary journal.

> **Answers**
> Learners' own answers.

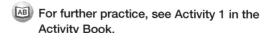 **For further practice, see Activity 1 in the Activity Book.**

4 Listen 14

• Tell learners they are going to listen to two children talking about where they live.

• Focus on the two pictures and ask learners to describe what they see in them. What do they think the children will say about these places? Elicit a few ideas as preparation for the listening activity.

• Play the audio at least twice. Learners listen and identify the place each child is talking about.

• Then elicit the answer from learners.

• Ask them to look at the adjectives in the box and ask learners to give examples using the adjectives to check the meaning.

• Play the audio again, and ask learners to classify the adjectives the children use to describe the places and find the adjective they both use to describe where they live.

• **Critical thinking:** What adjectives would learners use to describe the place where they live? Ask them to explain their answer, e.g. *I live in a city. It's noisy because there are a lot of cars and buses.*

> **Audioscript:** Track 14
>
> **Boy:** This is my city – Shanghai in China. It's on the East China coast and is one of the most crowded cities in the country. It's quite a noisy city but I love the colourful streets and the sound of busy people. It's very modern too with high-rise office buildings and spectacular towers. There is also an ancient part of the city, which is very popular with tourists.
>
> **Girl:** This is a photo of my village, Orta San Giulio in Italy. It is a beautiful, peaceful place located on the banks of the Orta lake. I love walking with my family and there are amazing mountains, forests and green hills – we often have picnics in the summer. It has a very small, pretty centre, which is very popular with tourists.

For further practice, see Activity 2 in the Activity Book.

5 Use of English

- Focus on the **Use of English** box and read the examples with the class.
- Read the questions one at a time and ask learners to reflect on the answers.
- Elicit the answers as a class and copy them on the board.
- **Study skills:** Encourage learners to write the answers in their notebooks as rules and to supply more examples. Give cues for learners to make sentences using the comparative and superlative.

 For further practice, see Activities 3 and 4 in the Activity Book.

6 Talk

- Ask learners to look at the pictures. Ask them where the places are (Ireland) and ask them to locate Ireland on a map of the world.
- If you have a map of Ireland, locate the two places on it too – Dublin and the Cork coast.
- Ask learners to describe the pictures using adjectives from the box in **Activity 4**.

7 Write

- Ask learners to describe and compare the pictures. Tell them to use the map to write about the location and to use comparatives and superlatives.
- Learners may also print a map of Ireland to accompany their work.
- **Informal assessment opportunity:** Circulate, asking learners questions about their work. Make notes about performance and mistakes for future remedial work.
- **Portfolio opportunity:** When learners have finished, ask them to write their name and the date, and file their writing in their portfolios.

8 Talk

- In pairs, learners discuss which place they would prefer to visit. Insist that they justify their answers.
- **Informal assessment opportunity:** Circulate listening to learners' interactions and noting strong points and mistakes for remedial work.
- **Critical thinking:** This is a good opportunity for learners to give opinions, to compare and contrast the places and also justify their answers.

☞ Wrap up

- When they have finished, learners share their preferences with the class. Then they can carry out a survey to see which place is the most popular and why.

Activity Book

1 Vocabulary

- Learners look at the pictures and complete the words.
- Check the answers as a class.

2 Vocabulary

- Learners circle the adjectives which best describe the city or the country.
- Check the answers as a class.

3 Read

- Learners read the text about visiting Buenos Aires in Argentina.
- They write the adjectives in their comparative or superlative form.

- Check the answers as a class.
- Ask learners if they would like to visit Buenos Aires. Why?

Answers
1 largest
2 most beautiful
3 best
4 colder
5 hotter
6 more humid
7 heavier
8 faster
9 cheaper
10 biggest

4 Challenge

- Learners compare their city or town to Buenos Aires in Argentina.
- They use comparatives and superlatives and the prompts.
- Check the answers as a class.

Answers
Learners' own answers.

Differentiated instruction

Additional support and practice

- Ask learners to compare the places in Learner's Book **Activity 2** and write some sentences about them using **Activity 7** as a model. Tell them to use comparative and superlative adjectives.

Extend and challenge

- Learners do **Photocopiable activity 5**. When learners have finished the activities, ask them to look for pictures to accompany their page. They can also add a map of the world and locate the cities on it.
- Ask learners to label their work with their name and the date and file it in their portfolios.

Lesson 2: Our carbon footprint

Learner's Book pages: 38–39
Activity Book pages: 30–31

Lesson objectives

Speaking: Talk about energy and the carbon footprint.

Reading: Read an information text, scan a text.

Critical thinking: Give opinions.

Language focus: Subordinate clauses

Vocabulary: *carbon, footprint, emissions, pole*

Materials: Copies of **Photocopiable activity 6**.

Warm up

- Remind learners of the new words they learned in **Lesson 1**.
- Ask learners how they think big cities affect the environment, e.g. clean air, space, noise.

1 Talk about it

- Ask learners to work in pairs. They look at the pictures and discuss the questions. Ask them to make notes of their answers.

Answers
Learners' own answers.

Reading strategy

- Scanning is a very useful reading strategy. Read the strategy with learners and explain how it can help them (they don't need to read the whole text to find the information they need).

[AB] For further practice, see Strategy check! in the Activity Book.

2 Read

- Ask learners to read the text and check if their ideas were correct.
- **Study skills:** Tell learners to look at the headings. How can headings help them locate the information they need?

Answers
Learners' own answers.

[AB] For further practice, see Activity 1 in the Activity Book.

3 Read

- Ask learners to re-read the text and identify any new words. Ask them to work out the meaning of new words from the context.
- When they have finished, they read the sentences and decide if they are true or false. Encourage them to give reasons for their answers and to indicate the parts in the text where they found the information.
- **Study skills:** Ask learners to look up the new words in the dictionary. Then, they copy the words that they find most difficult and the definitions in their Vocabulary journal.

Answers
1 true   2 true   3 true   4 false

4 Do a survey

- Individually, learners answer the questions.
- Then, in pairs, they discuss their answers. Encourage them to give reasons for their answers.
- You may ask them to make some notes of their ideas and have a class discussion afterwards focusing on how big or small the class' carbon footprint is.

> **Answers**
> Learners' own answers.

 For further practice, see Activities 2 and 3 in the Activity Book.

5 Use of English

- Read the explanation of subordinate clauses in the **Use of English** box. Provide more examples.
- Focus on the activity and ask learners to match the beginnings and endings of the sentences.
- Check the answers as a class. Ask learners to provide more examples.

> **Answers**
> Suggested answers:
> **1** b **2** a **3** d **4** c

 For further practice, see Activities 4 and 5 in the Activity Book.

6 Talk

- In pairs, learners discuss how energy is used at school and make notes of their ideas.
- Ask learners to consider the following: Is energy used correctly? Can they think of ways to improve the school's energy use? How?

> **Answers**
> Learners' own answers.

Wrap up

- As a class, learners discuss their lists and suggestions. They can vote for which suggestion is the easiest to carry out.
- **Home–school opportunity:** Learners tell their family about the carbon footprint. They make notes about energy use in their family. They may also ask parents how they use energy in their workplace.

Activity Book

Strategy check! Scanning

- Learners reflect on the strategies and tick those that will help them scan a text.
- Check the answers as a class.

> **Answers**
> Read the text quickly in order to locate information. ✓

1 Read

- Learners read the text and find two reasons why it's important to plant trees.
- Discuss as a class and ask learners to justify their choices.

> **Answers**
> Options:
> Because trees release oxygen making our air cleaner
> They make homes for animals
> They make the countryside look beautiful.
> They help us make a greener world.

2 Read

- Learners read and circle the correct answer.
- Check the answers as a class.

> **Answers**
> **1** less carbon dioxide
> **2** the air is cleaner
> **3** more than half
> **4** two hundred thousand
> **5** enjoyed

3 Use of English

- Ask learners to read the sentences and underline the subordinate clause in each sentence.
- Check the answers as a class.

> **Answers**
> **1** She decided to plant the tree **because it would help the environment**.
> **2** The children hope **that their campaign will help the environment**.
> **3** Scientists know **that planting more trees produces more oxygen for us to breathe**.

4 Use of English

- Tell learners to make sentences that are true for them using the words in the box.
- Ask them to share their sentences with the class.

> **Answers**
> Suggested answers:
> **1** I hope that we can reduce global warming.
> **2** I know that glaciers are melting.
> **3** I think that we should plant more trees
> **4** I believe that we should walk and cycle more instead of using the car.

Differentiated instruction

Additional support and practice

- Give each learner a copy of **Photocopiable activity 6**.
- Before doing this activity, review the information about the El Trapiche tree-planting project from page 30 of the Activity Book in Argentina and ask learners if they could do something similar in their city or neighbourhood.
- Elicit some ideas and supply additional vocabulary if necessary.

Extend and challenge

- Learners work in pairs and, using the notes they have made in this lesson and information they can collect from the Internet or reference books, they make a poster about energy use and ways of saving it.

Lesson 3: Past and present

Learner's Book pages: 40–41

Activity Book pages: 32–33

Lesson objectives

Listening: Listen and identify opinions.

Speaking: Speak about changes in a city or town, make a presentation.

Writing: Make notes for a presentation.

Critical thinking: Classify information, evaluate information.

Language focus: Past simple regular and irregular verbs; sequencing words; expressing opinion: *I think … , I (definitely) prefer … , I really like … , In my opinion …*

Vocabulary: *traffic lights, underground, horse-drawn carriage, washing machine, microwave, fridge, dishwasher, mobile phone, television, iron, cooker*

Materials: Photographs or pictures of cities now and in the past, Internet access, reference books.

Learner's Book

Warm up

- Show learners some photographs of cities in the past and today. Elicit some ideas on how they have changed. Are there more or fewer buildings? Are the buildings bigger or smaller? What about green areas?

1 Talk about it

- Ask learners to talk about the place where they live, how long they have lived there and how it has changed over the years.
- Then, they focus on the pictures of London and discuss how the city has changed.

Answers
Learners' own answers.

Listening strategy

- Focus on the expressions of opinion and tell learners that they should listen for these when they try to identify a speaker's opinion.
- Tell them that they would also use these expressions when giving their own opinion.
- Elicit examples by asking learners to say how they think London or their home town has changed.

(AB) For further practice, see Strategy check! in the Activity Book

2 Listen 15

- Ask learners to listen to the first part of Mia's presentation about her city and say what she prefers – the past or the present.
- Play the audio at least twice and elicit the answers from the class.
- What helped them decide on their answer?

Audioscript: Track 15

Part 1

Mia: I'm going to talk about my city, London. These are two photos of central London, past and present.

This is a photo from the year 1910. We can see the first cars, quite a lot of them! There is also a double-decker bus on the left hand side of the photo. If you look closely you can see the spiral stairs that the passengers climb to get to the top deck. I think I prefer these to modern day buses. The top deck has no roof, so it must have been great on a sunny day!

Part 2

In the present day photo we can see a lot of differences. There is a bicycle and some big, black taxis called Hackney cabs. There are double-decker buses in this photo too, but they are more modern. There is also an underground station in this photo which means the streets aren't as crowded as in the older photo. And there are traffic lights, which means it's easier to control the traffic.

I definitely prefer modern London because it's easier to travel around now as we have the underground, although I really like the old cars and buses.

Answer
In the present

3 Listen 15

- Focus on the words in the box. Check that learners understand the meaning.
- Ask learners to listen to the recording again and find out which vehicles and places are different in past- and present-day London.

- Play the audio at least twice again. Check the answers as a class.
- Ask learners to compare with their home town. Which of these things can they find in it? Is there an underground system?

Answers

	Past	Present
traffic lights	✗	✓
cars	✓	✓
buses	✓	✓
underground	✗	✓

 For further practice, see Activity 1 in the Activity Book.

4 Word study

- Focus on the pictures and the words in the box. Learners point to the things they can see in the picture.
- Ask learners which of these appliances they have at home.

Answers
1 fridge
2 mobile phone
3 television
4 iron
5 washing machine
6 cooker
7 dishwasher
8 microwave

 For further practice, see Activity 2 in the Activity Book.

5 Talk

- In pairs, learners discuss which of the appliances they think people used in 1910.
- Encourage learners to give their opinions using *I think that …, I'm sure that …, I know that …*

Answers
Learners' own answers.

6 Listen 16

- Tell learners to listen to the audio recording and check their answers to **Activity 5**.
- Play the audio again and check the answers as a class.

Audioscript: Track 16
Part 3

Mia: A hundred years ago English homes were very different from homes today. There was no electricity, so people cooked on stoves powered by oil or wood. There weren't any dishwashers to wash the pots and pans or microwaves to heat food quickly either, so life was much more difficult than it is today. There were no televisions – imagine that! And no mobile phones! People washed clothes by hand because there weren't any washing machines and some homes had oil irons to press clothes.

 For further practice, see Activities 3, 4 and 5 in the Activity Book.

7 Pronunciation 17

- Tell learners they are going to listen to the pronunciation of regular verbs in the past simple. Play the audio once. Ask them if they notice any difference in the final sounds.
- Explain that there are three different endings to regular verbs in the past. Ask them to listen again and put the verbs in the correct column.
- Play the audio a few more times.
- Check the answers as a class. Ask learners to help you copy the lists on the board.
- You may wish to ask learners to listen once again and say the verbs.

Audioscript: Track 17
needed
painted
cooked
washed
walked
travelled
cleaned
used

Answers

/id/	/t/	/d/
needed	cooked	travelled
painted	washed	cleaned
	walked	used

Speaking tip

- Write the sequencing words *first, then, next* and *finally* on the board.
- Ask learners what they think they can use these words for. Elicit ideas from the class.
- Focus on the explanation and the examples. Ask learners to give some examples of their own.

Present it!

- Tell learners that they are going to make a presentation about their town.
- Focus on the steps outlined in the box and tell learners to use them to organise their work.
- Give learners plenty of time to prepare their presentations.
- When they have finished, they rehearse their presentation with a partner.
- Then, they perform the presentation in front of the class.
- **Informal assessment opportunity:** Circulate, listening to learners and asking them questions while they are preparing the presentation. Make notes of their performance while they are making their presentation. You may wish to set up some remedial work on the most common mistakes you have observed.

> **Answers**
> Learners' own answers.

☞ Wrap up

- When learners have finished, ask the class to vote for the best presentation.

Activity Book

Strategy check!

- Learners read the sentences and tick the ones that express opinions.
- Check the answers as a class.

> **Answers**
> I prefer travelling by bus than by car. ✓
> I really like the old buses in my town. ✓

1 Listen 59 [CD2 Track 28]

- Learners listen to Cheung describe his city in the past and the present.
- They match the sentence halves to make sentences that express his opinions.
- Check the answers as a class.

Audioscript: Track 59

Cheung: Hi! I'm Cheung and I live in Beijing. One hundred years ago my city was very different to how it is today. In old Beijing, entire families lived together around a courtyard called a *Siheyuan*. Around the yard were small houses – one for the older family members, and another for the younger family members. There was also a sitting room and eating area for everyone to meet and eat. However, these houses didn't have proper kitchens, bathrooms or toilets, so I don't think life was very easy.

People walked or rode their bicycles to get around the city instead of going in the cars we see on the roads today. Today there are thousands and thousands of cars on the city streets. However, in my opinion we should ride our bikes more because the air in the city is very polluted.

Nowadays, many families live in small, high-rise apartment blocks. My apartment has all kinds of modern appliances. We've got a fridge, a microwave, a dishwasher, a television and mobile phones. I really like going out with my friends and we have lots of shopping malls and cinemas nearby, so there's lots to do in modern Beijing. I think that living in Beijing now is probably better than 100 years ago.

> **Answers**
> 1 b   2 d   3 a   4 e

2 Vocabulary 59 [CD2 Track 28]

- Learners listen again to Track 59 and tick the appliances Cheung mentions.
- Then they write the words under the pictures.
- Check the answers as a class.

> **Answers**
> microwave, television, dishwasher, mobile phone, fridge

Use of English

- Read the notes about regular and irregular verbs in the past simple. Ask learners to provide more examples of regular verbs in sentences.
- Write the infinitive of some irregular verbs on the board. Ask learners if they know the past tense forms for them. Elicit answers and write the correct forms on the board.
- Ask learners to write some sentences as examples in their notebooks.

3 Use of English

- Tell learners to match the present and the past simple of the verbs.
- Check the answers as a class.

> **Answers**
> have – had
> be – was/were
> ride – rode
> live – lived
> cook – cooked
> walk – walked

4 Use of English

- Learners complete the sentences with the correct form of the verb.
- Check the answers as a class.

> **Answers**
> 1 didn't have
> 2 walked, was
> 3 weren't
> 4 rode
> 5 lived
> 6 didn't use

5 Use of English

- Ask learners to read and complete the text with the correct form of the verbs in brackets.
- Check the answers as a class.

Answers
1 lived
2 didn't have
3 worked
4 didn't drive
5 walked
6 rode
7 didn't have
8 weren't

Differentiated instruction

Additional support and practice

- Offer extra opportunities to practise the affirmative and negative form of regular and irregular verbs. Write some verbs on the board. Learners make sentences about themselves using these verbs.
- In lower-level classes, ask learners to look for verbs in **Lessons 1** to **3** and write them in their notebooks with their past tense forms.

Extend and challenge

- Ask learners to write a few sentences using correct past tense forms about their memories of school a few years ago.

Lesson 4: Favourite fictional places

Learner's Book pages: 42–43
Activity Book pages: 34–35

Lesson objectives

Speaking: Speak about a favourite fictional place.

Reading: Read a descriptive essay.

Writing: Write a descriptive essay.

Language focus: Descriptive adjectives

Vocabulary: *magical, scary-looking, huge, enchanting, mysterious, colourful, exciting, exotic*

Materials: Dictionaries.

Learner's Book

Warm up

- Ask learners what kind of books they like reading, e.g. fantasy, science fiction, adventure, comics.
- Elicit a few book titles from them and ask what they are about.

1 Talk about it

- In pairs, learners talk about the last book or story they have read. Encourage them to speak about where the story is set and why it was special or unusual.
- You may wish to elicit a few book titles from the class after they have finished.

- **Informal assessment opportunity:** Circulate, listening to learners. Make notes of their performance. You may wish to set up some remedial work on the most common mistakes you have noticed.

Answers
Learners' own answers.

2 Talk

- Focus on the photos and ask learners if they recognise the places. Elicit the names from the class.
- In pairs, learners talk about the questions. Ask them to write down the adjectives they think they can use to describe the places shown in the photos.
- Elicit adjectives from the class. Write them on the board.

Answers
Learners' own answers.

3 Word study

- Ask learners to look at the pictures and the descriptive adjectives in the box.
- Ask them to look up the words they don't know in the dictionary. They write down the definitions in their Vocabulary journals.
- Which adjectives would they use to describe each place in **Activity 2**? Elicit answers as a class.

Answers
Learners' own answers.

[AB] **For further practice, see Activity 1 in the Activity Book.**

4 Word study

- Ask learners to read the sentences and choose adjectives from **Activity 3** to complete the sentences.
- Check the answers as a class.

Answers
1 scary-looking, magical, mysterious
2 magical, enchanting, mysterious, colourful/exotic, magical, colourful, scary-looking
3 exciting

[AB] **For further practice, see Activity 2 in the Activity Book.**

5 Talk

- Ask learners to talk about their favourite fictional place. Encourage them to give reasons for their answer and tell them to use words from the box.
- You may wish to ask learners to share their favourite fictional place with the class. Make a list on the board.

Answers
Learners' own answers.

6 Read

- Tell learners to read the text and decide which fictional place is being described.
- How do they know? Encourage them to justify their answers.

> **Answer**
> Pandora

 For further practice, see Activity 3 in the Activity Book.

7 Read

- Ask learners to read and answer the questions. These questions require learners to reflect on the structure and style of the text.
- You may ask them to work in pairs and discuss their answers.
- When they have finished, discuss the answers as a class.

> **Answers**
> 1 **Paragraph 1** Location
>   **Paragraph 2** Description
>   **Paragraph 3** Opinion
> 2 smaller, beautiful, exotic, lush, blue, purple, green, magical, tall, blue-skinned, scary.
> 3 I think that...
>   I'm not very keen on...

 For further practice, see Activities 4, 5 and 6 in the Activity Book.

Writing tip

- Focus on the writing tip about paragraphs and ask learners to organise their texts in the same way.

Write

- Tell learners that they are going to write a descriptive essay about their favourite fictional place.
- Go through the notes with the class and explain the steps to follow.
- Learners write their essay on a sheet of paper.
- They may search the Internet for images to accompany their essay.

> **Answers**
> Learners' own answers.

 For further practice, see Activity 7 in the Activity Book.

Wrap up

- Learners read their essay to the class. How many learners have chosen the same place? Are there places learners have never heard about?
- **Portfolio opportunity:** Collect the pages and file them in the learners' portfolios.
- **Home–school opportunity:** Learners take their essay home and share it with the family.

Activity Book

1 Vocabulary

- Learners look and match the adjectives to the picture they best describe.
- Check the answers as a class.

> **Answers**
> **Picture A**: magical, exciting, enchanting
> **Picture B**: huge, mysterious, scary-looking

2 Vocabulary

- Tell learners to substitute the words in bold with an adjective with a similar meaning from **Activity 1**.
- Check the answers as a class.

> **Answers**
> 1 huge
> 2 scary-looking
> 3 enchanting
> 4 mysterious
> 5 magical
> 6 exciting

3 Read

- Learners read the text and match the description to the correct picture.
- Check the answers as a class.

> **Answer**
> Picture B

4 Read

- Tell learners to re-read the text in **Activity 3** and answer the questions.
- Check the answers as a class.

> **Answers**
> 1 Paragraph 3
> 2 Paragraph 1
> 3 Paragraph 2

5 Read

- Ask learners to answer the questions about the text.
- Check the answers as a class.

> **Answers**
> 1 King Landorf, an army of beasts, gigantic black crows, lizard-like creatures.
> 2 dark clouds, a pale sun
> 3 Learners' own answers.

6 Read

- Ask learners to find words in bold in the text that mean the same as the definitions.
- Check the answers as a class.

Answers
1 miserable
2 strange
3 scary
4 gigantic
5 pale
6 desolate

7 Challenge

- Ask learners to draw a picture of their favourite fictional place.
- Tell them to think of adjectives to describe it and to organise their writing into three paragraphs.
- When they have finished, ask them to read their text to the class.
- **Portfolio opportunity:** File the texts in learners' portfolios.

Answers
Learners' own answers.

Differentiated instruction

Additional support and practice

- Learners write sentences in their Vocabulary journal using the new words in **Activity 3**.

Extend and challenge

- Learners work in pairs and create their own fictional place. They write a description using **Activity 6** in the Learner's Book as a model.

Lesson 5: Literature: *The Lost City*

Learner's Book pages: 44–47
Activity Book pages: 36–37

Lesson objectives

Listening: Listen to a story
Speaking: Speak about looking after the environment.
Reading: Read a story.
Writing: Answer questions.
Critical thinking: Give opinions.
Values: Looking after the environment.

Vocabulary: *valley, wondrous, ancient, trade route, bamboo, starving, roar, sparkle, jade, ivory, gold, silver, rubies, gong, chirp, magical, reward, precious, riches*

Materials: Dictionaries.

Learner's Book

Warm up

- Ask learners if they like stories about journeys. Have they read any? Elicit some names of stories from the class.

1 Talk about it

- Ask learners to talk about their travelling experiences. Have they ever been on a journey? Ask them to describe where they went and what they did.

Answers
Learners' own answers.

2 Talk about it

- Tell learners to look at the pictures and discuss the questions.
- Tell them to make some notes of their ideas.

Answers
Learners' own answers.

About the author

Margo Fallis was born in Edinburgh, Scotland. When she was seven, her family emigrated to Australia and three years later to the USA. Margo wrote for most of her life and drew her own illustrations. She loved travelling. She had a large family, so she started writing stories to read to her children. Then she started selling her stories to magazines and got a job writing children's stories. She ended up writing children's stories for Electric Scotland: http://www.electricscotland.com/kids/childrens_stories.htm

3 Listen and read 18

- Tell learners they are going to listen to the story.
- Tell the class to ignore any unknown vocabulary for the time being. They should concentrate on the general meaning of the story.
- Tell them to read and listen and see if their answers to the questions in **Activity 2** are correct.
- Play the audio at least twice. Check the answers as a class.

Audioscript: Track 18
See Learner's Book pages 44–47.

Answers
Learners' own answers.

4 Read

- Ask learners to read the first part of the text again and choose the correct answer for the questions.
- Check the answers as a class.
- Ask learners to guess the meaning of unfamiliar words from the context. Some words may be more difficult to guess, i.e. *wondrous*. Give a simpler adjective as a synonym (e.g. *amazing*).
- Proceed in the same way with the remaining sections of the text (**Activities 4** to **6**). Discuss the answers as a class.

- When learners have finished, ask them to write the words they have found the most difficult in their Vocabulary journal. They can draw a picture or write a definition to help them remember.
- **Critical thinking:** Ask learners to justify their choices when selecting an answer. What information in the text reflects their choice?
- Discuss the meaning of the story with the class. What was more important for Yong-Hu, the riches or the bamboo? Why?

> **Answers**
> **Activity 4: 1** a   **2** b   **3** c   **4** c   **5** b

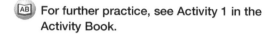 For further practice, see Activity 1 in the Activity Book.

5 Word study

- Ask learners to match the words in blue in the text with the definitions.
- Ask them to find the words and read the whole sentence they are in before deciding. This will help them contextualise the word.
- Check the answers as a class.

> **Answers**
> **1** chirp
> **2** bamboo
> **3** rubies
> **4** roar
> **5** jade
> **6** gong

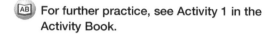 For further practice, see Activities 2, 3 and 4 in the Activity Book.

6 Word study

- Tell learners to read the story again and find the past simple forms of the verbs listed.
- They copy the verbs and the past forms in their notebooks.
- Check the answers as a class.
- Ask the class to make their own sentences using the verbs.

> **Answers**
> walked, heard, found, smiled, forgot, stood, ran, climbed, took, arrived

7 Word study

- Ask learners to complete the sentences with a verb from **Activity 8** in the past simple.
- Check the answers as a class.

> **Answers**
> **1** heard   **2** ran   **3** climbed   **4** forgot   **5** stood

 For further practice, see Activity 5 in the Activity Book.

8 Values

- Ask learners to think about the story. In pairs, they discuss the questions and make notes of their answers.

> **Answers**
> Learners' own answers.

 For further practice, see Activity 6 in the Activity Book.

Wrap up

- As a class, learners share their ideas on how to make cities cleaner.

Activity Book

1 Read

- Learners read the story again and match each sentence to the picture it describes.
- Check the answers as a class.

> **Answers**
> **1** c   **2** d   **3** a   **4** b

2 Read

- Ask learners to read the text and decide if the sentences are true or false.
- Then they correct the false sentences in their notebook.
- Check the answers as a class.

> **Answers**
> **1** true
> **2** false. Ho-Shing knows more about the Lost City.
> **3** true
> **4** false. It takes several hours.
> **5** false. He has a rest.
> **6** true

3 Vocabulary

- Complete each sentence with the correct word from the box.
- Check the answers as a class.

> **Answers**
> **1** chirp   **2** ruby   **3** reward   **4** roar   **5** sparkle

4 Read

- Learners answer the questions about the text.
- Check the answers as a class.

> **Answers**
> Suggested answers:
> 1 To find all the magical surprises.
> 2 The roar of a lion.
> 3 It takes several hours.
> 4 They have jewels on top.
> 5 A gong, a lot of bamboo and two lion statues.

5 Pronunciation 60 [CD2 Track 29]

- Tell learners you are going to play an audio recording.
- They listen and circle the verb that sounds different.
- Check the answers as a class.
- Play the audio again and ask learners to repeat.

> **Audioscript:** Track 60
> 1
> cooked
> watched
> started
> 2
> lived
> played
> needed
> 3
> painted
> washed
> talked

> **Answers**
> 1 started   2 needed   3 painted

6 📝 Values

- Learners look at the pictures and write about ways in which we can look after our environment.
- Then they share their ideas with the class.

> **Answers**
> Learners' own answers.

Differentiated instruction

Additional support and practice

- 💬 In small groups, learners choose one part of the story and act it out.

Extend and challenge

- 💬 In small groups, ask learners to make a poster about things they can do to look after the environment. Then, they make a presentation.

Lesson 6: Choose a project

Learner's Book pages: 48–49
Activity Book pages: 38–39

Lesson objectives

Listening: Listen to class presentations.
Speaking: Present your project to the class.
Reading: Read questions, instructions.
Writing: Write notes for a presentation.

Language focus: Unit 3 Review

Materials

1 **Design a poster:** writing/drawing supplies, A3 sheets of paper or large sheets of paper for the poster, Internet access.

2 **A presentation: How to become an eco-school:** writing supplies, A3 sheet of paper for the poster.

Learner's Book

📩 Warm up

- Ask learners what they have enjoyed most in the unit. What new information have they learned?
- Ask them what part of the story in **Lesson 5** they liked most.

Choose a project

- Learners choose an end-of-unit project to work on. Help them choose. Provide materials.

1 Design a poster

- Tell learners to read the steps outlined in the Learner's Book and use them to organise their project.
- Encourage them to look for and include in their poster any additional information they may find on the Internet or in reference books.

2 A presentation: How to become an eco-school

- Tell learners to follow the steps. This will help them organise their project.
- Learners prepare their presentation. They make a poster to accompany the presentation.

📩 Wrap up

- Learners present their work to the class.
- **Portfolio opportunity:** If possible, leave the student projects on display for a short while, then consider filing the projects, photos or scans of the work, in students' portfolios. Write the date on the work.

🗣 Reflect on your learning

- Learners answer the questions in their notebooks or on a separate sheet of paper. Learners consider the Big question for the unit: *Where would be an ideal place to live and why?*
- **Informal assessment opportunity:** Circulate as learners work. Informally assess their receptive and productive language skills. Ask questions. You may want to take notes on their responses.

Answers
Learners' own answers.

Look what I can do!

- **Aim:** to check that learners can do all the things from **Unit 3**.
- Review the *I can …* statements.
- Learners reflect on what aspects of the unit they have found most difficult and why.
- Do they have any ideas about how to overcome these difficulties? Encourage learners to think of strategies that may help them improve.
- Have they noticed an improvement in any aspect of their learning?
- Elicit what learners liked most about this unit and encourage them to explain why.

Answers
Learners' own answers.

Activity Book

Unit 3 Revision

1 Crossword

- Learners read the clues and complete the crossword.
- Check the answers as a class.

Answers
Down
1 dishwasher
2 ancient
3 pavement
6 recycle
8 fridge
Across
4 peaceful
5 fresh
7 scary-looking
8 forest
9 huge

My global progress

- Tell learners to read the questions and think about what they have studied in this unit.
- Ask them to answer the questions. Encourage them to take time to reflect on their learning and give honest answers.
- **Portfolio opportunity:** If you have been filing learners' work all along this unit, you may find it useful to put all the work of this unit together. You may ask learners to make a cover for their unit work, decorating it with an image that represents what they have learned.

4 Celebrations

Big question Is your culture really that different from others?

Unit overview

In this unit learners will:
- talk about celebrations
- read and learn about a celebration
- listen to children from different cultures describing a celebration
- read and perform a poem
- talk and write about the future
- write an email.

Learners will build communication and literacy skills as they read and listen to texts about different celebrations around the world; solve maths problems; speak about celebrations in their country and in their family and compare them to those in other cultures; learn about symbols and recipes and plan a party; develop vocabulary study skills; speak about the future; and learn to use defining relative clauses and linkers of addition.

At the end of the unit, they will apply and personalise what they have learned by working in small groups to complete a project of their choice: designing a poster for a celebration or writing an article.

Language focus
Defining relative clauses

Future with *will*

Linkers of addition: *and, both, too, also, as well*

Vocabulary topics: celebration words, telling the time, age groups, symbols, food, antonyms

Critical thinking
- Analysing information
- Giving opinions
- Predicting
- Comparing and contrasting.

Self-assessment
- I can talk about celebrations in my country.
- I can understand an account of a celebration.
- I can give a presentation about a 'coming of age' celebration in my culture.
- I can talk and write about the future.
- I can write about a celebration.
- I can understand and perform a poem.

Teaching tip

When doing a writing activity, writing a description or a story, encourage learners to follow the steps outlined in the activity as these will help them organise their text. Point out to learners how important it is that texts are well organised and divided into paragraphs.

Review learners' work, noting areas where they demonstrate strength and areas where they need additional instruction and practice. Use this information to customise your teaching as you continue to **Unit 5**.

Lesson 1: Celebrations

Learner's Book pages: 50–51

Activity Book pages: 40–41

Lesson objectives

Listening: Listen to descriptions of celebrations in different cultures.

Speaking: Practise theme vocabulary, speak about celebrations.

Reading: Read about celebrations in different countries.

Write: Complete notes and sentences.

Critical thinking: Problem solving, analyse, make inferences.

Language focus: Telling the time; useful phrases: … *is celebrated in …, it lasts for …, people decorate/have/go …, the festival celebrates …*

Vocabulary: *costumes, fireworks, feast, decorations, parades, lantern, symbol, light, paint*

Materials: Dictionaries, globe or map of the world.

Learner's Book

👉 Warm up

- Ask learners what celebrations are popular in their country. Write the names on the board.
- Ask them if they know the names of celebrations in other countries.
- What do they know about celebrations in other countries? How different or similar are they? Discuss briefly as a class.

1 🗨 Talk about it

- In pairs, learners talk about celebrations and holidays that are important in their family. They say which their favourite celebration is and why.
- Circulate, helping with additional vocabulary if necessary.
- **Critical thinking:** Encourage learners to give opinions and justify them.

Answers
Learners' own answers.

2 Word study

- Ask learners to look at the photos and describe what they see.
- Tell them to look at the words in the box and look up the ones they don't know in the dictionary.
- Ask them how many of the words in the box they can find in the pictures.
- **Study skills:** Elicit the definitions from learners and ask them to write the words and the meanings in their Vocabulary journal.

Answers
costumes, decorations, parades, lanterns, symbols, paint

 For further practice, see Activities 1 and 2 in the Activity Book.

3 Listen 19

- Tell learners they are going to listen to a girl describing a celebration. They listen and identify the relevant photo in **Activity 1**. They also listen and find what she likes about the celebration.
- Play the audio at least twice. Then elicit the answers from learners. Which words helped them decide?

Audioscript: Track 19

Girl: My favourite part of the New Year celebrations in my country is the lantern festival. We hang the lanterns from the windows in our houses and we carry them along the street too. Everywhere looks so pretty and magical! In my town we have a dragon dance as well which marks the end of the New Year. A dragon, which is made of paper and silk, is carried along the street by boys who dance underneath it. It's great fun!

Answers
Photo b: Chinese New Year.
She likes the lantern festival because everything looks so pretty and magical.

4 🗨 Talk

- Ask learners to look at the pictures again. Ask them which celebration they would like to go to and why.
- **Informal assessment opportunity:** Circulate, listening to learners' interactions and noting strong points and mistakes for remedial work.

Answers
Learners' own answers.

5 🔢 Problem solving

- Draw some clock faces and review telling the time, e.g. *It's 10 o'clock, half past …, quarter to …*
- On a map or globe, ask learners to find the cities listed in the activity.
- Explain that with am/pm the day is divided into the 12 hours before noon (the am hours) and the 12 hours after noon (the pm hours). 12 noon is followed by 12.01 pm while 12 midnight is followed by 12.01 am.
- With more advanced classes you may tell learners that am and pm stand for the Latin expressions 'ante meridiem' and 'post meridiem', meaning before and after midday respectively.
- Focus on the activity and ask learners to change the times in the 24-hour clock to the 12-hour clock time.
- **Critical thinking:** This problem-solving activity will require learners to analyse and make inferences in order to solve the problem. Allow plenty of time for learners to work independently.

For further practice, see Activity 3 in the Activity Book.

6 Problem solving

- Ask learners what time New Year is celebrated around the world (midnight, 12 o'clock or 00:00)
- Focus on the questions. Ask learners to work in pairs or small groups.
- They look at **Activity 5** and find what the time difference is between cities.
- Then they answer the questions.

Answers
1 04:00
2 02:00

7 Listen

- Tell learners that they are going to listen to a description of two different festivals and they are going to complete the notes. Tell them to write the notes in their notebooks.
- Before listening, write the name of the festivals on the board (*Diwali* and *Sham el Nessim*) as these will be difficult for learners to spell out from the pronunciation in the audio recording.
- Play the audio a few times. Pause after each festival to give learners time to complete the notes.
- Check the answers as a class.

Audioscript: Track 20

Speaker 1: *Diwali* is celebrated between mid-October and mid-November. It is the Hindu festival of lights. It lasts for five days. People decorate their homes in bright reds, greens and yellows and they light lots of oil lamps in their homes and gardens and in public places. Although the actual legends that go with the festival are different in different parts of India.

Speaker 2: *Sham el Nessim* is celebrated at the beginning of spring in Egypt. It lasts for one day and means 'the smell of spring'. Egyptians go to gardens and parks bringing the traditional food of the day with them, which is usually salted fish, coloured eggs and onions. The festival celebrates the start of spring and it was also celebrated by the ancient Egyptians.

Answers
1 *Diwali* is celebrated in **October–November**. It lasts for **five days**. People decorate **their homes in bright colours**.
2 *Sham el Nessim* is celebrated **at the beginning of spring**. It lasts for **one day**. Egyptians **go to gardens and parks**. The festival celebrates the **start of spring**.

 For further practice, see Activity 4 in the Activity Book.

8 Talk

- In pairs, learners use the phrases in **Activity 7** and the vocabulary in **Activity 2** to describe a festival or celebration in their own country.
- **Informal assessment opportunity:** Circulate, listening to learners' interactions and noting strong points and mistakes for remedial work.

For further practice, see Activity 5 in the Activity Book.

Wrap up

- When they have finished, learners share their chosen festival with the class.
- Then they can carry out a survey and see which celebration or festival is the most popular and why.

Activity Book

1 Vocabulary

- Ask learners to find and circle nine celebration words in the word search.
- Check the answers as a class.

Answers

C	O	S	T	U	M	E	S	C	F	U	D
N	T	G	O	C	D	K	Q	W	E	R	D
F	R	K	Q	T	E	L	Y	K	A	S	F
X	A	X	Z	A	C	A	D	S	S	S	I
I	D	R	L	L	O	N	Y	E	T	Y	R
C	I	P	O	W	R	T	I	M	P	M	E
N	T	A	J	L	A	E	A	U	M	B	W
G	I	R	H	I	T	R	Q	T	O	O	O
O	O	A	Q	G	I	N	A	S	Y	L	R
Q	N	D	D	H	O	S	O	O	B	M	K
N	S	E	N	T	N	I	G	C	R	Q	S
Z	R	S	M	S	S	E	Z	J	B	H	P

2 Vocabulary

- Learners complete the sentences with a word from **Activity 1**.
- Check the answers as a class.

> **Answers**
> 1 fireworks 2 feast 3 symbol 4 lanterns 5 parades 6 traditions

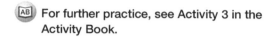 For further practice, see Activity 3 in the Activity Book.

3 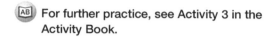 Problem solving

- Learners convert the clock times and write the time.
- Check the answers as a class.

> **Answers**
> 1 It's half past nine.
> 2 It's quarter to six.
> 3 It's quarter past four (in the morning).
> 4 It's twenty-five past six.
> 5 It's quarter to twelve (midnight).
> 6 It's twenty five to one (in the morning).

4 Read

- Learners read the text and complete the notes about the festival.
- Check the answers as a class.

> **Answers**
> **Name of festival:** Holi
> **When/celebrated?** end of February or early March
> **What it/celebrates?** that 'good' is better than 'bad'
> **How/long?** one day
> **How people celebrate:** light a bonfire, spray coloured water over each other, break a pot of buttermilk, form a human pyramid, eat traditional food.

5 Challenge

- Ask learners to think about a celebration they have been to.
- Then, they complete in their own words a description of this celebration.

> **Answers**
> Learners' own answers.

Differentiated instruction

Additional support and practice

- Ask learners to write a paragraph about the festival or celebration they spoke about in **Activity 8** of the Learner's Book.
- Tell them to look for pictures to illustrate their text.

Extend and challenge

- Learners search the Internet for information about the cities mentioned in this lesson. In pairs or small groups, they choose one and prepare a short presentation about it.

Lesson 2: The Rio Carnival

Learner's Book pages: 52–53

Activity Book pages: 42–43

Lesson objectives

Speaking: Talk about Carnival.

Reading: Read an information text.

Write: Complete sentences, join sentences.

Critical thinking: Visualise context.

Language focus: Defining relative clauses

Vocabulary: *carnival, colourful, parade, carnival float, costume, amazing, fabulous, rhythmic*

Materials: Drawing supplies, copies of **Photocopiable activity 7**.

Learner's Book

Warm up

- Remind learners of the celebrations and festivals they learnt about in **Lesson 1**.
- Ask them to look back at the pictures. Do they like the costumes the people are wearing in those festivals?
- Ask them if they like dressing up for celebrations.

1 Talk about it

- Ask learners to work in pairs. They look at the pictures and discuss the questions. Ask them to make notes of their answers.

> **Answers**
> Learners' own answers.

2 Read

- Ask learners to read the text and check if their ideas were correct.
- Ask learners to re-read the text and identify any new words. Ask them to work out the meaning of new words from the context.
- **Study skills:** Ask learners to look up the new words in the dictionary. Then, they copy the words that they find most difficult and the definitions in their Vocabulary journal.

> **Answers**
> Rio de Janeiro, Brazil Carnival

Reading strategy

- Read the strategy with learners and discuss how visualising can aid understanding.

 For further practice, see Strategy check! in the Activity Book.

3 Read

- Ask learners to read the text again and then close their eyes. Ask them to try and visualise the scene, i.e. create a mental picture.
- Then, they use this picture in their mind to answer the questions.
- **Critical thinking:** Visualising the scene while reading is a strategy that requires practice and continuity. It excites learners' imagination so it would be desirable for learners to do this simple exercise every time they encounter a text, especially a narrative or a description.

> **Answers**
> Suggested answers:
> 1 It's hot and sunny.
> 2 Yes, thousands of people.
> 3 Spectacular costumes.
> 4 They are singing, dancing, playing the drums, watching the Carnival and having fun.
> 5 You can hear samba music and drums.
> 6 Learners' own answers.

4 Read

- Tell learners to make a note of the words in the text that helped them make the mental picture.
- You may ask learners what other words evoke images for them.

> **Answers**
> Learners' own answers.

 For further practice, see Activity 1 in the Activity Book.

5 Use of English

- Read the explanation of defining relative clauses in the **Use of English** box. Ask learners to identify the sentences in the text and find more examples.
- Tell learners to match the sentence halves.

> **Answers**
> 1 b   2 c   3 d   4 a

 For further practice, see Activities 2 and 3 in the Activity Book.

6 Create it!

- Ask learners to imagine they are going to take part in the Carnival.
- Tell them to design the costume they are going to wear.
- When they have finished, they may write a few sentences to describe it.

> **Answers**
> Learners' own answers.

 For further practice, see Activity 4 in the Activity Book.

Wrap up

- When they have finished, learners show their costume design to the class.
- Learners vote for the most original, the prettiest, etc.

Activity Book

Strategy check!

- Tell learners to read and tick the strategies that will help them visualise a context.

> **Answers**
> Create a picture in your mind about what you are reading. ✓
> Use your imagination. ✓

1 Read

- Learners read Marco's account of the carnival in his city.
- Tell them to visualise the context as they read and then tick the picture that matches the celebration.
- Check the answers as a class.

> **Answer**
> Picture B

2 Use of English

- Learners read and circle the correct answer.
- Check the answers as a class.

> **Answers**
> 1 which   2 which   3 that   4 which   5 which

3 Use of English

- Learners join these sentences with a defining relative clause.
- Check the answers as a class.

> **Answers**
> 1 That's the giant **which** I saw yesterday.
> 2 That's the girl **who** was the Carnival queen.
> 3 I stayed in a hotel **which** was very expensive.
> 4 Venice is a famous city in Italy **which** also has a big Carnival celebration.
> 5 Those are the special cakes **which** we eat during Carnival.

4 Challenge

- Learners design and describe their own giant for the Carnival parade.
- **Home–school opportunity:** Learners take their costume design home and show it to the family.

Differentiated instruction

Additional support and practice

*   Give each learner a copy of **Photocopiable activity 7**. When they have finished, ask learners to write their sentences for the class on the board.
*   Ask the class to give the correct answers.

Extend and challenge

*   Choose a piece of music that is evocative, e.g. Celtic music, soft Brazilian or classical music. Tell learners that you are going to play the music and they are going to listen with their eyes closed.
*   Tell them to visualise images that the music evokes for them.
*   Then, they share with the class the images that the music inspired. They may also write a short paragraph about the images.

Lesson 3: Personal celebrations

Learner's Book pages: 54–55

Activity Book pages: 44–45

Lesson objectives

Listening: Listen and compare information, listen and complete a table.

Speaking: Speak about family celebrations, make a presentation.

Writing: Make notes for a presentation.

Critical thinking: Compare and contrast.

Language focus: Future simple: *will*

Vocabulary: *eat, light, receive, get, blow-out, sing, birthday, song, blessing, candles, cake, food, present*

Materials: Map of the world, Internet access.

Learner's Book

☞ Warm up

*   Ask learners how they celebrated their last birthday. Do they have any plans for the next one? What clothes did they wear?

1 ☁ Talk about it

*   Ask learners to talk about what age is special in their family. Do they celebrate the 18th birthday or a different age? Ask learners to talk about the sort of celebration they have in their family.

Answers
Learners' own answers.

Listening strategy

*   Read the strategy about making connections with the class.
*   **Critical thinking:** Ask learners to reflect on how this strategy may help them understand what they hear, e.g. they can anticipate the content and vocabulary they will hear, they will remember the content because they can relate to it personally.

2 Listen 21

*   Tell learners they are going to listen to three children from different cultures talking about their *coming of age* celebrations.
*   Ask learners what they think *coming of age* means.
*   Ask them to listen and find out if any of the celebrations are similar to the ones celebrated in their culture. You may ask them to make some notes to help them remember.
*   Play the audio at least twice and elicit the answers from the class.
*   Ask learners what words helped them understand.

Audioscript: Track 21

Speaker 1: My *Quinceañera* celebration

As a Mexican girl I will celebrate my coming of age when I am 15 years old. It's called the *Quinceañera* celebration and it celebrates the time when a girl becomes a young woman. For the ceremony I'll wear a beautiful ball dress and a tiara (a pretty headband) which will be a present from my family for my birthday. There will be a ceremony with family and friends and afterwards a reception (a type of party) where I will receive my gifts and celebrate with traditional food and music. I'm really excited because I'm having mine next year.

Speaker 2: My 21st birthday

Although some families in England celebrate the 18th birthday, in my family we like to celebrate the special age of 21. So, I won't have a big party when I'm 18, but I'll have a big birthday party with lots of family and friends when I'm 21. My birthday is in the summer so I'll probably have a party in the garden. My mum will make a big birthday cake and I'll get a birthday present that I will keep forever to remind me of my big day. Everyone will sing *Happy Birthday* and I'll blow out candles on my cake! I'm looking forward to the party – it'll be really good fun.

Speaker 3: My coming of age day

When I am 20 I will celebrate my 'coming of age' day. In Japan, this is the second Monday of January. I won't be a teenager anymore – I'll be an adult! On this special day I'll receive my first kimono (a traditional dress for Japanese women). Kimonos are very expensive and so I'll use it throughout my life for different ceremonies. During the ceremony I'll receive a blessing – my family will be there and they will sing songs and dance. After this, I'll go with my family to a restaurant and eat traditional food like sushi, noodles and rice. I'm looking forward to celebrating with my family and friends.

Answers
Learners' own answers.

3 Listen 21

- Focus on the pictures. Ask learners who they think the people in the pictures are.
- Tell them to listen to the recording again and match the pictures to the speakers.
- Play the audio at least twice again. Check the answers as a class.

> **Answers**
> Speaker 1 – b
> Speaker 2 – c
> Speaker 3 – a

4 Listen 21

- Tell learners to copy the table in their notebooks.
- Tell them to listen to the recording again and complete the table with the information they hear.
- Play the audio at least twice.
- Tell learners to compare their answers with a partner.
- Then, check the answers as a class.

> **Answers**
>
> | Country | A tradition | Age | Special clothes | A feast/ special food |
> |---------|-------------|-----|-----------------|------------------------|
> | Japan | Coming of age | 20 | kimono | sushi, noodles and rice |
> | Mexico | *Quinceañera* | 15 | ball gown and tiara | traditional feast |
> | England | 21st birthday | 21 | none | birthday cake |

5 Word study

- Focus on the words in the boxes. Check that learners understand the meaning of the words. Tell them to look up the meaning in the dictionary if necessary.
- Ask learners to match the verbs to the nouns to form phrases.
- Check the answers as a class.

> **Answers**
> eat – a cake/food
> light – candles
> receive – a blessing/a gift
> get – a gift/a blessing
> make – a cake
> sing – a song

 For further practice, see Activities 1, 2 and 3 in the Activity Book.

6 Use of English

- Ask learners to look at the **Use of English** box and say if the form *will/won't* changes or not. Read the notes and the examples. Provide some more examples and ask learners to provide their own.
- Write them on the board and ask learners to make negative sentences. Highlight the use of *will/won't* + infinitive.

- Tell learners to copy the examples in their notebooks.
- **Note on the use of *shall*:** It is not common to talk about future facts using *shall*. It is very formal and old-fashioned. It is more common in a literary context. However, it *is* used to make an offer or suggestion (*Shall I cook dinner tonight? We'll ask him later, shall we?*) or to ask someone what to do (*Which restaurant shall we go to?*) (Source: *Cambridge English Dictionary online.*)

7 Use of English

- Ask learners to read the sentences and complete them with the words from the box.
- Check the answers as a class.

> **Answers**
> 1 For the ceremony **I'll wear** a beautiful ball gown.
> 2 **I'll celebrate** my coming of age when I am twenty.
> 3 **I'll receive** gifts from my family and friends.
> 4 My mum **will make** a big birthday cake.
> 5 It **will be** really good fun!

 For further practice, see Activity 4 in the Activity Book.

> ### Speaking tip
>
> - Focus on the **Speaking tip** and explain that we can use information about our own lives when we want to make a presentation more personal.

> ### Present it
>
> - Tell learners that they are going to make a presentation about their coming of age celebration.
> - Focus on the steps outlined in the box and tell learners to use them to organise their work.
> - Then, they make their presentation to the class.
> - **Home–school opportunity:** Give learners plenty of time to prepare their presentations as this may involve asking family members for information.
> - **Critical thinking:** Encourage learners to give their opinion of the celebration. How important is it for them and for their family? Ask them to give reasons for their opinions.
> - **Informal assessment opportunity:** Circulate, listening to learners and asking them questions while they are preparing their presentation. Make notes on their performance. You may wish to set up some remedial work on the most common mistakes you have observed.
>
> > **Answers**
> > Learners' own answers.

 For further practice, see Activity 5 in the Activity Book.

Wrap up

- When learners have finished making their presentations, ask the class to comment on the celebrations, e.g. Do they have the same celebrations in their families? Do they celebrate these occasions in the same way?

Activity book

1 Read

- Ask learners to read the text and match each child to the correct information.
- Check the answers as a class.

Answers
1 c   2 a   3 b   4 f   5 e   6 d

2 Read

- Ask learners to read and answer the questions about their own celebrations.
- **Critical thinking:** When they have finished, ask learners to compare and contrast their answers with the information they have read in **Activity 1**. How similar or different are the celebrations?

Answers
Learners' own answers.

3 Vocabulary

- Tell learners to read the sentences and complete them with the correct word.
- Check the answers as a class.

Answers
1 food   2 get, cake   3 lights   4 song   5 blow out   6 blessing

4 Vocabulary

- Learners write questions and answers about Jack's next birthday.
- Check the answers as a class.

Answers
Suggested answers:
1 Will Jack have a party? No, he won't.
2 Will Jack go to the cinema? Yes, he will.
3 Will Jack get some presents? Yes, he will.
4 Will Jack have a special meal? No, he won't.
5 Will Jack have a birthday cake? Yes, he will.

5 Challenge

- Ask learners to write about how they will celebrate their next birthday.

Answers
Learners' own answers.

Differentiated instruction

Additional support and practice

- Offer extra opportunities to practise the affirmative and negative form of the future with *will*. Write some verbs on the board. Learners make sentences about themselves using these verbs in the future.
- Ask learners to copy the phrases in Learner's Book **Activity 5** in their notebooks and write an example sentence for each.

Extend and challenge

- Ask learners to work in small groups and choose one of the countries mentioned in this lesson.
- They search the Internet or use reference books and find information about traditions in that country.
- They prepare a short summary with pictures and share it with the class.

Lesson 4: Favourite things

Learner's Book pages: 56–57

Activity Book pages: 46–47

Lesson objectives

Speaking: Speak about the food people eat during celebrations.

Reading: Read about traditional symbols and Pancake Day, read a recipe.

Writing: Write a description of a celebration.

Critical thinking: Problem solving.

Language focus: adding information: *both, and, as well, too, also*

Review: Quantifiers: *more, little, some, any, few, less, fewer, not as many, not as much*

Vocabulary: *mixture, flour, flip, pancake, frying pan, mix, cook, serve, sugar, jam, syrup, shamrock, clover, mythical, zodiac, cornucopia, harvest, horn-shaped*

Materials: Dictionaries.

Learner's Book

Warm up

- Ask learners what their favourite food is. Elicit some food vocabulary.
- Is there any food they particularly dislike?

1 Talk about it

- Ask learners what food they eat on special occasions. Does the family buy or make any special food on certain days in the year?
- Ask them if they like this special food and how it tastes.

- Elicit some vocabulary and supply any additional words as necessary.
- Ask learners to copy these words in their Vocabulary journals.

Answers
Learners' own answers.

2   Talk

- Focus on the pictures in the *Pancake Day* text and ask learners to describe what they see.
- Ask learners to read the text. Encourage them to guess the meaning of unfamiliar words from the context. If necessary, tell them to use their dictionaries.
- In pairs, learners discuss the questions. Ask them to make notes of their answers.
- Take advantage of this activity to review the use of *more, little, some, any, few, less, fewer, not as many, not as much.*
- Have learners ever eaten pancakes? Would they like to eat them? Is there anything similar in their country or region?
- **Critical thinking:** Question 3 in this activity requires learners to do some maths. You may also ask them to work out the necessary ingredients to make enough pancakes for the whole class.

Answers
1 Learners' own answers.
2 Learners' own answers.
3 55g plain flour, pinch of salt, 1 egg, 100ml milk mixed with 37.5ml water, 25g butter

 For further practice, see Activity 1 in the Activity Book.

Writing tip

- Read the notes and examples with the class. Add some more examples of your own and elicit some from learners.
- You may write gapped sentences on the board and ask learners to supply the correct word.

3 Read

- Ask learners to look at the pictures and read the sentences. Elicit the meaning of unfamiliar words.
- Ask them to look up the words they don't know in the dictionary. They write down the definitions in their Vocabulary journals.
- Then, tell learners to re-read the sentences and choose the correct word.

Answers
1 and   2 too   3 also   4 and   5 as well

 For further practice, see Activities 2 and 3 in the Activity Book.

Write

- Tell learners that they are going to write the description of a celebration.
- Go through the notes with the class and explain the steps to follow.
- Learners write their description and the recipe on a sheet of paper.
- They may search the Internet for images to accompany the essay.
- They present their work to the class.

Answers
Learners' own answers.

 For further practice, see Activity 4 in the Activity Book.

Wrap up

- After learners have read their description to the class, they carry out a survey to find out how many learners have chosen the same celebration and the same recipe. Are there celebrations and recipes learners have never heard about?
- **Portfolio opportunity:** Collect the pages and file them in the learners' portfolios.
- **Home–school opportunity:** Learners may ask family members for recipes to include in their descriptions. Then, they take their work home and share it with the family.

Activity Book

1 Read

- Learners read and write the name of the special food under each picture.
- Check as a class.

Answers
1 Ghana – yam
2 Vietnam – moon cakes
3 Korea – *Songphyun* (rice cakes)

2 Read

- Learners complete the sentences with the correct linker of addition.
- Check as a class.

Answers
1 and   2 as well/too   3 also   4 Both   5 as well/too

3 Read

- Learners read the recipe for mashed yams with boiled eggs and match each instruction to the correct picture.
- Check as a class.

Answers
a 1   b 3   c 5   d 4   e 8   f 2   g 6   h 7

4 📝 Challenge

- Learners draw and describe a food they like to eat during harvest festival. Tell them to illustrate their text.
- Learners share their work with the class.

Answers
Learners' own answers.

Differentiated instruction

Additional support and practice

- 💬 Learners work in pairs. They write sentences using linkers of addition on slips of paper.
- They cut them up in halves and pass them to another pair. They try to match the sentence halves. Then they copy them in their notebooks.

Extend and challenge

- Learners choose one of the symbols in Learner's Book **Activity 3** and search the Internet for more information about the festival it is associated with.
- Then, they write a short description of the festival and illustrate it with pictures.

Lesson 5: Literature: *Horrid Henry's Birthday Party*

Learner's Book pages: 58–61

Activity Book pages: 48–49

Lesson objectives

Listening: Listen to a story, listen and answer questions.

Speaking: Speak about inviting friends to your house, describe yourself, plan a party.

Reading: Read a story.

Writing: Answer questions, plan a party.

Critical thinking: Make predictions, give opinions.

Language focus: Adjectives, antonyms

Vocabulary: *clever, moody, jolly, tough, lazy, anxious, weepy, rude, weak, cheerful, hardworking, miserable, calm, stupid, polite, dry-eyed*

Materials: Dictionaries, copies of **Photocopiable activity 8**.

Learner's Book

🗩 Warm up

- Ask learners if they have a favourite story character. Who is this character? What is he/she like? Elicit some information from the class.
- Tell them about your favourite story character.

1 🗩 Talk about it

- Ask learners if they invite friends to their house. If so, when do they invite them and what do they do?

Answers
Learners' own answers.

2 Listen and read 22

- **Critical thinking:** Focus on the illustrations. Ask learners to predict what the story is going to be about. Who do they think is the main character in the story? Why do they think so? What kind of person is Horrid Henry?
- Tell learners they are going to listen to a story about Horrid Henry.
- They listen to the recording and read the text. Ask them to find out what Horrid Henry is organising.

Audioscript: Track 22
See Learner's Book pages 58–59.

Answer
a birthday party

About the author

Francesca Simon, the author of Horrid Henry books, was born in the US. She attended Yale and Oxford universities where she majored in medieval studies and Old English. She also worked as a journalist. In 1989, she started to write children's books. She is one of the UK's best-selling children's writers and she has published over 50 different books, including the popular *Horrid Henry* series.

Henry has a brother called Perfect Peter, who is the exact opposite of Henry and is always respectful of other people.

For more information, visit: http://www.francescasimon.com/ http://www.horridhenry.co.uk/

3 Listen 22

- Tell learners they are going to listen to the story again and answer the questions.
- You may wish to ask them to answer without listening first to see how much they remember from the story.
- Then, play the audio a few times. Encourage learners to make notes.
- Then they answer the questions in their notebooks. Tell learners to compare their answers with their partners and then check the answers as a class.

Answers
1 13
2 the girls – Margaret, Susan, Clare and Linda
3 because he's no fun
4 no
5 because Ralph didn't invite Henry to *his* party
6 his brother
7 Henry has no guests on his list
8 annoyed because he won't get any presents

 For further practice, see Activity 1 in the Activity Book.

4 Word study

- Ask learners to match the words with the definitions.
- First, ask them to find the words in the text and read the sentence they are in. The context will help them understand the meaning.
- If learners still have difficulties, they may use their dictionaries.
- Check the answers as a class.
- Tell learners to write the words they have found the most difficult in their Vocabulary journal. They add a definition and an example.

Answers
1 c   2 e   3 f   4 a   5 g   6 h   7 b   8 d

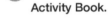 **For further practice, see Activities 2 and 3 in the Activity Book.**

5 Antonyms

- Tell learners to read the words and match the opposites.
- Tell them to use their dictionaries if they have difficulties with the meanings of words.
- Check the answers as a class.

Answers
weak – tough
clever – stupid
rude – polite
lazy – hardworking
jolly – moody
dry-eyed – weepy
cheerful – miserable
anxious – calm

 For further practice, see Activities 4 and 5 in the Activity Book.

6 Read

- Ask learners to read the text again and match the descriptive clues with the children on Henry's guest list.
- Check the answers as a class.

Answers
1 Jolly Josh
2 Clever Clare
3 Rude Ralph
4 Moody Margaret
5 Weepy William
6 Lazy Linda

7 Talk

- Ask learners to look at the adjectives again and decide which they would use to describe themselves.
- They compare their choices with their partners.

Answers
Learners' own answers.

8 Pronunciation 23

- Focus on the activity and tell learners that they are going to listen to the pronunciation of these words.
- Ask them if they know how they are pronounced.
- Play the audio a few times. Were they right?
- Tell them that you are going to play the audio again. In their notebook, they have to group the words that sound the same. Tell them that there are three different sounds.
- Play the audio at least twice again and check the answers as a class.
- Then, ask learners to read the words aloud. Check for correct pronunciation.

Audioscript: Track 23
1 tough
2 enough
3 bought
4 dough
5 rough
6 though
7 thought

Answers
Group 1: **1** tough **2** enough **5** rough
Group 2: **4** dough **6** though
Group 3: **3** bought **7** thought

 For further practice, see Activity 6 in the Activity Book.

9 Write

- Tell learners to write a guest list for their birthday.
- They have to explain why they want to invite each person. Tell them to use positive adjectives to describe each person.

Answers
Learners' own answers.

10 💬 Over to you

- Tell learners to plan a party in pairs.
- They use the questions to plan what they are going to do.
- When they have finished writing their plans (games, food, etc.) they make a poster advertising the party.
- They put up the poster in the classroom.
- They look at their classmates' posters and decide which party they would like to go to and why.
- **Informal assessment opportunity:** While learners are preparing their plans for the party, circulate asking questions and making notes on performance and mistakes.

☞ Wrap up

- Learners vote for the best/most original party and give reasons for their choice.

Activity book

1 Read

- Tell learners to read the extract on pages 58–59 of the Learner's Book again and say why Henry doesn't want these classmates to come to his party.
- Check the answers as a class.

> **Answers**
> 1 Because she's too moody.
> 2 Because she's too crabby.
> 3 Because he's no fun.
> 4 Because he doesn't like him.
> 5 Because he's weepy.
> 6 Because he wasn't invited to Ralph's party.

2 Read

- Learners unjumble the adjectives and match them to the classmates they describe on Henry's list.
- Tell learners to use the text in the Learner's Book to help them.
- Check the answers as a class.

> **Answers**
> Clever Clare
> Moody Margaret
> Anxious Andrew
> Rude Ralph
> Tough Toby
> Weepy William
> Jolly Josh
> Greedy Graham

3 Read

- Tell learners to re-read the text and decide which sentences are fact (F) or opinion (O).
- Check the answers as a class.

> **Answers**
> 1 F   2 O   3 F   4 F   5 O   6 F   7 F

4 Read

- Learners read the clues and do the crossword.
- Check the answers as a class.

> **Answers**
> **Down**
> 1 jolly   4 rude   5 lazy   6 tough
> **Across**
> 2 moody   3 clever   7 anxious   8 weepy

5 Vocabulary

- Learners choose the opposite adjectives to complete the sentences.
- Check the answers as a class.

> **Answers**
> 1 tough 2 rude 3 anxious 4 bad-tempered 5 jolly 6 hardworking

6 Pronunciation 61 [CD2 Track 30]

- Learners listen and cross out the word that has a different sound.
- Check as a class.

> **Audioscript:** Track 61
> 1
> tough
> bought
> enough
> 2
> dough
> rough
> though
> 3
> thought
> bought
> enough

> **Answers**
> 1 bought   2 rough   3 enough

> ### Differentiated instruction
>
> **Additional support and practice**
>
> - Give learners copies of **Photocopiable activity 8**. When they have solved the wordsearch, they make another wordsearch using vocabulary from the whole unit.
>
> **Extend and challenge**
>
> - 💬 In small groups, learners choose one part of the story and write what Henry actually said to himself as he was crossing out the names.

Lesson 6: Choose a project

Learner's Book pages: 62–63

Activity Book pages: 50–51

Lesson objectives

Listening: Listen to class presentations.

Speaking: Present your project to the class.

Reading: Read questions and instructions.

Writing: Write an article, create a poster.

Language focus: Unit 4 Review

Materials:

1 Design a poster for a celebration: writing/drawing supplies, A3 sheets of paper or large sheets of paper for the poster, Internet access.

2 Write an article: writing supplies.

Learner's Book

Warm up

- Ask learners what they have enjoyed most in the unit. What new information have they learnt?

Choose a project

- Learners choose an end-of-unit project to work on. Help them choose. Provide materials.

1 Design a poster for a celebration

- In groups, learners design a poster for a celebration at their school.
- Tell learners to read the steps and use them to organise their project.
- When they have finished, they prepare a poster.

2 Write an article

- In groups, learners write an article for their school magazine on similarities between different cultures. The topic is festivals and celebrations.
- Tell learners to follow the steps. This will help them organise their project.

Wrap up

- Learners present their work to the class.
- **Portfolio opportunity:** If possible, leave the learner projects on display for a short while, then consider filing the projects, photos or scans of the work, in learners' portfolios. Write the date on the work.

Reflect on your learning

- Learners think about what they have studied in the unit and answer the revision questions 1–7.
- Learners consider the Big question for the unit: *Is your culture really that different from others?*
- **Informal assessment opportunity:** Circulate as learners work. Informally assess their receptive and productive language skills. Ask questions. You may want to take notes on their responses.

Answers
Learners' own answers.

Look what I can do!

- **Aim:** to check that learners can do all the things from **Unit 4**.
- Review the *I can …* statements. Learners reflect on what aspects of the unit they have found most difficult and why.
- Do they have any ideas about how to overcome these difficulties? Encourage learners to think of strategies that may help them improve.
- Elicit what they liked most about this unit and encourage them to explain why.
- Ask learners what new things they have learned about festivals and celebrations. Elicit what they found most interesting about this unit and encourage them to explain why.

Activity Book

Unit 4 Revision

- Learners do the multiple-choice activity which revises the language covered in **Unit 4**.
- Learners choose the correct word to complete the sentences.

Answers
1 b 2 c 3 b 4 b 5 b 6 c 7 c 8 a 9 c 10 c 11 c 12 b

My global progress

- Tell learners to read the questions and think about what they have studied in this unit.
- Ask them to answer the questions. Encourage them to take time to reflect on their learning and give honest answers.
- **Portfolio opportunity:** If you have been filing learners' work all through this unit, you may find it useful to put all the work of this unit together. You may ask learners to make a cover for their work, decorating it with an image that represents what they have learned.

Review 2

Learner's Book pages: 64–65

1 Vocabulary

- Learners label the places with words from the box.

Answers
1 office buildings   2 traffic lights   3 vehicle
4 underground train station   5 forest   6 mountains
7 path   8 lake

2 Use of English

- Learners write sentences comparing the city and the country using the adjectives in the box.

Answers
Learners' own answers.

3 Vocabulary

- Tell learners to read the clues and guess the words.

Answers
1 carbon footprint
2 fridge
3 decorations
4 candles
5 global warming
6 learners' own answers
7 ancient

4 Listen 24

- Tell learners to listen and look at the picture.
- Then, they write down the things that were used and the things that weren't used in the past.

Audioscript: Track 24

Old lady: When I was a child life was different from the life we live today. In the streets, rich people used horses and carriages to get about. There were a few cars but not many. There were some buses, but much slower than the ones in the city today. We rode our bikes most of the time. It was the cheapest form of transport and it was good exercise too!

Our houses didn't have all the electrical appliances we have today. We didn't have electric irons or dishwashers and we certainly didn't have a microwave! We cooked our food on wood stoves!

Answers
were used: a, c, d, e, f
weren't used: b, g, h

5 Use of English

- Ask learners to choose the correct word to complete the sentences.

Answers
1 costume
2 who
3 feast
4 made
5 traditional
6 also
7 which
8 received
9 best
10 will

6 Write

- Tell learners to write an email to a friend describing how they celebrated their birthday.
- They use the words in the box to help them.

Answers
Learners' own answers.

7 🗩 Talk

- Learners work in pairs and ask their partner their opinion about life in the future.
- They use the prompts shown as help.

Answers
Learners' own answers.

Photocopiable resources 7 and 8

Answers
A dance <u>which</u> people like in Brazil. Samba
A festival <u>which</u> takes place in February. Carnival
A strong person <u>who</u> can carry an elephant. Super Samson Simpson
A gas <u>which</u> can be a problem. CO2
A part of the earth <u>which</u> has melting ice. Poles
A boy <u>who</u> has no friends. Henry
A festival <u>which</u> is celebrated in India. Holi

Answers
calm, stupid, cheerful, lazy, polite, tough, jolly, weepy

5 Famous people

Big question How can we become better citizens?

Unit overview

In this unit learners will:
- speak about jobs
- read about famous people and their humanitarian work
- prepare an interview with a famous person
- write a biography
- understand extracts from a novel
- talk about qualities people have.

Learners will build communication and literacy skills as they read and listen to texts about jobs, famous people and their humanitarian work; speak about people they admire; make presentations; develop study and vocabulary study skills; learn to use modals of speculation, question tags and their correct intonation, and conjunctions.

At the end of the unit, they will apply and personalise what they have learned by working in small groups to complete a project of their choice: designing a poster about a special person or writing a biography.

Language focus
Modals of speculation

Question tags

Conjunctions: *so, and, but, because*

Vocabulary topics: jobs, adjectives, personal qualities, parts of a ship

Critical thinking
- Analysing information
- Giving opinions
- Predicting
- Comparing and contrasting.

Self-assessment
- I can talk about famous people and their jobs.
- I can understand a text about a famous person.
- I can give a presentation about a famous person.
- I can write a biography of my idol.
- I can understand an extract from a novel.
- I can talk about personal qualities people have.

Teaching tip
When doing a writing activity, writing a description or a story, learners tend to use the same adjectives every time. Encourage learners to use a variety of descriptive adjectives to make their writing more interesting. If they are keeping a Vocabulary journal, tell them to refer to the vocabulary they have recorded there for help.

Review learners' work, noting areas where they demonstrate strength and areas where they need additional instruction and practice. Use this information to customise your teaching as you continue to **Unit 6**.

Lesson 1: Famous people

Learner's Book pages: 66–67

Activity Book pages: 52–53

Lesson objectives

Listening: Listen for information, listen and complete notes.

Speaking: Practise theme vocabulary, speak about jobs and personal qualities.

Reading: Read about personal qualities.

Writing: Complete notes and sentences.

Critical thinking: Speculating.

Language focus: Modals of speculation: *must, can't, could, might*

Vocabulary: *artist, explorer, scientist, inventor, entrepreneur, composer, brave, kind, caring, positive, intelligent, determined, fun, creative, writer, actress, film, director, singer*

Materials: Dictionaries, map of the world, copies of **Photocopiable activity 9**.

Learner's Book

👉 Warm up

- Ask learners what famous people they know about. Why are they famous?
- Work with the class to come up with a list of words for jobs.
- Write the word *citizen* on the board. Encourage learners to think about its meaning. Elicit some ideas.
- Ask learners if they think they are a good citizen. Why do they think this?

1 💬 Talk about it

- In pairs, learners talk about five famous people in their country. What are their professions?
- Circulate, helping with additional vocabulary if necessary.

> **Answers**
> Learners' own answers.

2 💬 Word study

- Ask the class to look at the photos. Ask them if they know who these people are.
- In pairs, learners read the words in the box. Encourage them to look up any words they don't know in the dictionary.
- In pairs, they match the jobs to the photos.
- **Study skills:** Elicit the definitions of the professions from learners and ask them to write the words and the meanings in their Vocabulary journal.

> **Answers**
> 1 Alexander Graham Bell – inventor
> 2 Frida Kahlo – artist
> 3 Captain Cook – explorer
> 4 JS Bach – composer
> 5 Marie Curie – scientist
> 6 Steve Jobs – entrepreneur

3 Listen 🔊25

- Tell learners they are going to listen to a recording about the people in the photos. Say the names aloud before playing the audio recording so that learners are familiar with the pronunciation.
- They listen and check their answers.
- Play the audio at least twice. Then elicit the answers from learners. Which words helped them decide?

> **Audioscript:** Track 25
>
> **1**
> Alexander Graham Bell was a famous inventor. He was born in Edinburgh, Scotland in 1847. Like his father, Bell was a teacher. In 1870 he started research on sending sound over a wire. In 1876 he sent the first message over a telephone. Bell changed the world with his invention. He died at his home in Canada in 1922.
>
> **2**
> Frida Kahlo was born in Mexico in 1907. She started painting after she was hurt in a bus accident and was soon one of Mexico's most famous artists. She died in 1954 after many years of health problems.
>
> **3**
> Captain Cook was born in 1728 in Marton, England. He was an explorer who sailed most of the South Pacific. He was famous for his navigating and map-making skills. Cook was killed by the natives of the Hawaiian islands in 1779.
>
> **4**
> Johann Sebastian Bach was a famous classical composer from the Baroque period. He was born in Germany in 1685 into a family of musicians and he composed many famous classical pieces including *Air on a G-String* and the *St. Matthew Passion*. He died in 1750.
>
> **5**
> Marie Curie was a famous scientist. She was born in Warsaw, Poland in 1867. She made history in 1903 when she became the first woman to win the Nobel prize for physics for her work on radioactivity alongside her husband Pierre Curie. She died in 1934.
>
> **6**
> Steve Jobs was born in Wisconsin, USA in 1955. He was an entrepreneur, inventor and the co-founder of Apple computers, which developed a series of revolutionary technologies: the iPod, the iPhone and the iPad. He died in 2011.

> **Answers**
> See **Activity 2**.

 For further practice, see Activity 1 in the Activity Book.

4 Listen

- Ask learners to listen to the recording again. Tell them to take notes about when and where these people were born.
- Ask learners what kind of information they will be looking for, e.g. names of countries, years, dates.
- Play the audio at least twice. Allow time for learners to take their notes.
- Check as a class.

> **Answers**
> 1 Bell (Scotland/1847)
> 2 Frida Kahlo (Mexico/1907)
> 3 Captain Cook (England/1728)
> 4 JS Bach (Germany/1685)
> 5 Marie Curie (Warsaw, Poland/1867)
> 6 Steve Jobs (Wisconsin, USA/1955)

5 Word study

- Focus on the words in the box. Elicit the meaning from learners.
- Encourage them to look up the words they don't know in the dictionary.
- Then, ask them to decide which words they think describe each of the people in the photos.
- **Critical thinking:** Encourage learners to speculate what these people are like. Ask them to explain their opinions.

> **Answers**
> Learners' own answers.

 For further practice, see Activities 2 and 3 in the Activity Book.

6 Use of English

- Ask learners how sure they are about their opinions in **Activity 5**.
- Explain that they can use certain words to show that they are making a speculation about something.
- Focus on the **Use of English** box and read the examples together. Explain the degrees of certainty shown by the modal verbs: *could* and *might* are used when we are not too sure about something, *must* and *can't* when we are sure about what we are saying.
- Explain that *can't* is the opposite of *must* in this context.
- Ask them to focus on the structure of the sentences and answer the question.
- Then, they choose the correct meaning **a** or **b** for each sentence, **1** and **2**.
- Elicit more examples from learners and write them on the board.

> **Answers**
> The infinitive
> **1** b   **2** a

For further practice, see Activity 4 in the Activity Book.

7 Talk

- In pairs, learners use the modal verbs and the words in the box to talk about the photos. They speculate about the jobs the people do.
- **Informal assessment opportunity:** Circulate, listening to learners' interactions and noting strong points and mistakes for remedial work.

> **Answers**
> Michelle Yeoh – actress
> Nancy Ajram – singer
> Arundhati Roy – writer
> Hayao Miyazaki – film director

8 Listen 26

- Tell learners that they are going to listen to information about the people in the photos. They take notes in their notebooks and check if their speculations were correct.
- Play the audio a few times. Pause after each description to give learners time to complete their notes.
- Check the answers as a class.

> **Audioscript:** Track 26
>
> Michelle Yeoh was born in Malaysia in 1962. She is a famous actress known for her roles in action and martial arts films such as Ang Lee's *Crouching Tiger, Hidden Dragon*.
>
> Nancy Ajram is a pop star from Lebanon. She was born in 1983 in Beirut. She released her first album when she was only 15 years old. Her music video for *Fi Hagat* was the most viewed Arabic music video on the Internet – it had 31 million views on Youtube.
>
> Hayao Miyazaki is a Japanese film director and manga artist. He was born in Tokyo in 1941 and is famous for producing and directing Japan's most successful film, *Spirited Away*, in 2001.
>
> Arundhati Roy is a famous Indian writer. She was born in Shillong in 1961 and is best known for her novel *The God of Small Things*.

> **Answers**
> See **Activity 7**

Wrap up

- When they have finished, learners discuss who they think the most interesting person is.

Activity Book

1 Word study

- Ask learners to complete the sentences with a profession.
- Check the answers as a class.

Answers
1 composer
2 inventor
3 explorer
4 entrepreneur
5 singer
6 film director
7 scientist
8 artist

2 Word snake

- Learners find and circle seven adjectives in the word snake.
- Check the answers as a class.

Answers
caring positive determined clever fun creative brave

3 Vocabulary

- Learners look at the people in the photos and choose an adjective from **Activity 2** to describe them.
- Check the answers as a class. Ask them to give reasons for their choice.

Answers
Suggested answers:
a caring/kind
b positive
c brave/determined
d clever/creative/determined
e kind/caring
f creative

4 Use of English

- Learners complete the sentences with the correct modal verb.
- Check the answers as a class.

Answers
2 could/might
3 can't
4 must
5 could/might
6 can't

Differentiated instruction

Additional support and practice

- Learners do **Photocopiable activity 9**. First they fill the blanks with the correct modal verb. Then they look at the pictures and speculate about the people in them. They can do the second part independently or in pairs.

Extend and challenge

- Learners search the Internet for information about famous people in their country. They make a file using **Activity 8** in the Learner's Book as a model.

Lesson 2: Famous people and their work

Learner's Book pages: 68–69
Activity Book pages: 54–55

Lesson objectives

Listening: Listen to numbers.

Speaking: Talk about famous people who help others.

Reading: Read and match headings.

Write: Complete sentences, answer questions.

Critical thinking: Identify the main idea in a paragraph.

Vocabulary: *songwriter, pop star, extremely, awards, record deal, successful, release, foundation, nutritious, fame*

Materials: Copies of **Photocopiable activity 10**.

Learner's Book

👉 Warm up

- Ask learners if they know what a charity is. Remind them of 'Malaria no more', the organisation they read about in **Unit 2**.
- Ask them if there are any similar organisations they know about, i.e. that help people in need in different ways such as the Red Cross.
- Elicit from learners what sort of work these associations do, e.g. advancement of education and health, human rights, child protection. You may wish to introduce the expression *humanitarian work*.

1 💬 Talk about it

- Ask learners to work in pairs. Ask them to make a list of famous people who use their fame to help others, e.g. Angelina Jolie, Lionel Messi, Bill and Melinda Gates.
- Tell them to look at the picture and say who the person is. Is she popular in their country? How do they think she helps others?
- Ask learners to make a few notes of their answers.
- **Informal assessment opportunity:** Circulate, listening to learners' interaction. Take notes of common mistakes for remedial work.

Answers
Learners' own answers.

2 Read

- Ask learners to read the text and check if their ideas were correct.
- Ask learners to re-read the text and identify any new words. Ask them to try to work out the meaning of new words from the context.
- **Study skills:** Ask learners to look up the new words in the dictionary. Then, they copy the words that they find most difficult in their Vocabulary journal, along with the definitions.

Reading strategy

- Read through and discuss the strategy with learners.

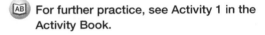 For further practice, see **Strategy check!** in the Activity Book.

3 Read

- Ask learners to read the text again.
- **Critical thinking:** Ask learners to read each paragraph and identify the main idea in each, i.e. what the paragraph is about. Then they choose the heading that best describes this main idea.
- **Informal assessment opportunity:** Circulate, asking questions and encouraging learners to explain how they are doing the activity.
- **Study skills:** Explaining how they are doing an activity helps learners to reflect on their own learning.

Answers
1 Quick facts
2 Early life and career
3 Humanitarian work
4 Personal life

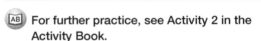 For further practice, see Activity 1 in the Activity Book.

4 Read

- Tell learners to read the sentences and choose the correct option to complete each one.
- Tell them to re-read the text in **Activity 2** if they need help.
- Check as a class and ask learners to explain their answers.

Answers
1 b   2 b   3 b   4 c   5 a

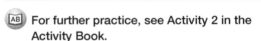 For further practice, see Activity 2 in the Activity Book.

5 Pronunciation 27

- Tell learners that they are going to listen to some large numbers.
- Play the audio. Stop after each number for learners to repeat.

- Ask individual learners to read the numbers without the audio to check pronunciation.

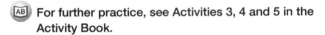
Audioscript: Track 27
1 twenty-eight thousand
2 fifty million
3 five million
4 one hundred and thirty thousand
5 five hundred and forty-five thousand

6 Talk

- Ask learners to talk about the questions in their group.
- **Informal assessment opportunity:** Circulate, listening to learners' interaction. Take notes of common mistakes for remedial work.

Answers
Learners' own answers.

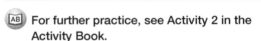 For further practice, see Activities 3, 4 and 5 in the Activity Book.

Wrap up

- When they have finished, learners share their ideas with the class.

Activity Book

Strategy check!

- Learners tick the strategies that will help them match headings to paragraphs.

Answers
Look at the visual clues. ✓
Look for key words in each paragraph. ✓

1 Read

- Learners read the text and match headings **a–d** to each paragraph.
- Ask them to explain what helped them decide.

Answers
1 b   2 a   3 d   4 c

2 Read

- Learners read the text again and answer the questions.
- Check the answers as a class.

Answers
1 No, they don't.
2 They are very brave, determined people who enjoy danger.
3 You can't sit down, walk or lie in bed.
4 It travels at 27,700 kmph.
5 It's used to carry the astronauts when they are outside.
6 He is famous for being the astronaut who has spent the most time in space.

3 Pronunciation 62 [CD2 Track 31]

- Learners match the large numbers (**a–f**) to the words (**1–6**).
- Check the answers as a class.

Answers
1 b   2 e   3 c   4 a   5 d   6 f

4 Listen 62 [CD2 Track 31]

- Learners listen and repeat the numbers from **Activity 3**.

Audioscript: Track 62
1 one hundred and fifty-five thousand
2 sixteen thousand, eight hundred and sixty-five
3 twelve million
4 twenty-seven thousand, seven hundred
5 one hundred and eighty-eight million
6 four hundred and seventy-six thousand

5 Challenge

- Learners read and answer the questions.
- Discuss as a class.
- **Portfolio opportunity:** Learners write the answers as a paragraph on a separate sheet of paper. They write their name and the date. File it in their portfolios.
- **Home–school opportunity:** Learners ask the questions in **Activity 5** to a family member and write a short paragraph with their answers.

Answers
Learners' own answers.

Differentiated instruction

Additional support and practice

- Give each learner a copy of **Photocopiable activity 10**. They read a text about footballer Lionel Messi and match titles to paragraphs. Then they give their opinion of Messi using modals.

Extend and challenge

- In groups, learners search the Internet and find information about famous people in their country who do charity work. They write a summary using the text about Shakira in Learner's Book **Activity 2** as a model.

Lesson 3: A presentation about a famous person

Learner's Book pages: 70–71
Activity Book pages: 56–57

Lesson objectives

Listening: Listen and complete notes.
Speaking: Speak about famous people, make a presentation.
Writing: Make notes for a presentation.
Critical thinking: Give opinions.
Study skills: Reflecting on learning.

Language focus: Question tags
Vocabulary: *beautiful, remarkable, amazing, exotic, extraordinary*

Materials: Map of the world, Internet access.

Learner's Book

⤷ Warm up

- Remind learners of the famous people they read about in **Lesson 1**. Ask them who impressed them most and why.

1 💬 Talk about it

- Ask learners to talk about who they admire and why. Ask them to explain what makes that person special.
- Circulate, helping with additional vocabulary if necessary.

Answers
Learners' own answers.

2 💬 Talk about it

- Ask learners to look at the photos and say who they think these people are and what they think they do. Are these two people famous in their country?
- Remind learners to use modals to show how sure they are of what they are saying.

Answers
Learners' own answers.

3 Listen 28

- Tell learners they are going to listen to two children making presentations about the two famous people in the photos.
- They listen and check if their ideas in **Activity 2** were right.
- Play the audio at least twice and elicit the answers from the class.
- Ask learners which words helped them understand.

Audioscript: Track 28

Child 1: Today, I am going to talk about my favourite actor, Jackie Chan. I think he's amazing. He was born on April the 7th 1954, in China. His parents named him Chan Kong-Sang which means 'born in Hong Kong'.

When he was very young, he started to practise kung fu with his father every morning. When he was seven, he started to study at the China Drama Academy where he learned martial arts, singing, acting and acrobatics.

His martial arts skills are brilliant. I went to the cinema to see *The Karate Kid*. It was fantastic!

Child 2: For my presentation, I am going to talk about Jane Goodall because I think she is a remarkable woman who has led an extraordinary life. She was born in London on 3rd April 1934 and lived between London and the beautiful city of Bournemouth by the sea. When Jane was a child, she liked watching the animals and birds in her garden, but she dreamed of travelling to Africa to observe exotic animals in their natural habitat. Jane became famous for her amazing work on the behaviour of chimpanzees in Tanzania.

Answers

Jane Goodall – animal behaviour expert
Jackie Chan – film actor, martial arts expert

Listening strategy

- Tell learners they are going to listen to the first presentation again and complete the notes.
- Focus on the strategies and explain that these strategies will help them complete the notes.

 For further practice, see Strategy check! in the Activity Book.

4 Listen

- Focus on the notes and encourage learners to think about the information they will need to listen for in the audio recording, e.g. a year, a noun, a verb.
- Tell them to listen to the recording of the first presentation again and complete the notes about Jackie Chan.
- Play the audio a few times. Check the answers as a class.

Answers

1 I am going to talk about **my favourite actor, Jackie Chan.**
2 He was born on **April 7th 1954 (in China)**.
3 When he was very young, he started to **practise kung fu** with his father.
4 At the China Drama Academy he learned **martial arts, singing, acting** and acrobatics.
5 I went to the cinema to see *The Karate Kid*. (**It was fantastic!**)

 For further practice, see Activity 1 in the Activity Book.

5 Read

- Tell learners that one of the things that helps make a presentation more interesting is the use of adjectives.

- **Critical thinking:** Look at the presentation about Jane Goodall and ask learners to read it as it is. What do they think about it? Does the word *nice* give any special information about the nouns it accompanies? What adjectives could they use instead?
- Ask learners to replace the word *nice* (in blue) with an adjective from the box.
- Tell learners to use their dictionaries to help them.
- Has the presentation improved?
- Ask learners to copy the adjectives they found the most difficult in their Vocabulary journals and add a definition or an example.

Answers

Learners' own answers.

 For further practice, see Activity 2 in the Activity Book.

6 Listen

- Tell learners to listen again to the recording of the presentation about Jane Goodall and check their answers.
- Play the audio at least twice and check the answers as a class.

Answers

1 remarkable
2 extraordinary
3 beautiful
4 exotic
5 amazing

 For further practice, see Activity 2 in the Activity Book.

Use of English

- Read the notes and the examples. Provide some more examples and ask learners to provide their own.
- Insist on the use of the correct intonation.

7 Use of English

- Ask learners to read the sentences with the correct intonation.
- Play the audio and ask learners to check if their intonation was right.
- Play each sentence again, pausing after each for learners to repeat.

Audioscript: Track 29

1 Jane Goodall is British, isn't she?

2 She lived in London, didn't she?

3 She dreamed of travelling to Africa, didn't she?

4 Jackie Chan's real name means 'born in Hong Kong', doesn't it?

5 *The Karate Kid* was fantastic, wasn't it?

Answers
Learners' own answers.

 For further practice, see the Use of English box and Activity 3 in the Activity Book.

Present it!

- Tell learners that they are going to make a presentation about a famous person they admire.
- Focus on the steps outlined in the box and tell learners to use them to organise their work.
- Then, they perform the presentation in front of the class.
- Encourage the rest of the class to ask questions about the famous person.
- **Informal assessment opportunity:** Circulate, listening to learners and asking them questions while they are preparing their presentation. Make notes of their performance while they are making their presentation. You may wish to set up some remedial work on the most common mistakes you have observed.

 For further practice, see Activity 4 in the Activity Book.

⇨ Wrap up

- When learners have finished, ask the class to find out how many of them have chosen the same person. Why do they think this has happened? Is this person very popular in their country? Why?

Activity book

Strategy check!

- Ask learners to read the strategies and decide which they will find useful for this activity.
- **Study skills:** Encourage them to give reasons for their answers. This will require them to reflect on best ways of learning and on the strategies they use when they learn.

> **Answers**
> Read the notes you have to complete before listening. ✓
> Think about the missing information: is it a verb, a noun, an adjective ...? ✓

1 Listen 63 [CD2 Track 32]

- Ask learners to listen and complete the notes on Nelson Mandela.
- Check the answers as a class.

Audioscript: Track 63

Boy: Today I am going to talk about a remarkable man, Nelson Mandela. He was born in South Africa in 1918 and had a happy childhood. When he began his studies to be a lawyer he learnt about the apartheid system in South Africa. Mandela believed in racial equality and decided to fight for the rights of black people in his country. He was put in prison for 27 years and wasn't released until 1990. He became the first black president of South Africa in 1994.

Answers
1 Nelson Mandela
2 respected
3 1918
4 lawyer
5 believed
6 prison
7 1990
8 president

2 Word study

- Ask learners to match the adjectives to the meanings.
- Check the answers as a class.

Answers
1 caring
2 generous
3 determined
4 brave
5 remarkable

3 Listen 64 [CD2 Track 33]

- Tell learners to read the sentences and complete them with the correct question tag.
- Then listen, check and repeat with the correct intonation.

Audioscript: Track 64

1 Nelson Mandela was born in 1918, wasn't he?
2 He studied to be a lawyer, didn't he?
3 He was one of the most respected people in the world, wasn't he?
4 Mother Teresa dedicated her life to helping others, didn't she?
5 She was very generous with her time and love, wasn't she?

Answers
1 wasn't he?
2 didn't he
3 wasn't he?
4 didn't she?
5 wasn't she?

4 Challenge

- Tell learners they are going to write a presentation about Mother Teresa.
- They use the prompts and adjectives from **Activity 2** to make their presentation more interesting.

- Ask them to exchange their presentation with a partner. Is the presentation interesting enough? Have they used a variety of interesting adjectives?
- **Portfolio opportunity:** Ask learners to write their names and the date on their presentation and file it in their portfolios.

> **Answer**
> Suggested answer:
> Mother Teresa was an extraordinary person who helped many people. At an early age she was generous and she helped the poor, the sick and children without parents. In 1950 she started the Missionaries of Charity in Calcutta, India. This remarkable woman visited many countries to help poor children. She won the Nobel Peace Prize in 1979 for her humanitarian work.

Differentiated instruction

Additional support and practice

- Offer extra opportunities to practise question tags. Write some sentences on the board and ask learners to supply the tags and say them using the correct intonation.

Extend and challenge

- Ask learners to work in small groups. They write a description of a famous person following the model of **Activity 5** in the Learner's Book. They exchange their text with another group. They replace the adjective *nice* with suitable, more descriptive ones.

Lesson 4: A short biography

Learner's Book pages: 72–73
Activity Book pages: 58–59

> ## Lesson objectives
> **Speaking:** Speak about personal qualities and achievements.
> **Reading:** Read a short biography.
> **Writing:** Write a short biography.
> **Critical thinking:** Give opinions, analyse, problem solving.
>
> **Language focus:** Conjunctions: *so, and, but, because*
> **Vocabulary:** *outer space, capsule, skydiver, fulfil a dream, helicopter, stratosphere, brave, determined*
>
> **Materials:** Dictionaries, Internet access, photos of dangerous sports.

Learner's Book

Warm up

- Ask learners what dangerous sports they know the names for in English for, e.g. *mountaineering, skydiving, bungee jumping*.

- Show some photos of dangerous sports and elicit the names. Ask learners if they would like to do any of those sports when they are older. What qualities do they think people need to have to do these activities?

1 Talk about it

- Ask learners to look at the photos. They talk about what they know about Felix Baumgartner. Why has he become famous? Would they like to do something similar?
- **Critical thinking:** Ask the class if they would like to be famous. Why? Why not? What are the advantages and the disadvantages of being famous? Elicit a few ideas and help with additional vocabulary as necessary.

> **Answers**
> Learners' own answers.

2 Read

- Ask learners to read the text and check if their ideas were correct.
- Encourage them to guess the meaning of unfamiliar words from the context. If necessary, tell them to use their dictionaries.
- Tell learners to choose the words that seem more difficult and copy them in their Vocabulary journals. They add a definition or an example sentence.

3 Read

- Ask learners to re-read the article and match the paragraphs to the words (**a**–**d**).
- Remind learners to look for the main idea in each paragraph to help them decide.
- Tell them that it may be useful to highlight the words or phrases that help them decide.
- Check the answers as a class. Ask them to justify their choices.

> **Answers**
> paragraph 1 – c
> paragraph 2 – b
> paragraph 3 – a
> paragraph 4 – d

 For further practice, see Activity 1 in the Activity Book.

> ### Writing tip
> - Read the notes with the class. Add some examples of your own and elicit some from learners.
> - You may write gapped sentences on the board and ask learners to supply the correct conjunction.

4 Read

- Ask learners to read the sentences and complete them with a suitable conjunction from the **Writing tip** box.
- Check the answers as a class.

- Ask learners if any of these sentences could be true of them.

> **Answers**
> **1** because **2** so **3** and **4** but

[AB] **For further practice, see Activity 2 in the Activity Book.**

5 ⟨💬⟩ Talk

- In pairs, learners think about one achievement of their own and say why it was so special.
- You may ask learners to share their partner's achievements with the class.

[AB] **For further practice, see Activities 3 and 4 in the Activity Book.**

6 ⟨📝⟩ Write

- Tell learners that they are going to write about people they admire and explain why.
- Ask them to copy the table and to think about three people and write what they admire about them.
- Tell them to write as many details about these people as they can remember.

> **Answers**
> Learners' own answers.

Write

- Learners choose one person they admire from **Activity 6** and use their notes to write a short biography.
- Tell them to divide their writing into four paragraphs. Remind them to use conjunctions.
- They may do some research on the Internet and print some pictures to illustrate the biography.

> **Answers**
> Learners' own answers.

[AB] **For further practice, see Activity 5 in the Activity Book.**

⟨➡⟩ Wrap up

- Learners share their biography with the class.
- Display the biographies around the classroom.
- **Portfolio opportunity:** Collect the pages and file them in the learners' portfolios.
- **Home–school opportunity:** Learners take their work home and share it with the family. They may ask family members whom they admire and why.

Activity Book

1 Read

- Learners match the sentences to the correct pictures.
- They compare their choices with a partner.
- Check the answers as a class.

> **Answers**
> **1** f **2** a **3** d **4** b **5** e **6** c

2 Use of English

- Learners complete the sentences with the correct conjunction.
- Check the answers as a class.

> **Answers**
> **1** because **2** so **3** because **4** but **5** and

3 ⟨📝⟩ Write

- Learners complete the sentences about themselves using conjunctions from **Activity 2**.
- Then, they share them with the class.

> **Answers**
> Learners' own answers.

4 ⟨📝⟩ Write

- Learners complete the chart with a more detailed list of their personal achievements.
- Tell them to use the ideas listed in the box.

> **Answers**
> Learners' own answers.

5 ⟨📝⟩ Challenge

- Learners write their own short biography using the notes they made in the table in **Activity 4**.
- Tell them to use linking words to join ideas.
- They may add photos of their achievements or illustrate their biography in some way.

Differentiated instruction

Additional support and practice

- ⟨💬⟩ Learners work in pairs. They write pairs of sentences and ask another pair to join the sentences using conjunctions.

Extend and challenge

- ⟨💬⟩ Learners work in small groups and play a guessing game. They take turns to give some information about a famous person they have read about in this unit. The other group members have to guess who it is.

Lesson 5: Literature: Extracts from *The Stowaway*

Learner's Book pages: 74–77
Activity Book pages: 60–61

Lesson objectives

Listening: Listen to a summary of a story, listen and answer questions.

Speaking: Speak about the characters in a story.

Reading: Read a summary of a story, distinguish between old and modern English.

Writing: Answer questions.

Values: Showing the best of ourselves.

Vocabulary: *rigging, anchor, mast, sails, deck, ship's bell, crew, ropes, prow, independent, brave, determined, foolish, strict, kind, worthless, caring*

Materials: Dictionaries.

Learner's Book

Warm up

- Ask learners if they have read any stories about journeys. Elicit some names, e.g. *Sinbad the sailor, Sandokan, 20,000 Leagues Under the Sea.*
- Do they like these stories? Why?

1 Talk about it

- Ask learners to talk about their experiences of journeys. Have they ever been on a difficult journey?
- Elicit from them the meaning of *stowaway* (someone who hides on a ship).

> **Answers**
> Learners' own answers.

2 Read 30

- Tell learners they are going to listen to a summary of the story.
- Play the audio at least twice.

> **Audioscript:** Track 30
> See Learner's Book page 74.

About the author

- Karen Hesse was born in Baltimore, Maryland. She graduated with a degree in English and minors in psychology and anthropology. Her first book, *Wish on a Unicorn*, was published in 1991. She's well known for writing historical fiction. Her characters are diverse, e.g. Mila, the girl raised by dolphins, or Nicholas Young, the stowaway on Captain Cook's ship. For more information, visit: http://karenhesseblog.wordpress.com/

3 Read and listen 31

- Tell learners they are going to listen to and read Nicholas's diary entries.
- Ask them to look at and compare the language of the summary and the language of the diary.
- Play the audio a few times. Encourage learners to make notes.
- Then discuss as a class. Is the language formal or informal? How do they know? Is it modern or old? What words or phrases show this?

> **Audioscript:** Track 31
> See Learner's Book pages 74–76.

> **Answers**
> The language of the summary is modern and formal.
> The language of the diary is old. It is more informal and personal than the summary.
> Examples of old-fashioned language: *It's a wonder ... ; for when I sent the letter, I hardly knew my plans myself; Father thinks me worthless.*

4 Read and listen 31

- Tell learners to read the text again and answer the questions after each section.
- Play each section at least twice. Pause and give learners time to answer.
- Check the answers as a class. Encourage learners to justify their answers, saying where in the text they have found the answer.

> **Answers**
> 1 true
> 2 true
> 3 true
> 4 false
> 5 true
> 6 false
> 7 true
> 8 true
> 9 true
> 10 true

[AB] **For further practice, see Activities 1, 2 and 3 in the Activity Book.**

5 Read

- Ask learners to match the old English phrases with the modern English ones.
- First, ask them to find the words in the diary text and read the sentence they are in. This will help them understand the meaning.
- Check the answers as a class.

Answers
1 c   2 a   3 d   4 b

6 Talk

- Tell learners to discuss Nicholas's personality in pairs. Why do they think he decided to stow away on the ship?
- You may ask pairs to share their ideas with the class. Encourage them to justify their answers.

Answers
Learners' own answers.

7 Read

- Ask learners to read the text again and find words to match the definitions.
- Ask them to start by finding the words in the text and reading the sentence they are in. This will help them understand the meaning.
- Check the answers as a class.

Answers
1 courageous
2 perilous
3 cluck, bleat
4 stern
5 scholar
6 worthless
7 quitter

8 Word study

- Ask learners to find the words in blue in the text and try to work out their meaning.
- Then they identify the parts of the ship.
- They compare their work with their partners.

Answers
a sails
b deck
c rigging
d ship's bell
e mast
f ropes
g prow
h anchor
i crew

 For further practice, see Activities 4 and 5 in the Activity Book.

9 Talk

- Tell learners to discuss if they would like to read this book and why/why not.
- **Informal assessment opportunity:** While learners are talking about the book, circulate asking questions and making notes on common mistakes.

Answers
Learners' own answers.

10 Values

- Ask learners to look at the words in the box and to use them to discuss the questions.
- Circulate, listening to learners' interactions. Help with additional vocabulary as necessary.
- You may ask some questions to help learners reflect on their own strengths, especially if you notice that some learners may have a rather negative self-image.
- Encourage them to reflect on what aspects of their personality they could improve.

Answers
Learners' own answers.

 For further practice, see Activity 6 in the Activity Book.

Wrap up

- Learners share their ideas about **Activity 10** with the class. Do they all agree? If they don't, encourage learners to discuss and justify their ideas.

Activity Book

1 Read

- Tell learners to read the extracts from *The Stowaway* again and decide if the sentences are true or false.
- Then, they correct the false sentences.
- Check the answers as a class.

Answers
1 true
2 false. Some of the crew knew he was on board.
3 true
4 false. It's a good hiding place.
5 false. It clangs on the hour and every half hour.
6 true
7 true
8 true
9 false. All his brothers are scholars.
10 true

2 Vocabulary

- Learners circle the adjectives that best describe Nicholas.
- Encourage them to explain why they think so.
- Check the answers as a class.

Answers
brave, determined, foolish

3 Write

- Ask learners what advice they would give to Nicholas.
- They write their suggestion.
- Compare answers as a class.

Answers
Learners' own answers.

4 Vocabulary

- Learners complete the sentences with a word from the box.
- Check the answers as a class.

> **Answers**
> 1 anchor 2 sails 3 ship's bell 4 rigging 5 prow

5 Vocabulary

- Learners match the words to their meanings.
- Check the answers as a class.

> **Answers**
> 1 e 2 c 3 a 4 b 5 d

6 Values

- Learners circle the word which they think is a good quality in a person.
- Then, they complete the sentences saying which qualities they think they have themselves and giving reasons for their answers.

> **Answers**
> Learners' own answers.

> ### Differentiated instruction
>
> #### Additional support and practice
>
> - Ask the class to imagine they are on board the ship. Tell them to write a diary entry for one day describing what happens on the ship.
>
> #### Extend and challenge
>
> - Bring in some books about journeys suitable for the age and level of the learners.
> - In small groups, learners choose one and make a file card about it: title, author, publisher. Then they read the book and make a summary of the plot.
> - Then they prepare a presentation, trying to persuade the class to read their chosen book.

Lesson 6: Choose a project

Learner's Book pages: 78–79
Activity Book pages: 62–63

> ### Lesson objectives
>
> **Listening:** Listen to class presentations.
>
> **Speaking:** Present your project to the class.
>
> **Reading:** Read questions and instructions.
>
> **Writing:** Write a biography.
>
> **Language focus: Unit 5** Review

> **Materials**
> 1 **Special people:** Roll of paper big enough to draw the outline of a volunteer's body, pieces of chalk or pencils of different colours.
> 2 **A biography:** Internet access or reference books, writing supplies.

Learner's Book

⮕ Warm up

- Ask learners what they have enjoyed most in the unit. What new information have they learned?
- What words did they find the most interesting/useful/difficult?

Choose a project

- Learners choose an end-of-unit project to work on. Help them choose. Provide materials.

1 Special people

- Learners work in groups of five. Give groups the necessary materials for the project.
- Tell learners to read and follow the steps of the project.

2 A biography

- In groups, learners search the Internet or use reference books to find information about a famous person in their country.
- Tell learners to follow the steps outlined in the Learner's Book. This will help them organise their project.
- They write the biography and illustrate it with pictures of the person they are writing about.

⮕ Wrap up

- Learners present their work to the class.
- **Portfolio opportunity:** If possible, leave the learner projects on display for a short while, then consider filing the projects, photos or scans of the work, in learners' portfolios. Write the date on the work.

🗨 Reflect on your learning

- Learners think about what they have studied in the unit and answer the questions in their notebooks or on a separate sheet of paper.
- Learners consider the Big question for the unit: *How can we become better citizens?* Encourage them to explain their answers. Can they think of one or two actions they can actually take to become better citizens?
- **Informal assessment opportunity:** Circulate as learners work. Informally assess their receptive and productive language skills. Ask questions. You may want to take notes on their responses.

Look what I can do!

- **Aim:** to check that learners can do all the things from **Unit 5**.
- Review the *I can* ... statements.
- Learners reflect on what aspects of the unit they have found most difficult and why.
- Do they have any ideas about how to overcome these difficulties? Encourage learners to think of strategies that may help them improve.
- Elicit what they liked most about this unit and encourage them to explain why.

Answers
Learners' own answers.

Activity Book

Unit 5 Revision

1 Vocabulary

- Learners complete the sentences with the correct word. They can use the words more than once.

Answers
Suggested answers:
1 scientist
2 film director
3 singer
4 writer
5 entrepreneur
6 caring
7 skilled
8 determined

2 Use of English

- Learners read and circle the correct answer.
- Check the answers as a class.

Answers
1 might be
2 might be
3 could be
4 wasn't he?
5 didn't she?
6 wasn't it?
7 haven't we?

3 Over to you

- Learners complete the sentences with their own ideas.

Answers
Learners' own answers.

My global progress

- Tell learners to read the questions and think about what they have studied in this unit.
- Ask them to answer the questions. Encourage them to take time to reflect on their learning and give honest answers.
- **Portfolio opportunity:** If you have been filing learners' work all along this unit, you may find it useful to put all the work of this unit together. You may ask learners to make a cover for their unit work, decorating it with an image that represents what they have learned.

Photocopiable activity 9

Answers
1 must; 2 could; 3 can't; might 4 must; 5 can't

Photocopiable activity 10

Answers
1 Quick fact; 2 Career; 3 Humanitarian work; 4 Personal life

6 Myths and fables

Unit overview

In this unit learners will:
- listen to fables from around the world
- describe mythical creatures
- tell an anecdote
- read and understand simple proverbs
- write a short story
- read a poem about a mythical creature.

Learners will build communication and literacy skills as they read and listen to texts about legends and fables and mythical creatures; talk about proverbs and their meaning; tell anecdotes and write stories; develop vocabulary study skills; and learn to use conjunctions, narrative tenses and punctuation in direct speech.

At the end of the unit, they will apply and personalise what they have learned by working in small groups to complete a project of their choice: creating their own mythical creature and writing a short story

Language focus
Conjunctions: *if, and, but, where, so, when*

Past simple and past continuous

Punctuation of direct speech

Vocabulary topics: mythical creatures, negative prefixes, world proverbs.

Critical thinking
- Personalising information
- Activating background knowledge
- Giving opinions
- Predicting.

Self-assessment
- I can talk about and describe mythical creatures.
- I can understand fables from around the world and the lessons they teach us.
- I can tell an anecdote about a personal experience.
- I can write a short story.
- I can understand simple proverbs.
- I can understand a poem about a mythical creature.

Teaching tip

Provide opportunities for personalisation so that learners can relate to the content they are learning. In this way this content will become more memorable and learners will be able to apply their recently acquired knowledge to different aspect of their lives.

Review the learners' work, noting areas where they demonstrate strength and areas where they need additional instruction and practice. Use this information to customise your teaching as you continue to **Unit 7.**

Lesson 1: Myths and fables

Learner's Book pages: 80–81

Activity Book pages: 64–65

Lesson objectives

Listening: Listen for information, listen and check.

Speaking: Practise theme vocabulary, speak about mythical creatures.

Reading: Read about mythical creatures.

Writing: Complete notes and sentences.

Language focus: Conjunctions: if, and, but, where, so, when

Vocabulary: *myth, abominable, snowman, Cyclops, unicorn, creature, pool, slither, spit, die, gallop*

Materials: Dictionaries, map of the world, Internet access or reference books, pictures of fairies, sheets of paper, drawing supplies.

Learner's Book

👉 Warm up

- Show learners a picture of a fairy and ask them if they like stories with fairies in them. Ask them if fairies exist.
- Ask them what other creatures appear in stories, e.g. dwarves, elves, witches, wizards.
- Elicit the names of some stories with these characters in them.
- Ask learners what we can learn from these stories. Do they have a teaching? What is it?

Answers
Learners' own answers.

1 💬 Talk about it

- Write the word *myth* on the board and ask the class if they know what a myth is. Elicit some ideas.
- Then ask them to read the explanation in the book and check if they were right.
- Do learners know any myths? Are there any local myths that they know? Encourage learners to tell the class what they are about.

Answers
Learners' own answers.

2 💬 Talk

- Ask learners to look at the mythical creatures and match the names to the pictures.
- Ask learners what they know about each of the creatures. Ask them if they think people were afraid of them. Would learners be afraid of them? Encourage the class to explain their answers.

Answers
a Medusa b Cyclops c the Abominable Snowman d unicorn

3 Listen 32 [CD2 Track 1]

- Tell learners that they are going to listen to an audio about these four mythical creatures.
- Tell them to listen and check their answers.

Audioscript: Track 32
Mythical creatures

1

In Greek mythology the cyclops were huge, one-eyed monsters which liked to eat humans. They were locked in the underworld because of their horrible features. The legend says that the cyclops only had one eye because they gave one away so they could see into the future.

2

People know Medusa for her hair made of snakes and because she could turn men into stone. The legend says that Medusa was a beautiful young girl, but she was also vain and also wanted to look in the mirror and see how beautiful she was. When she met the goddess Athena, the goddess punished her for being vain. She twisted Medusa's hair into terrible snakes and sent her to live with the blind monsters at the end of the Earth.

3

He's about 2–3 metres tall and he is hairy – you don't want to run into him at night! He has been a mystery creature of the woods for hundreds of years and there have been recorded sightings of him all over the world. He sleeps in the day and looks for food at night. The creature is known by many names – Bigfoot, Sasquatch and Yeti. He is known as the Yeti or Abominable Snowman in the Asian mountain range of the Himalayas, but in the American Northwest he's called Bigfoot and the Sasquatch in Canada. But does he really exist?

4

The unicorn is similar to a horse with a white body and a long spiral horn. Its horn is thought to protect people from poison. In fact people hunted unicorns because they thought they could protect them from disease. Unicorns are gentle, friendly creatures.

 For further practice, see Activities 1 and 2 in the Activity Book.

4 💬 Talk

- Ask learners which of these creatures they think is the most frightening and which they would like to find out more about.
- Ask them to explain their answers. You may need to help them with additional vocabulary, e.g. adjectives.
- Remind them of the opinion clauses *I think that/I don't think that ..., I know ..., I believe ...*
- **Informal assessment opportunity:** Circulate, listening to learners' interactions and noting strong points and mistakes for remedial work.

Answers
Learners' own answers.

5 Read

- Ask learners to read about the unicorn and find out how it helped the animals.
- Check the answer as a class.
- **Study skills:** Ask learners to choose the words in the reading text that they found the most difficult to remember the meaning of. Ask them to write these words in their Vocabulary journals with a definition. They may add a drawing.

> **Answers**
> The unicorn dipped his horn in the poisoned water. Then the water was good and the thirsty animals could drink.

 For further practice, see the Use of English box and Activity 3 in the Activity Book.

6 Talk

- In pairs, learners use the cues to talk about the mythical creatures on the page using the conjunctions in the **Use of English** box.
- **Informal assessment opportunity:** Circulate listening to learners' interactions and noting strong points and mistakes for remedial work.

> **Answers**
> 1 The Cyclops has only got one eye **so** it can see into the future.
> 2 **When** Medusa entered the temple, the goddess Athena punished her.
> 3 It is called the Abominable Snowman in the Himalayas, **but** it is called Bigfoot in the American Northwest.
> 4 **If** the animals hadn't been thirsty, they wouldn't have drunk from the pool.
> 5 The snake spat in the pool **where** the animals went to drink.

 For further practice, see Activity 4 in the Activity Book.

Wrap up

- When they have finished, learners vote for the scariest creature.

Activity Book

1 Read

- Ask learners to read and match the descriptions to the mythical sea monsters.
- Check the answers as a class.

> **Answers**
> 1 b   2 a   3 c

2 Read

- Learners read the descriptions again and write A (Aspidochelone), K (Koshi) or Kr (Kraken).
- Check the answers as a class.

> **Answers**
> 1 A 2 K 3 A 4 Kr 5 A 6 K 7 A 8 K

3 Use of English

- Tell the class to complete the sentences about the mythical creatures using the conjunctions in the **Use of English** box.
- Check the answers as a class.

> **Answers**
> 1 when   2 so   3 and/but   4 if   5 where   6 but

4 Challenge

- Tell the class to draw their own mythical creature.
- Then, they describe it and write about what it did.

> **Answers**
> Learners' own answers.

Differentiated instruction

Additional support and practice

- In pairs, ask learners to write sentences about the mythical creatures that appear in this lesson beginning *I think that/I don't think that ..., I know ..., I believe ...*
- You may wish to replay the audio from **Activity 3** in the Learner's Book and ask the class to take notes on each mythical creature. Then learners can extend the conversation in **Activity 6** adding more information.

Extend and challenge

- Learners search the Internet for information about other mythical creatures in their country or in other countries, e.g. Nessie, Mokèlé-mbèmbé. They write a short text and add pictures to it.

Lesson 2: Fables

Learner's Book pages: 82–83
Activity Book pages: 66–67

Lesson objectives

Listening: Listen to fables, listen and match.

Speaking: Talk about fables, talk about the moral of a fable.

Reading: Read for information.

Write: Complete sentences, answer questions.

Critical thinking: Use background knowledge, identify key ideas.

Language focus: Negative prefixes

Vocabulary: *grasshopper, tiny, store, starving, beg, advice, hungry*

Materials: Internet access, storybooks.

Learner's Book

Warm up

- Ask learners if they know the story of the hare and the tortoise. If they do, ask them to tell it. If they don't, tell them the story.
- Write the words *myth* and *fable* on the board. Ask the class what they think is the difference is between the two. Elicit some ideas.
- **Critical thinking:** This activity helps learners activate their background knowledge of the subject. The more background knowledge they have, the easier comprehension becomes.

1 Talk about it

- Ask learners to read the explanation of what a fable is. Were they right?
- In pairs, they talk about any fables they know. Ask them to write down a few notes of the names of the fables, the animals who feature in it and what the fable is about.

> **Answers**
> Learners' own answers.

Reading strategy

- Ask learners to think about what they would like to find out before they read the text.

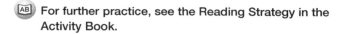 For further practice, see the Reading Strategy in the Activity Book.

2 Read

- Ask learners to look at the picture and write three questions about information they hope to find in the text.

> **Answers**
> Learners' own answers.

3 Talk

- Tell learners to read the text.
- Then, with a partner, they look at their questions and try to find the answers in the text.
- Ask learners to re-read the text and identify any new words. Ask them to work out the meaning of any new words from the context.
- **Study skills:** Ask learners to look up the new words in the dictionary. Then, they copy the words that they find most difficult in their Vocabulary journal along with the definitions.

> **Answers**
> Learners' own answers.

4 Read

- Tell learners that one of the characteristics of fables is that they always teach something.
- Explain that this teaching is called the *moral* of the fable.
- Ask learners to read the text again and then choose what they think is the moral of the story.
- Check the answers as a class.
- **Critical thinking:** In order to do this activity, learners have to read, analyse and find the key ideas. Ask them to explain what they did. This helps them to become aware of the strategies they use.

> **Answer**
> **b** It is best to plan for the future.

 For further practice, see Activities 1, 2 and 3 in the Activity Book.

5 Listen 33 [CD2 Track 2]

- Tell learners that they are going to listen to two more fables.
- Ask them to look at the pictures and say what they think the fables might be about. Encourage them to explain their answers.
- Focus on the titles and ask learners to match them to the correct picture.
- Play the audio at least twice. Ask learners if their ideas were right.

> **Audioscript:** Track 33
>
> 1 Once there was a young shepherd boy who looked after his sheep at the bottom of a mountain near a dark forest. It was lonely for him all day, so he thought of a plan so he could get some friends to talk to. One day, he rushed down towards the village shouting, 'Wolf, Wolf,' and the villagers came out to meet him. This made the boy happy, so a few days afterwards he tried the same trick again. Once again the villagers came to his help. But shortly after this a wolf came out from the forest, and began to walk around the sheep. The boy cried out, 'Wolf, Wolf,' louder than before. But this time the villagers, who had been fooled twice before, thought the boy wasn't telling the truth again, and nobody came to help him. So the wolf made a good meal of the boy's flock of sheep. When the boy complained, the wise man of the village said, 'A liar will not be believed, even when he speaks the truth.'
>
> 2 One day, while Mat Jambol was out fishing, a large wave smashed into his boat. He hit his head and fell into the water. When he woke up, two turtles were helping him. The larger one helped him up to the surface of the water by swimming under him, and the smaller one bit him gently from time to time to keep him awake. Together, the turtles brought him to the shore near his village. When Mat Jambol told his friends what had happened, none of them believed him. He just smiled to himself.
>
> A few weeks later, a terrible storm came to the island. When the rain stopped, Mat Jambol went out to look at the sea. The beach was covered with turtles! There were turtles from one end of the beach to the other. They were very large and had strange markings on their grey shells.

A little boy came running up the beach to Mat Jambol. 'Mat Jambol,' he said, 'Look at the turtles! What kind are they? What are they doing? Where did they come from?'

Mat Jambol smiled. 'You ask so many questions,' he said. "These are leatherback turtles. They don't usually lay their eggs here, but perhaps, because of the storm, they have come here instead. Just think, they have come all the way from the Indian Ocean.'

Everyone in the village came to watch the turtles lay their eggs. The turtles dug holes in the sand and laid their eggs in the holes. 'Why don't we dance on the turtles for good luck?' said one village woman. Mat Jambol laughed, 'That's just a myth,' he said. 'Also, you might hurt the turtles.' Soon the turtles had finished laying their eggs. They covered the eggs with sand and then went back into the sea.

One good turn deserves another.

> **Answers**
> 1 a   2 b

6 Talk

- Ask learners to match one of the morals with each story.
- Ask them to think of other situations in life where these morals are good.
- **Informal assessment opportunity:** Circulate, listening to learners' interaction. Take notes of common mistakes for remedial work.

> **Answers**
> 2 Be honest – The Shepherd's Boy and the Wolf
> 3 Be kind – Mat Jambol and the Turtles
> Learners' own answers.

7 Word study

- Tell learners to use their dictionary to find out how to make the adjectives (in blue) negative by adding the correct prefix.
- Check the answers as a class.

> **Answers**
> 1 irresponsible   2 unkind   3 dishonest

8 Word study

- Ask learners to match the correct prefix to each adjective.
- Check the answers as a class.

> **Answers**
> unfair, unfriendly, unreliable, dislike, distrust, irregular, disagree

 For further practice, see Activity 4 in the Activity Book.

9 Talk

- Ask learners to use the adjectives in **Activity 8** to talk about situations in their own life.

> **Answers**
> Learners' own answers.

 For further practice, see Activities 5 and 6 in the Activity Book.

Wrap up

- Learners discuss their answers to **Activity 9** to see whether there are situations common to many of them.

Activity Book

Strategy check!

- Learners tick the strategies which will help them find specific information in a text

> **Answers**
> Think about what you want to find out before you read a text. ✓
> Scan for key words in a text. ✓

1 Read

- Tell learners to read the fable about the Ant and the Dove and decide which picture doesn't represent the story.

> **Answer**
> Picture B

2 Read

- Learners answer the questions about the text. Then, they compare their answers with a partner or partners.
- Check the answers as a class.

> **Answers**
> 1 He went to have a drink.
> 2 She threw him a branch.
> 3 He wanted to shoot the dove.
> 4 The ant stung the hunter on the foot.

3 Read

- Learners think what the fable is about and circle the correct moral.
- They discuss their ideas in a small group.
- Check the answers as a class.

> **Answer**
> Being kind

4 Vocabulary

- Learners match the words to the correct prefix in order to make the negative.
- Check the answers as a class.

> **Answers**
> fair – unfair, kind – unkind, trust – distrust, responsible – irresponsible, honest – dishonest, agree – disagree, regular – irregular, reliable – unreliable, friendly – unfriendly

5 Vocabulary

- Ask learners to do the questionnaire with a friend or someone in their family.
- They write an example of what they do to be like this and tick how often they do it.
- **Home–school opportunity:** Encourage learners to do this activity with family members.

6 📝 Challenge

- Learners write a report about the person they interviewed in **Activity 5**.

> **Answers**
> Learners' own answers.

Differentiated instruction

Additional support and practice

- Provide additional practice of negative prefixes.

Extend and challenge

- 💬 In small groups, ask learners to search the Internet or visit the library and look for fables that are popular in their country. They choose one and tell the fable to the class. Then, they ask the class what they think the moral of the fable is.

Lesson 3: Telling an anecdote

Learner's Book pages: 84–85
Activity Book pages: 68–69

Lesson objectives

Listening: Listen to an anecdote.

Speaking: Tell an anecdote.

Writing: Make notes, complete sentences.

Critical thinking: Make predictions.

Language focus: Past simple and past continuous; connectors: *when, as*

Vocabulary: *camping, forest, bear, mountain, noise, scared*

Materials: Map of the world, Internet access, copies of **Photocopiable activity 11**.

Learner's Book

🗩 Warm up

- Remind learners of what they read and learned about mythical animals. Elicit from them information that they have found curious and interesting.

> **Answers**
> Learners' own answers.

1 💬 Talk about it

- Ask learners what they remember about the Abominable Snowman. Ask them to describe it.
- Elicit the different names it has. Where does the Abominable Snowman live? Where is that place? Can learners locate it on a map?

> **Answers**
> Learners' own answers.

Listening strategy

- Focus on the **Listening strategy** and ask learners how it might help them in this case, e.g. anticipate what the story is about, the vocabulary they will hear.
- **Critical thinking:** Predicting content from questions and pictures helps learners to anticipate the kind of information and vocabulary they will find in a reading or listening text. This knowledge helps learners approach the text in a more relaxed way.

---

2 💬 Talk about it

- Ask learners to look at the pictures and try to work out the story. They can use the words in the box to help them.
- Ask them to discuss in small groups and then share their ideas with the class.

> **Answers**
> Learners' own answers.

3 Listen 34 [CD2 Track 3]

- Tell learners they are going to listen to Sophie's anecdote. They listen and check if their ideas were right.
- Play the audio at least twice. Ask the class to take a few notes as they listen.
- Write *Blue Ridge* and *Georgia* on the board and explain that they are the names of a mountain chain and of a state in the US.

> **Audioscript:** Track 34
>
> **Sophie:** When I was seven I went camping with my family. We drove from Florida to Georgia and went camping in the Blue Ridge Range in Georgia. There were lots of great things to do – we went hiking, fishing and mountain biking.
>
> One day, I was walking in the mountains with my dad when we heard a strange noise in the trees. We thought it was an animal – deer and black bears live in the Blue Ridge mountain range. We stopped to listen but the noise stopped, but as we were walking again we saw something behind a tree. We were very scared and as we were looking for somewhere to hide, the creature ran off into the forest. I tried to get my camera, but it was too late. Was it just a bear or was it Bigfoot?

[AB] For further practice, see Activities 1 and 2 in the Activity Book.

4 💬 Talk

- Ask learners to think about what other animals live in the forest. Write the names on the board.
- Ask the class what they think the girl saw. Encourage them to explain their answers.

> **Answers**
> Learners' own answers.

5 Use of English

- Ask learners to look at the sentences in the **Use of English** box and discuss the questions.
- Give some more examples. Write them on the board and ask learners which verb describes an action in progress and which describes an action that interrupts the first.

> **Answers**
> Learners' own answers.

 For further practice, see Activities 3, 4 and 5 in the Activity Book.

Speaking tip

- Focus on the **Speaking tip** and give some examples using connectors.
- Ask learners to come up with some examples of their own.

6 💬 Talk

- In pairs, learners retell Sophie's anecdote.
- They can use the notes they made in **Activity 3** and make notes of words they remember.
- They use the illustrations as a guide.
- Remind learners to use the past simple and the past continuous.
- **Informal assessment opportunity:** Circulate, listening to learners' interaction. Take notes of common mistakes for remedial work.

> **Answers**
> Learners' own answers.

💬 Telling an anecdote

- Tell learners that they are going to tell an anecdote to the class.
- First they choose a situation.
- Then, they write answers to the questions. These will help them organise their work.
- When they have finished, learners tell their anecdote to their group.
- **Informal assessment opportunity:** Circulate, asking questions while learners are preparing their anecdote. Make notes of their performance while they are telling their anecdote. You may wish to set up some remedial work on the most common mistakes you have observed.

🡒 Wrap up

- When learners have finished, ask each group to vote for the most interesting anecdote.
- **Home–school opportunity:** Learners tell their anecdote to the family.

Activity Book

1 Write

- Ask learners to look at the pictures, which illustrate the story and use the prompts to summarise what's happening in each picture.
- Remind learners to use the past simple.
- Check the answers as a class.

> **Answers**
> 1 The family arrived at the hotel.
> 2 They went to the beach.
> 3 They had dinner.
> 4 They went to bed.
> 5 Mum fed the baby.
> 6 She saw something.
> 7 The young girl pointed to something in the corridor.

2 Write

- Ask learners to say what they think the girl saw in the corridor.
- Ask them to justify their answers.

> **Answers**
> Learners' own answers.

3 Use of English

- Tell learners to complete the sentences about the anecdote using the past simple or the past continuous form of the verb in brackets.
- They use the pictures to help them.
- Check the answers as a class.

> **Answers**
> 1 dropped, was walking
> 2 blew, was swimming
> 3 was feeding, saw
> 4 were leaving, saw

4 Write

- Tell the class to write the anecdote using their answers from **Activities 1** and **3** and the time phrases in the box.
- Check the answers as a class.

> **Answers**
> Learners' own answers.

5 Challenge

- Tell learners to complete these sentences as if they were writing their own anecdote.
- They use the past simple or past continuous.
- Check the answers as a class.

Differentiated instruction

Additional support and practice

- Offer extra opportunities to practise the past simple and past continuous. Learners do **Photocopiable activity 11**.

Extend and challenge

- 💬 Ask learners to work in small groups. They look for information and write an anecdote about the first sighting of the Loch Ness monster.

Lesson 4: Lessons in life

Learner's Book pages: 86–87
Activity Book pages: 70–71

Lesson objectives

Speaking: Speak about proverbs, speak about a story.

Reading: Read a story, read and complete.

Writing: Use correct punctuation, write a short story.

Critical thinking: Reflect and personalise.

Language focus: Review of past simple; review of the use of direct speech; punctuation – speech marks, question and exclamation marks, commas

Vocabulary: *gossip, cushion, throw, feathers, out of sight, take back, do harm, characters, setting, resolution*

Materials: Dictionaries, copies of **Photocopiable activity 12**.

Learner's Book

📖 Warm up

- Remind learners of the moral of the fables they read in **Lesson 2**. Which they have found the most inspiring?

1 💬 Talk about it

- Explain what a proverb is. Ask them if they can think of a proverb.
- Learners are unlikely to know proverbs in English, so elicit some proverbs from them in their own language and encourage them to explain in English the advice that they give.

Answers
Learners' own answers.

2 Read

- Ask learners to read the story and choose the appropriate proverb.
- Encourage them to guess the meaning of unfamiliar words from the context. If necessary, tell them to use their dictionaries.
- Discuss the story with learners as a class or ask them to work in small groups.
- They discuss what they think about the girl's behaviour. Encourage them to justify their opinions.
- Ask them to reflect on how gossiping can hurt people. Elicit examples.

Answer
Think before you speak.

3 Read

- Ask learners to re-read the text and complete the information in their notebook.
- Ask learners about the meaning of the words in bold. Explain that most stories can be broken down into these components.
- Check the answers as a class.

Answers
1 The story has got two characters: the teacher and the girl.
2 The setting is in the classroom and outside.
3 The problem is that the girl gossips about other people.
4 What happens in order to resolve the problem? The teacher asks her to go outside, to cut open the cushion and to throw all the feathers into the wind. Then the teacher asks her to bring all the feathers back.
5 The resolution is 'Think before you speak.'

4 💬 Word study

- Ask learners to look at the proverbs and discuss what they mean.
- They also discuss how the proverbs could apply in their own life.
- **Critical thinking:** In this activity, learners are required to understand the meaning of the proverbs, reflect on them and decide how this information relates to their own life.

📖 For further practice, see Activities 1 and 2 in the Activity Book.

Writing tip

- Ask learners to look at the explanation and examples in the box. Ask them what they think 'direct speech' means.
- Ask learners to look at the punctuation marks in the sentences and how they are used.

- Ask them to look for more examples in the reading text. You may also ask them to look back at the text about the grasshopper and the ant in **Lesson 2**.
- Tell them to circle the punctuation marks they find.

 For further practice, see Activities 3 and 4 in the Activity Book.

Write

- Tell learners that they are going to write a short story based on one of the proverbs in **Activity 4**.
- They choose they proverb they like best and make notes using **Activity 3** as a model.
- Tell them to follow the steps outlined to organise their work.
- When they have finished writing the story, they read it to a partner. The partner guesses which proverb it matches.

 For further practice, see Activities 3 and 4 in the Activity Book.

Wrap up

- Ask learners to read their story to the class. Can they guess the proverb it matches?
- **Portfolio opportunity:** Collect the stories and file them in the learners' portfolios.
- **Home–school opportunity:** Learners take their work home and share it with the family.

Activity Book

1 Read

- Learners read the proverbs from around the world and match them to the pictures.
- Check the answers as a class.

> **Answers**
> 1 b 2 e 3 a 4 d 5 c

2 Read

- Learners match the meanings to the proverbs. They discuss in pairs or small groups first.
- Check the answers as a class.

> **Answers**
> 1 Practice makes perfect.
> 2 A leopard can't change its spots.
> 3 A trouble shared is a trouble halved
> 4 Think before you act
> 5 Many hands make light work.

3 Read

- Learners read the story and punctuate the missing sentences.
- Then, they use the sentences to complete the story.
- Learners compare their work with a partner's and discuss any differences.
- Check the answers as a class.

> **Answers**
> 1 b 'Where am I going to find something to eat?' he cried to himself.
> 2 c 'Marvellous!' he said,
> 3 d 'Tee-hee-hee!'
> 4 a 'You'll just have to stay there until you get thin again.'

4 Read

- Learners read the complete story again and decide which proverb from **Activity 1** it matches.
- Check the answers as a class. Ask learners to justify their choice.

> **Answers**
> Think before you act.

5 📝 Challenge

- Ask learners to write their own short story based on one of the proverbs in **Activity 1**.
- Before learners start writing, tell them to come up with a list of ideas for their story using the questions as a prompt.

> **Answers**
> Learners' own answers.

Differentiated instruction

Additional support and practice

- 💬 Give learners a copy of **Photocopiable activity 12**. They punctuate the sentences correctly. Then they write their own sentences and exchange these with a partner. They punctuate each other's sentences.

Extend and challenge

- Ask learners to look for popular sayings in English. They choose a few of them and try to find equivalents in their own language. How similar or different are the sayings?

Lesson 5: Poem: *The Lambton Worm*

Learner's Book pages: 88–91
Activity Book pages: 72–73

Lesson objectives

Listening: Listen to a poem, listen and complete a summary.

Speaking: Discuss a poem, recite a poem.

Reading: Read a poem, read and match, read and answer questions.

Writing: Answer questions.

Critical thinking: Predict content from visual clues.

Values: Being courageous.

Language focus: Review of past simple and past continuous

Vocabulary: *worm, knight, tough, awful, browse, scary, fast asleep, brave, harm*

Materials: Dictionaries.

Learner's Book

Warm up

- Play a vocabulary game to review the vocabulary learned so far.
- Ask learners to work in small groups. They choose five words and write definitions.
- Groups take turns to read the definitions and guess the words they describe.

1 🗨 Talk about it

- Ask learners to look at the pictures and describe the animal.
- Tell them this is a poem about a monstrous animal. Ask them to talk about similar legends in their country.

> **Answers**
> Learners' own answers.

2 Listen and read 35 [CD2 Track 4]

- **Critical thinking:** Focus on the illustrations. Ask learners to predict what the story is going to be about. Who do they think is the main character in the story? Why do they think so? What's the title of the poem?
- Tell learners they are going to listen to a poem and match the pictures to the correct verse.
- Tell them to ignore the new words (in blue) for the time being.
- Play the audio at least twice.
- Check the answers as a class.

> **Audioscript:** Track 35
> See Learner's Book pages 88–89.

> **Answers**
> Paragraph 1: c, Paragraph 2: e, Paragraph 3: a, Paragraph 4: b, Paragraph 5: d, Paragraph 6: f

[AB] For further practice, see Activity 1 in the Activity Book.

3 Listen and read 35 [CD2 Track 4]

- Tell learners to listen to the poem again and complete the summary. They use verbs in the past simple and the past continuous.
- Check the answers as a class.

> **Answers**
> **1** was fishing **2** threw **3** was fighting **4** forgot **5** ate **6** came **7** was

[AB] For further practice, see Activities 2 and 3 in the Activity Book.

4 Read

- Ask learners to re-read the poem and answer the questions.
- You could ask them to work in pairs or small groups and discuss the questions.
- Check the answers as a class.

> **Answers**
> Suggested answers:
> **1** Learners' own answer.
> **2** It could have been a huge eel.
> **3** It liked to eat calves, lambs and little kids.
> **4** It was big and fat with big teeth, a big mouth and great big goggly eyes.
> **5** He was brave.
> **6** He cut it in half.

[AB] For further practice, see Activity 4 in the Activity Book.

5 Use of English

- Ask learners to match the highlighted words in the poem with words of a similar meaning.
- **Study skills:** This poem includes a significant number of new words. Encourage learners to first understand the meaning of the poem without focusing on the unknown vocabulary. Then, they look at the words in context and try to guess the meaning. If there are words that they still don't understand, tell them to use their dictionaries for help.

> **Answers**
> **1** brave **2** tough **3** scary **4** awful
> **5** browse **6** harm **7** fast

6 Pronunciation 36 [CD2 Track 5]

- Explain what stress is, i.e. the way that a word or syllable is pronounced with greater force than other words or other syllables.
- Tell learners to listen to the stressed and unstressed words in the lines of the poem.
- Play the audio a few times.

> **Audioscript:** Track 36
> He <u>caught</u> a <u>fish</u> upon his <u>hook</u>.
> But <u>Lambton</u> had no <u>fear</u>.

7 🗨 Talk

- Ask learners to take turns and practise a verse of the poem.
- Tell them to identify where the stressed words are.
- **Informal assessment opportunity:** Circulate, checking for correct pronunciation. Note down learners' strengths and weaknesses.

> **Answers**
> Learners' own answers.

8 Listen 37 [CD2 Track 6]

- Tell learners to listen to the verse and check their answers.
- Play the audio a few times.

> **Audioscript:** Track 37
>
> Just <u>what</u> kind of <u>fish</u> it was
>
> Young <u>Lambton</u> could not <u>tell</u>
>
> He <u>couldn't</u> be <u>bothered</u> to <u>carry</u> it <u>home</u>
>
> So he <u>threw</u> it down a <u>well</u>.

 For further practice, see Activity 5 in the Activity Book.

9 Talk

- Ask learners to practise reading the poem aloud.
- Remind them to stress important words to add rhythm and rhyme to the verse.
- **Informal assessment opportunity:** Circulate, checking for correct pronunciation. Note down learners' strengths and weaknesses.

> **Answers**
> Learners' own answers.

10 Values

- In the story, Sir John was courageous. Ask learners to discuss why.
- Then, they talk about how we can be courageous in life. Ask them to make a few notes of their ideas.

> **Answers**
> Learners' own answers.

11 Talk

- As a class, ask learners to look at the pictures and discuss how the people in them show courage and why.
- Ask learners if they have ever been in similar situations and what happened. What kind of courage do these situations require?

> **Answers**
> Learners' own answers.

 For further practice, see Activity 6 in the Activity Book.

Wrap up

- Learners read the poem as a class.

Activity book

1 Read

- Tell learners to read the poem again and put the sentences in order.
- They compare their answers with a partner and discuss any differences.
- Then check the answers as a class.

> **Answers**
> 1 He threw it in the well. – 3
> 2 The worm ate calves, lambs and sheep … even kids! – 5
> 3 He caught a strange fish. – 2
> 4 John went fishing. – 1
> 5 The worm grew and grew. – 4
> 6 He came home and killed it. – 8
> 7 When it was full, it fell asleep wrapped around Penshaw Hill. – 6
> 8 Sir John heard news of the terrible worm. – 7

2 Read

- Learners match the rhyming words.
- Check the answers as a class.

> **Answers**
> size – eyes, tell – well, sheep – asleep, hill – fill

3 Read

- Ask learners to complete the lines of the poem with the rhyming words.
- Then they re-read the poem to check their answers.

> **Answers**
> 1 Young Lambton could not **tell**
>   So he threw it down a **well**.
> 2 And grew an awful **size**
>   And great big goggly **eyes**.
> 3 On calves and lambs and **sheep**.
>   When they were fast **asleep**.
> 4 And it had had its **fill**
>   Ten times round Penshaw **Hill**.

4 Read

- Learners read the description of the Lambton Worm in the Learner's Book and draw a picture of it.
- They compare their drawing with other learners' pictures and discuss the differences.

> **Answers**
> Learners' own answers.

5 Pronunciation 65 [CD2 Track 34]

- Learners listen to and mark the stressed and unstressed words in the lines of the poem.
- Then they practise saying the verse.
- Check the answers as a class.

> **Audioscript:** Track 65
>
> This <u>scary</u> worm would often <u>feed</u>
>
> On calves and lambs and sheep.
>
> And <u>swallow</u> little <u>kids</u> alive
>
> When <u>they</u> were <u>fast</u> asleep.

> **Answer**
> See audioscript.

6 Values

- Learners answer the quiz questions and work out their scores.

> **Answers**
> Learners' own answers.

Differentiated instruction

Additional support and practice

- Ask learners to look for a poem they like. They mark the stressed words and say the poem aloud. Then, they read it to the class.

Extend and challenge

- Ask learners to find information about a monstrous animal in their country or region. They write a short story about it, including a courageous character.

Lesson 6: Choose a project

Learner's Book pages: 92–93
Activity Book pages: 74–75

Lesson objectives

Listening: Listen to class presentations.

Speaking: Present your project to the class.

Reading: Read questions and instructions.

Writing: Write a short story.

Language focus: Unit 7 Review

Materials:
1 **My mythical creature:** drawing supplies.
2 **A short story:** writing supplies.

Learner's Book

☞ Warm up

- Ask learners what they have enjoyed most in this unit. What new information have they learned?
- What words did they find the most interesting/useful/difficult?
- Which monster do they like best?

Choose a project

- Learners choose an end-of-unit project to work on. Help them choose. Provide materials.

1 My mythical creature

- Learners work in groups. They look at the creatures they have read about in the unit.
- They decide what kind of creature they are going to create.
- Tell learners to read and follow the steps of the project.
- They write the description of the creature.
- Tell them to check that they have included all the information mentioned in the steps.

2 A short story

- In groups, learners write a story about how *Practice makes perfect*.
- They follow the steps outlined in the Learner's Book.
- Tell them to use their dictionaries for help.
- Tell them to check that they have included all the information mentioned in the steps.

☞ Wrap up

- Learners present their work to the class or publish it in the school magazine.
- **Portfolio opportunity:** If possible, leave the learner projects on display for a short while, then consider filing the projects, photos or scans of the work, in learners' portfolios. Write the date on the work.

🗨 Reflect on your learning

- Learners think about what they have studied in the unit and answer the questions. Learners consider the Big question for the unit: *What lessons can we learn about life from myths and fables?*
- **Informal assessment opportunity:** Circulate as learners work. Informally assess their receptive and productive language skills. Ask questions. You may want to take notes on their responses.

> **Answers**
> 2 dishonest, unkind, unfair, disagree, irresponsible, unfriendly
> 5 1 when/because 2 so 3 where 4 so
> 7 'Think before you speak'

Look what I can do!

- **Aim:** to check that learners can do all the things from **Unit 6**.
- Review the *I can …* statements. Learners reflect on what aspects of the unit they have found most difficult and why.
- Do they have any ideas about how to overcome these difficulties? Encourage learners to think of strategies that may help them improve.
- Remind them of the morals of the fables they have read.

Activity Book

Unit 6 Revision

1 Crossword

- Learners read the clues and complete the crossword

> **Answers**
> **Across**
> 5 perfect 6 think 8 unfriendly 9 saw 10 feeding
> **Down**
> 1 honest 2 tentacles 3 reading 4 serpent 7 disagree

My global progress

- Tell learners to read the questions and think about what they have studied in this unit.

- Ask them to answer the questions. Encourage them to take time to reflect on their learning and give honest answers.
- **Portfolio opportunity:** If you have been filing learners' work all through this unit, you may find it useful to put all the work of this unit together. You may ask learners to make a cover for their work, decorating it with an image that represents what they have learned.

Photocopiable activity 12

Answers
1 "What is your name?", asked the teacher.
2 Paul said you must be Dave's sister. Hello!
3 Jill asked: "Is lunch ready mum?"
4 I am so hungry said Paul. I could eat a horse.
5 "Do you know where the post office is?", the lady asked the policeman.
6 The teacher asked: "has anyone seen Dianne and Yasmine?"

Review 3

Learner's Book pages: 94–95

1 Listen 38 [CD2 Track 7]

- Learners look at the pictures. Then they listen to the recording and match the speakers to the pictures.
- Play the recording at least twice.

Audioscript: Track 38

1 Explorer: I like to discover and find out about different parts of the world. In my profession you need to be brave and determined to succeed.

2 Artist: At school I used to win competitions for my drawings and paintings, so I knew from an early age what I wanted to be when I was older. You need to be very creative in my profession.

3 Scientist: I like to spend hours doing experiments and observing things in order to find solutions to different problems. You need to be very determined and intelligent in my profession.

4 Film director: I direct large groups of actors and actresses during filming. We have to do lots of takes to get a part of the film just right. In my profession you need to be positive, creative and fun to work with.

Answers
1 a   2 b   3 d   4 c

2 Listen 38 [CD2 Track 7]

- Learners copy the table and listen again to the audio.
- Then they write the profession in the table and complete the notes.

Answers
Suggested answers:
1 Explorer – brave and determined
2 Artist – creative
3 Scientist – determined and intelligent
4 Flim director – positive, creative, fun to work with

3 Use of English

- Tell learners to choose the correct words to make logical conclusions.

Answers
1 must be
2 can't be
3 must be
4 can't be

4 Vocabulary

- Tell learners to read the clues and guess the word.

Answers
1 composer   2 beautiful   3 unfriendly   4 dishonest
5 caring   6 fable

5 💬 Talk

- Ask learners to use question tags to check information.
- Circulate, checking for correct intonation.

Answers
Learners' own answers.

6 Use of English

- Tell learners to read the text and choose the correct word to complete the sentences.

Answers
1 went   2 When   3 arrived   4 First   5 spectacular
6 was walking   7 so   8 Then   9 lay down   10 so   11 patient

7 📝 Punctuation

- Learners write the sentences in their notebooks using correct punctuation.

Answers
1 "I'd love to be an explorer," he said.
2 "I passed my piano exam!" she said, happily.
3 "For your homework, please do some research about Medusa," the teacher said.
4 a "What do you think about Billy?" the football captain asked.
   b "He's a great player and very reliable," replied the manager.
5 "Quick!" said the captain. "Drop the anchor."

8 📝 Write

- Learners write a short story about a day they visited a zoo, a farm or a safari park.
- They use the questions to generate ideas and organise their writing.

Answers
Learners' own answers.

9 💬 Talk

- In pairs, learners look through **Unit 6**. They discuss which fable or myth they liked best.
- Tell them to give reasons for their answer.

Answers
Learners' own answers.

7 Ancient civilisations

Big question What can we see of ancient civilisations in our culture today?

Unit overview

In this unit learners will:
- talk and find out about ancient civilisations
- read about the Egyptian pyramids
- give a presentation about life in ancient times
- interview a partner about a discovery
- write a newspaper report
- understand and talk about an extract from a book.

Learners will build communication and literacy skills as they read and listen to texts about ancient civilisations, ancient buildings and objects and discoveries; speak about life in ancient times and compare it with life in modern times in their country or region; make presentations, complete notes, read and write reports; develop vocabulary study skills; learn to use subordinate clauses to express opinion; use the past simple passive; and understand emotions through intonation.

At the end of the unit, they will apply and personalise what they have learned by working in small groups to complete a project of their choice: writing about a famous building or statue, or breaking codes.

Language focus

Subordinate clauses to express opinion

Past simple passive

Vocabulary topics: ancient buildings and objects, emotions

Critical thinking
- analysing information
- giving opinions
- comparing and contrasting.

Self-assessment
- I can understand and talk about ancient civilisations.
- I can read and understand a text about the Egyptian pyramids.
- I can give a presentation about life in my country in ancient times.
- I can interview my partner about a discovery.
- I can write a newspaper report.
- I can understand and talk about an extract from a book.

Teaching tip

Before doing a reading or a listening activity, and especially if learners have to deal with a lot of information, it is important to take time at the very beginning of the lesson to activate learners' experiences with and knowledge of the topic. Doing this engages their attention, gets them using English, and sets them up for more successful comprehension. Include visuals, realia, discussion and personalisation, open-ended questions and brainstorming activities.

Review the learners' work, noting areas where they demonstrate strength and areas where they need additional instruction and practice. Use this information to customise your teaching as you continue to **Unit 8**.

Lesson 1: Ancient civilisations

Learner's Book pages: 96–97

Activity Book pages: 76–77

Lesson objectives

Listening: Listen for information, listen and match.

Speaking: Practise theme vocabulary, speak about ancient buildings.

Reading: Read about ancient buildings

Write: Complete notes and sentences.

Language focus: Subordinate clauses

Vocabulary: *Colosseum, sphinx, pyramid, aqueduct, tomb, creature, shape, organs, mummification, numerals, mummy, slave, digits, liver, stomach, lungs, heart, preserved*

Materials: Dictionaries.

Learner's Book

Warm up

- Ask learners what famous buildings there are in their country. Why are they famous?
- Ask them if they have ever been to a museum. If so, what sort of museum was it? What did they see?

1 Talk about it

- Focus on the photos and ask the class if they know these buildings. Elicit as much information from learners as possible – where the buildings are, who built them and what for.

> **Answers**
> Learners' own answers.

2 Listen 39 [CD2 Track 8]

- Tell learners they are going to listen to a recording of two children talking about the buildings in the photos. They listen and match the names of the buildings to the photos.
- Play the audio at least twice. Then elicit the answers from learners. Which words helped them decide?

> **Audioscript:** Track 39
>
> **1:** There's lots of information about ancient Egypt on this page. Look, it says that ancient Egypt was one of the greatest civilisations of the past. Egypt is in north-east Africa and the ancient Egyptians lived on the banks of the River Nile. It says here that the pyramids were the stone tombs of Egypt's kings – the 'pharaohs'.
>
> **2:** Look, here it is! It says it's a huge stone sculpture of a creature with the body of a lion and the head of a human. 'It is believed that the Great Sphinx of Giza guarded the tomb of the King from tomb raiders!'

> **3:** In ancient Rome, they had some incredible buildings! It says that as cities got bigger in ancient Rome, fresh water was a problem and people started to die because they were drinking dirty water from the rivers. So, they started to build long, stone channels called aqueducts to carry clean water from the hills nearby to the towns.
>
> **4:** Amphitheatres were places where the Romans went for entertainment. They had a central stage with rows of seats around it. They are quite similar to a modern football stadium. People used to watch fights between gladiators and wild animals such as lions and bears. Look, this was the largest amphitheatre in the Roman Empire – the Colosseum.

> **Answers**
> the pyramids – photo a
> the Sphinx – photo b
> the Colosseum – photo c
> an aqueduct – photo d

📖 **For further practice, see Activity 1 in the Activity Book.**

3 Listen 39 [CD2 Track 8]

- Tell learners to read the sentences and match them with a building from **Activity 1**.
- Ask them to look for unfamiliar vocabulary and guess the meaning from the context. They can also use their dictionaries for help.
- When they have finished, play the audio again and ask learners to check their answers.
- **Study skills:** Discuss as a class how many they got right and which words in the audio helped them decide.

> **Answers**
> **1** the pyramids
> **2** the Sphinx
> **3** the Colosseum
> **4** an aqueduct
> **5** the Colosseum

4 Use of English

- Focus on the **Use of English** box about subordinate clauses and read the examples together.
- Give some more examples and write them on the board.
- Ask learners to look at the box and match the sentence halves to reflect their own opinion.

> **Answers**
> Learners' own answers.

5 Talk

- In pairs, learners read the facts in the box. They discuss the meaning of unfamiliar words and use their dictionaries if necessary.
- Then they decide if the facts are true or false. Ask them to use the drawings in **Activity 6** to help them.
- Tell them to use the clauses *I think that/I don't think that ..., I know ..., I believe ...*

- **Informal assessment opportunity:** Circulate, listening to learners' interactions and noting strong points and mistakes for remedial work.

> **Answers**
> Learners' own answers.

 For further practice, see Activity 2 in the Activity Book.

6 Word study

- Focus on the definitions. Ask learners to match them to the pictures.
- When they have finished, ask them to compare their answers with a partner.
- Check the answers as a class.
- **Study skills:** Ask learners what helped them decide on their answers, e.g. *Have you seen these things before? Were there words in the definitions that helped you?*
- Ask learners to choose the words that they found the most difficult to remember the meaning of and write them in their Vocabulary journals with a definition. They may add a drawing.

> **Answers**
> 1 d 2 b 3 f 4 a 5 e 6 c
> 1 Roman baths
> 2 gladiator
> 3 Roman numerals
> 4 canopic jar
> 5 hieroglyphics
> 6 mummy

 For further practice, see Activity 3 in the Activity Book.

Wrap up

- When they have finished, learners discuss which they think is the most interesting building. Would they like to visit it?

Activity Book

1 Vocabulary

- Ask learners to complete the sentences and then match each one to a picture.
- Check the answers as a class.

> **Answers**
> 1 pyramids – a
> 2 gladiator – e
> 3 Roman baths – h
> 4 canopic jar – d
> 5 amphitheatre – f
> 6 mummy – i
> 7 aqueduct – b
> 8 Sphinx – c
> 9 Roman numerals – g

2 Read

- Learners read about Maya's description of the pyramids.
- They complete the sentences in their notebook.
- Check the answers as a class.

> **Answers**
> Suggested answers:
> 1 Maya thinks that the pyramids are amazing.
> 2 She knows that they are the tombs of the kings in ancient Egypt.
> 3 Archaeologists know that it took 100,000 men about 20 years to build the Great Pyramid of Giza.
> 4 Maya believes that the painting on the walls must be very interesting to see.
> 5 She knows that she'd love to visit the pyramids one day.

3 Challenge

- Ask learners to look at the hieroglyphic symbols and write words in hieroglyphs for their friend to guess.

> **Answers**
> Learners' own answers.

Differentiated instruction

Additional support and practice

- In pairs, ask learners to write sentences about famous buildings in their country beginning *I think that/I don't think that ..., I know ..., I believe ...*

Extend and challenge

- Learners search the Internet for information about famous buildings in their country. They write a short text and add pictures to it.

Lesson 2: Egyptian pyramids

Learner's Book pages: 98–99
Activity Book pages: 78–79

Lesson objectives

Speaking: Talk about the pyramids.

Reading: Read and answer questions.

Write: Complete sentences, answer questions.

Critical thinking: Use background knowledge.

Language focus: Past simple passive

Vocabulary: *tomb, pharaoh, queen, million, archaeologist, thousands, storage room, treasures, magnificent, chariot, royal, throne, statue, weapon, jewellery, mummified*

Materials: Map of the world, file cards, copies of **Photocopiable activity 13**.

Learner's Book

Warm up

- Ask learners about the ancient buildings they learned about in **Lesson 1**. Ask them to locate the relevant countries on the map.

- Ask learners to write their name using hieroglyphics (see Activity Book, page 77).

1 Talk about it

- Ask learners to look at the KWL chart. Tell them that they are going to use the chart to discuss and write notes about the pyramids.
- **Study skills:** Explain to learners that they can use this kind of chart for any topic they want to discuss and learn about.

> **Answers**
> Learners' own answers.

Reading strategy

- Focus on the first letter of the acronym – **Know**. Ask learners to discuss what they already know about the pyramids.
- Tell them to think of questions they would like to find an answer to in the text.
- **Critical thinking:** This strategy helps learners activate their background knowledge of a subject. This knowledge will provide them with context clues for better comprehension. The more background knowledge a learner possesses about a subject, the easier comprehension becomes.

For further practice, see Strategy check! and Activity 1 in the Activity Book.

2 Read

- Ask learners to read the text and try to find the answers to the questions they came up with in **Activity 1**.
- Ask learners to re-read the text and identify any new words. Ask them to work out the meaning of new words from the context.
- **Study skills:** Ask learners to look up the new words in the dictionary. Then, they copy the words that they find most difficult in their Vocabulary journal along with a definition.

> **Answers**
> Learners' own answers.

3 Read

- Ask learners to read the text again and then answer the questions.
- They work with a partner or in a small group and compare their answers.

> **Answers**
> 1 They were built for pharaohs and their queens and the objects they would need after they died.
> 2 It took 23 years to build.
> 3 On top of the pyramid was a block of gold.
> 4 They were filled with treasures and everyday objects.
> 5 Cats were mummified because people thought that they protected the Pharaohs.

4 Use of English

- Focus on the **Use of English** box and the examples. Explain the past passive.
- Write a few of the examples on the board and highlight the verb forms. Show the difference between the active and passive form.
- Ask learners to find more examples in the text. You may wish to ask them to copy these examples in their notebooks.
- Give some more examples of sentences using the past passive.

> **Answers**
> Learners' own answers.

For further practice, see Activities 2 and 3 in the Activity Book.

5 Use of English

- Tell learners to complete the information about how the pyramids were built using the correct form of the passive.
- Circulate, checking learners' work and helping if necessary.
- Check the answers as a class.

> **Answers**
> 1 was marked   2 were moved   3 were made
> 4 was (almost) finished   5 was placed

6 Talk

- Ask learners to talk about the questions and complete the *What I have learned* column of their KWL chart.
- **Informal assessment opportunity:** Circulate, listening to learners' interactions. Take notes of common mistakes for remedial work.

Wrap up

- When they have finished, learners share their ideas with the class.

Activity Book

Strategy check!

- Learners tick the strategies that will help them use their own knowledge.

> **Answers**
> Talk about what you know about the topic. ✓
> Think of questions before reading. ✓
> Think of questions you'd like to find the answer to in the text. ✓

1 Read

- Tell learners to look at the pictures. In pairs, they make a list of questions about Egyptian mummies that they would like to find out the answer to.

- Then tell them to read the text and try to find the answers.

> **Answers**
> Learners' own answers.

2 Use of English

- Learners complete the sentences about the mummy-making process using the past simple passive.
- Then they put the sentences in the correct order.

> **Answers**
> 1 was covered – 2
> 2 was dried out – 3
> 3 was preserved – 1
> 4 was wrapped – 6
> 5 were used – 4
> 6 was put – 8
> 7 was stuffed – 5
> 8 was wrapped – 7

3 Use of English

- Learners make questions with the prompts and then match them to the correct answer.
- Check the answers as a class.

> **Answers**
> 1 Why was salt used? c
> 2 How long was the body dried out for? a
> 3 What was used to preserve the skin? f
> 4 What was the mummy put in? b
> 5 What was the mummy stuffed with? e
> 6 What material was the mummy wrapped in? d

> **Differentiated instruction**
>
> **Additional support and practice**
>
> - Provide additional practice of the past passive. Write a few sentences in the past passive on the board.
> - Make some deliberate mistakes in some of the sentences, e.g. using the active form of the past instead of the passive. Ask learners to correct them.
>
> **Extend and challenge**
>
> - Give each learner a copy of **Photocopiable activity 13**. This provides further practice of the past passive.

Lesson 3: Everyday life in ancient times

Learner's Book pages: 100–101

Activity Book pages: 80–81

> **Lesson objectives**
>
> **Listening:** Listen, order and complete notes, listen for clues.
>
> **Speaking:** Make a presentation.
>
> **Writing:** Make notes for a presentation.
>
> **Critical thinking:** Give opinions.

> **Language focus:** *whereas, too, both*
>
> **Vocabulary:** *togas, tunics, bread, sandals, olives, meat, baths, chariot, gladiator, farmer, soldier, merchant, engineer, villas, Roman numerals*

> **Materials:** Map of the world, Internet access.

Learner's Book

☞ Warm up

- Remind learners of what they read and learnt about ancient Egypt in **Lesson 2**. Elicit from them information they have found curious and interesting.
- Ask them what other ancient civilisations they would like to learn about. Make a list on the board.

1 ☺ Talk about it

- Ask learners to discuss what everyday life is like in their town or city.
- Ask them to focus on the aspects listed in the box. Tell them to make some notes of their discussion.

> **Answers**
> Learners' own answers.

2 📝 Word study

- Ask learners to look at the picture of everyday life in ancient Rome and compare it with their town. They discuss as a class how similar or different it is.
- Ask the class to look at the picture. They match words from the box to elements in the picture.

> **Answers**
> Learners' own answers.

[AB] **For further practice, see Activity 1 in the Activity Book.**

3 Listen 40 [CD2 Track 9]

- Tell learners they are going to listen to the first part of Ryan's presentation about life in ancient Rome.
- Look at the **Listening strategy**. Tell learners that they should listen carefully for words that they already know from **Activity 2**. This will help them understand what they hear.
- Play the audio once and ask the class to put up their hands every time they hear a word from the box in **Activity 2**. Please note that not all the words appear.
- Then they listen again and order the different parts of the presentation.
- Play the audio a few times for learners to check their answers.

Audioscript: Track 40

Part 1

Ryan: Today I'm going to talk about life in ancient Rome. First of all, I'm going to describe the houses in ancient Rome. Most people lived in apartment buildings in noisy, narrow streets, but rich people lived in big, beautiful homes.

The very early Romans wore <u>togas</u>. They looked like a white sheet. Togas were arranged very carefully, in a stylish way. The Romans didn't like togas because they were difficult to wear and they were cold. So, they changed to more comfortable <u>tunics</u>, which looked like long t-shirts. They were far more practical. Roman boys wore a tunic down to their knees. Roman girls wore a simple tunic with a belt at the waist. When they went outside, they wore a second tunic that reached their feet.

There were lots of different jobs in Rome. The people who lived in the country were usually <u>farmers</u> and they made food for the people who lived in the city. In the city, there were craftsmen who made dishes, jewellery and weapons, and the more educated Romans who were teachers or <u>engineers</u>. Many men were part of the Roman army.

Typical food in ancient Rome was <u>bread</u>, beans, fish, dried fruit, vegetables and cheese. Poor Romans didn't eat a lot of <u>meat</u>, but they did eat some very strange things such as mice and snails!

Entertainment was very popular in ancient Rome and most events were free. The Romans liked <u>chariot</u> racing and watching plays in amphitheatres. The Romans also loved bathing and usually visited the local public <u>baths</u> once a day. There were about 900 public baths in ancient Rome!

Answers
a Typical food – 4
b Common jobs – 3
c Roman houses – 1
d Entertainment – 5
e Clothes – 2

 For further practice, see the Listening strategy in the Activity Book.

4 Talk

- Ask learners to discuss in pairs or small groups what differences and similarities there are between life in ancient Rome and life in their own city or town.
- Tell them to use the notes about their town that they made in **Activity 1**.
- You may wish to play the audio again and ask learners to make notes about Ryan's presentation under the headings **a–e** in **Activity 3**.
- Tell them to use *whereas, too* and *both*. Look at the example sentence with *whereas* and give some more examples using *too* and *both*.
- **Informal assessment opportunity:** Circulate, listening to learners' interactions. Take notes of common mistakes for remedial work.

Answers
Learners' own answers.

 For further practice, see Activity 2 in the Activity Book.

5 Listen 41 [CD2 Track 10]

- Tell the class that they are going to listen to the second part of Ryan's presentation.
- They listen and complete the sentences about how ancient Rome still affects modern culture.
- **Critical thinking:** Before listening, discuss the question as a class. Ask learners to give their opinions.
- Play the audio at least twice and allow time for learners to make notes and complete the sentences.

Audioscript: Track 41

Part 2

Ryan: The Romans were skilled <u>engineers</u> and builders. They showed us how to build straight roads and how to transport water via aqueducts (bridges that carry water). They were the very first civilisation to heat houses with central heating.

Children loved to play in ancient Rome and we still play many of the games they played today such as dice games, board games, marbles, and hide and seek. The Roman number system called Roman numerals is also still used around the world. We can still see them on clock faces, in kings' and queens' names and even in the Superbowl numbering.

Answers
1 straight roads
2 aqueducts
3 houses with central heating
4 dice games, board games, marbles, and hide and seek.
5 clock faces

 For further practice, see Activities 3, 4 and 5 in the Activity Book.

6 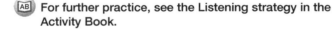 Word study

- Ask learners to look at the Roman numerals and their equivalent in numbers.
- Write a few numbers in Roman numerals on the board and ask learners to work them out.
- In pairs, learners write Roman numerals on a sheet of paper and give it to their partner to solve.

Answers
Learners' own answers.

 For further practice, see Activity 6 in the Activity Book.

Speaking tip

- Focus on the tip and explain that in order to make a presentation more interesting learners should talk about a variety of ideas.
- You may wish to point out that these ideas have to follow a logical order.

Present it!

- Focus on the steps outlined in the box and tell learners to use them to organise their work.
- First, they choose a period of history in their country and search the Internet for information about the topics listed.
- They look for pictures to make the presentation more attractive.
- Then, they perform the presentation in front of the class. Remind them to use time expressions.
- Set a time limit of three minutes to allow everyone in the class to give their presentation and keep the audience interested.
- **Informal assessment opportunity:** Circulate, asking questions while learners are preparing the presentation. Make notes of their performance while they are making their presentation. You may wish to set up some remedial work on the most common mistakes you have observed.

☞ Wrap up

- When learners have finished, ask the class to vote for what they think is the most interesting period in their country's history.
- **Portfolio opportunity:** Collect the pictures and the script of the presentation, write the learner's name and the date and file it in their portfolio.
- **Home–school opportunity:** Learners make their presentation to their family at home.

Answers
Learners' own answers.

Activity Book

1 Vocabulary

- Ask learners to label the things they see in the pictures using words from the box.
- Check the answers as a class.

Answers

a t-shirt	e baseball boots	i box chariot
b hamburger	f house	j sandals
c car	g tunic	k villa
d jeans	h olives	

2 Vocabulary

- Ask learners to complete the sentences using words from **Activity 1**.
- They use *whereas*, and *too* to compare and contrast.
- Check the answers as a class.

Answers
Suggested answers:
1 Romans wore tunics, whereas I wear jeans and a t-shirt.
2 Romans ate olives, whereas I eat hamburgers.
3 Romans lived in villas, whereas I live in a house.
4 Romans wore sandals, whereas I wear boots.
5 Romans used chariots, whereas I travel by car.

Strategy check!

- Learners read the strategies and tick the ones that will help them listen for clues.

Answers
Listen for words that you already know. ✓
Don't try to understand every word. Be selective. ✓

3 Listen 66 [CD2 Track 35]

- Tell learners to listen to Luis talking about an aspect of Roman life.
- They identify and circle the topic Luis talks about.
- Check the answer as a class.

Audioscript: Track 66

Luis: I've found out that the ancient Romans loved playing games in their leisure time. They played ball games and they enjoyed flying kites on windy days too. Boys liked to play war games and the girls played with dolls made of material or clay.

Both boys and girls loved to play a game called *Tali* (nowadays it's called *knucklebones*). In *Tali,* players roll four four-sided dice, with the sides marked 1, 3, 4 and 6. Most of the scoring was based on numerical value. The pieces were usually made from animal bones but were also made of silver, gold, marble, glass and wood. The four *Tali* were dropped from a height onto a table or the floor and the score was calculated from the numbers on the sides facing up.

Answer
entertainment

4 Listen 66 [CD2 Track 35]

- Tell learners they are going to listen again and tick the words that give clues about the topic.
- Check the answers as a class.

Answers
leisure time, kites, dolls, ball games

5 Listen

- Tell the class to read the sentences and circle the correct answer to complete each one.
- Check the answers as a class.

Answers
1 boys and girls 2 animals' bones 3 four
4 on the floor 5 facing up

6 Roman numerals

- Tell learners to look at the pictures and talk about ways in which Roman numerals are still used today.
- Learners write the numbers equivalent to the Roman numerals.
- Check the answers as a class.

Answers
1 8   2 45   3 4   4 2014

Differentiated instruction

Additional support and practice

- Offer extra opportunities to practise Roman numerals. Ask learners to work in small groups and write sums using Roman numerals on sheets of paper. They exchange papers with another group and do the Maths.

Extend and challenge

- Ask learners to work in small groups. They prepare a presentation about another ancient culture (e.g. ancient Greece, the Mayas, the Aztecs) using the Ryan's presentation about ancient Rome as a model.

Lesson 4: Discoveries

Learner's Book pages: 102–103
Activity Book pages: 82–83

Lesson objectives

Speaking: Speak about discoveries.

Reading: Read a newspaper report, read and complete a fact sheet.

Writing: Write a newspaper report.

Critical thinking: Distinguish between fact and opinion.

Language focus: Past simple and past simple passive

Vocabulary: *discovery, discover, mystery, infection, blow, amazed, time machine, treasures*

Materials: Dictionaries, map of the world, Internet access, photos of famous archaeological sites (e.g. Petra, the Mayan pyramids, the Chinese terracotta soldiers).

Learner's Book

Warm up

- Show learners photos of some famous archaeological sites and ask them what they think these places are and why they are famous.
- Explain the meaning of *discover* and *discovery*. Tell the class the names of these archaeological sites and locate them on a map.

1 Talk about it

- Ask learners to talk about a time when they discovered something important. What was it? Where did they discover it?
- If they haven't discovered anything they think is important, ask the class if they would like to be archaeologists and where they would like to go to find interesting things.

Answers
Learners' own answers.

2 Read

- Ask learners to look at the pictures and describe them. Where do they think these objects were found?
- Ask learners to read the newspaper report. They make notes about the objects that were found inside the tomb.
- Encourage them to guess the meaning of unfamiliar words from the context. If necessary, tell them to use their dictionaries.

Answers
hieroglyphics, a golden chariot, weapons, jewellery, a throne, a board game, a solid gold face mask

3 Read

- Ask learners to re-read the report and complete the fact sheet.
- Check the answers as a class.

Answers
1 on 24th November 1922.
2 by Howard Carter.
3 in the Valley of the Kings.
4 a golden chariot, weapons and jewellery.

4 Read

- Ask learners to re-read the text and decide which sentences are fact (F) and which are opinion (O).
- How do they know?
- **Critical thinking:** Encourage learners to look for clues that help them decide, e.g. the use of verbs such as *think* and *believe* to give an opinion.
- Check the answers as a class.

Answers
1 F   2 O   3 F   4 O   5 O

 For further practice, see Activities 1 and 2 in the Activity Book.

5 Write

- Ask learners to look at the categories in the box and find examples of each one in the newspaper report in **Activity 2**.
- Write the examples on the board.

- Then ask learners to read the sentences in the activity and match them to the correct category.
- Check the answers as a class.

> **Answers**
> 1 a headline
> 2 a quotation
> 3 an opinion
> 4 a fact

 For further practice, see Activity 3 in the Activity Book.

Writing tip

- Ask learners to look at the sentences in the **Writing tip** box. Ask them to decide which is in the past passive (the first sentence) and which is in the past simple (the second sentence).
- Explain that these tenses are used when telling a story.
- Ask learners to find more examples of each tense in the newspaper report in **Activity 2**.
- Elicit more examples from the class. Write them on the board and ask learners to copy them in their notebooks.

 For further practice, see Activity 4 in the Activity Book.

Write

- Tell learners that they are going to write a report on a discovery. It can be real or invented.
- First learners decide what was discovered and make notes about the object, the place, the date, and who discovered it.
- If they are writing about a real discovery, ask them to search the Internet for information and pictures.
- Tell them to follow the steps in the Learner's Book to organise their work.
- They write the report and display it in the classroom.

> **Answers**
> Learners' own answers.

 For further practice, see Activity 5 in the Activity Book.

➮ Wrap up

- Ask learners to share what they wrote in **Activity 5** in their Activity Book with the class.
- **Portfolio opportunity:** Collect the reports and file them in learners' portfolios.
- **Home–school opportunity:** Learners take their work home and share it with the family.

Activity Book

1 Read

- Learners read an article about the discovery of some surprising Roman artefacts in London. What do they think is surprising about the objects that have been found.
- Discuss the answers as a class.

> **Answers**
> The artefacts are 2000 years old. They are in excellent condition.

2 Read

- Learners complete the fact sheet about the discovery.
- Check the answers as a class.

> **Answers**
> 1 yesterday   2 archaeologists   3 central London
> 4 (some of the following) plates, bowls, coins, a bear's skull, an amphitheatre, and an entire Roman street

3 Read

- Learners re-read the text in **Activity 1** and find examples in the text of a quotation, a fact, an opinion and a headline.
- They compare their answers with a partner.
- Then check as a class.

> **Answers**
> Suggested answers:
> 1 'They are in excellent condition,' said the archaeologist.
> 2 They were discovered at a building site in central London.
> 3 'This is the best find in years!'
> 4 Surprising discovery in London well

4 📝 Read

- Learners change the sentences to the past simple or past simple passive.
- Check the answers as a class.

> **Answers**
> 1 Plates and bowls were discovered by an archaeologist.
> 2 Archaeologists found the plates and bowls at the bottom of the well.
> 3 Romans used the plates and bowls 2000 years ago.
> 4 The site was discovered by archaeologists in central London.
> 5 Coins, an amphitheatre and a bear's skull were found by the archaeologists too.

5 Challenge

- Check learners understand what a time capsule is and why it might be created. Ask learners to imagine that they live in the future and they have discovered a time capsule full of everyday objects they use now.
- Tell them to write an article about what they discover.
- They may do this activity in pairs or groups of three.

> **Answers**
> Learners' own answers.

Differentiated instruction

Additional support and practice

- 💬 In pairs or small groups, learners play a game to revise the past passive and the vocabulary they have learnt so far.
- Each group member writes three words for objects or people on a piece of paper.
- The other group members take turns to say things about the word. The author can only answer *yes* or *no* (e.g. *It was found in a tomb.* Author: *Yes.*) Then they have to guess the word.

Extend and challenge

- 💬 Bring in a few short newspaper or magazine articles suitable for the level of the learners. Ask learners to work in small groups and find examples of fact, opinion, quotations and headlines.

Lesson 5: Literature: *There's a Pharaoh in Our Bath!*

Learner's Book pages: 104–106
Activity Book pages: 84–85

Lesson objectives

Listening: Listen to an extract from a story, listen and answer questions, listen and identify tone in speech.

Speaking: Speak about the characters in a story, speak about the ending of a story.

Reading: Read a summary of a story, read and do a personality quiz.

Writing: Write answers to questions, write a short paragraph.

Critical thinking: Predict, speculate.

Values: Being patient.

Language focus: Subordinate clauses

Vocabulary: *moon-like, winged, hooded, hawk, tubby, pudgy, angry, excited, worried, impatient*

Materials: Dictionaries, Internet access, copies of **Photocopiable activity 14**, writing and drawing supplies, sheets of paper, card to make the covers of the album and the pyramid, sand and glue (optional).

Learner's Book

 Warm up

- Play a guessing game. Give a definition and ask the class to give the corresponding word, e.g. *What do you call the king of ancient Egypt?* (pharaoh) *What's the name of the ancient Egyptian 'alphabet'?* (hieroglyphics)
- Ask learners what they remember from **Lesson 4** about Tutankhamun and his tomb.
- Ask if they would like to go into the pyramids and see the tombs of pharaohs. Encourage them to explain their answers.

1 💬 Talk about it

- Ask learners to talk about famous discoveries that have been made in their country. If they don't know much about this, you could ask them to search the Internet for some information.

> **Answers**
> Learners' own answers.

2 Read and listen 42 [CD2 Track 11]

- **Critical thinking:** Focus on the illustrations. Ask learners to predict what the story is going to be about. Who do they think is the main character in the story? Why do they think so? What's the title of the story?
- Tell learners they are going to listen to an extract from a story. They answer the questions after each part.
- Play the audio once all the way through to give learners an idea of what the story is about. Then play each part at least twice and allow time for the class to answer the questions.
- Tell learners to look at the **Glossary** boxes to find out the meaning of unfamiliar words.
- Check the answers as a class.

> **Audioscript:** Track 42
> See Learner's Book pages 104–106.

> **Answers**
> 1 old mummy-cases, ancient skeletons and a stuffed rhinoceros
> 2 beautifully painted and ancient
> 3 the mummy of the missing Pharaoh
> 4 Grimstone
> 5 *Please keep this way up at all times. Not to be opened before Christmas.*
> 6 the clue to a fabulous treasure
> 7 the ancient Egyptian God of the Dead.

[AB] For further practice, see Activity 1 in the Activity Book.

3 💬 Talk

- Tell learners to read the text again and, working in small groups, discuss what they think happened when Professor Jelly opened the coffin.
- **Critical thinking:** Ask learners to speculate about different options and encourage them to explain their opinions. Reassure them that there is no 'correct answer'.

> **Answers**
> Learners' own answers.

4 Word study

- Ask learners to match the adjectives to the correct part of the body or face (according to their use in the story extract).
- Tell learners to use their dictionary and the illustrations in the story text to help them.

- Then ask them to find the words in the text and read the sentence they are in. This will help them fully understand the meaning and contextualise the word.
- Check the answers as a class.

> **Answers**
> 1 c   2 d   3 a   4 f   5 e   6 b

 For further practice, see Activities 2, 3 and 4 in the Activity Book.

5 Pronunciation 43 [CD2 Track 12]

- Tell learners to look at the adjectives in the box and elicit their meaning.
- Ask learners to say something with the correct intonation that shows that emotion.
- Tell learners to listen to the direct speech sentences from the story and match them with one of the emotions.
- Play the audio a few times.
- Check the answers as a class.

> **Audioscript:** Track 43
> 1 'But who's inside?'
> 2 'Of course I'm making it up.'
> 3 'This could be the discovery of the century. It could make our fortunes.'
> 4 'You're making this up, Jelly, aren't you?'

> **Answers**
> 1 impatient   2 angry   3 excited   4 worried

 For further practice, see Activity 5 in the Activity Book.

6 Use of English

- Review with learners the use of subordinate clauses to express opinion. They did some work on this in **Lesson 1**.
- Focus on the activity and ask learners to use affirmative and negative subordinate clauses to complete the sentences giving their opinion of the story.
- Check the answers as a class.

> **Answers**
> Learners' own answers.

7 ✏ Write

- Ask learners to think what happens when the professor opens the coffin and write a paragraph.
- They write this on a separate sheet of paper.
- When they have finished, ask learners to read it to the class.
- **Critical thinking:** Ask learners to write down their ideas in note form; then they choose the best ideas to include. Tell them that the events need to be consistent with what has happened so far and with the characters.
- **Portfolio opportunity:** Ask learners to write their name and the date on their text and file it in their portfolio.

8 Values

- In the story, Grimstone is very impatient. Ask the class to find examples of this in the text.
- Ask learners if they are impatient. How do they know? Elicit some examples.
- In pairs ask learners to read the quiz questions and answer them honestly to find out how impatient they are.
- When they have finished, ask them to work out the results and discuss their answers with their partner.

> **Answers**
> Learners' own answers.

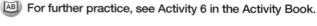 For further practice, see Activity 6 in the Activity Book.

☞ Wrap up

- Learners share their results with the class and, if necessary, make some resolutions to change their behaviour.

Activity Book

1 Read

- Tell learners to read the extract again and decide if the sentences are true or false.
- Ask them to identify the parts of the text that help them arrive at their answers.
- Check the answers as a class.

> **Answers**
> 1 true 2 false 3 false 4 true 5 false 6 true 7 false 8 true

2 Vocabulary

- Learners match the adjectives to the part of the body they describe in the story text.
- Check the answers as a class.

> **Answers**
> 1 pudgy 2 winged 3 tubby 4 moon-like 5 hawk 6 hooded

3 Vocabulary

- Ask learners to read the description of Grimstone's face.
- Then, they draw a picture of him in the box.

> **Answers**
> Learners' own answers.

4 Use of English

- Learners complete the summary of the extract using the verbs in the box either in the past simple passive or in the past simple.
- Check the answers as a class.

> **Answers**
> 1 was pushed   2 looked   3 were inspected   4 took
> 5 was becoming   6 thought   7 finished

5 Pronunciation 67 [CD2 Track 36]

- Learners listen to the examples of direct speech and match to an emotion (**a–d**).
- Check the answers as a class.

Audioscript: Track 67

1 'Shall I open the school report now?'
2 'Why did you do that?'
3 'Mum, are you ready now?'
4 'Open the door, it could be him.'

Answers
1 d   2 c   3 b   4 a

6 Values

- Learners write sentences about situations in which they need to be patient.
- Discuss learners' answers as a class.

Answers
Learners' own answers.

Differentiated instruction

Additional support and practice

Give learners copies of **Photocopiable activity 14**. They imagine they are part of Professor Jelly's expedition. They make an album of the discoveries they have made with captions explaining what they are. They make a simple card pyramid. For this you may wish to enlarge the copy to make a bigger pyramid. If you want to make it more 'real', you could ask learners to cover the faces of their pyramid with liquid glue and then dust it with sand. Then they write the mysterious message they found in the tomb using hieroglyphics. They challenge the rest of class to break the code.

Extend and challenge

- Ask learners to find information about the legend of Anubis. They write a short summary and share the information with the class.

Lesson 6: Choose a project

Learner's Book pages: 108–109
Activity Book pages: 86–87

Lesson objectives

Listening: Listen to presentations.

Speaking: Present your project to the class.

Reading: Read questions and instructions, research.

Writing: Write about a famous building.

Language focus: Unit 7 Review

Materials:

1 A famous building or statue: Internet access or reference books, drawing supplies or photos.

2 Egyptian hieroglyphics – Break the code! writing supplies.

Learner's Book

☞ Warm up

- Ask learners what they have enjoyed most in the unit. What new information have they learned?
- What words did they find the most interesting/useful/difficult?
- Which discovery or monument do they like most?

Choose a project

- Learners choose an end-of-unit project to work on. Help them choose. Provide materials.

1 A famous building or statue

- Learners work in groups. Supply reference books or Internet access.
- Tell learners to read and follow the steps of the project outlined in the Learner's Book.
- If possible, organise a visit to the building or statue and tell learners to take photos.

2 Egyptian hieroglyphics: Break the code!

- In groups, learners look at the hieroglyphics and break the code.
- Then they create their own coded messages using hieroglyphics or a code of their own.
- They write the coded messages on sheets of paper and give them to the class to break.

☞ Wrap up

- Learners present their work to the class.
- **Portfolio opportunity:** If possible, leave the learner projects on display for a short while, then consider filing the projects, photos or scans of the work, in learners' portfolios. Write the date on the work.

☉ Reflect on your learning

- Learners think about what they have studied in the unit and answer the questions.
- **Informal assessment opportunity:** Circulate as learners work. Informally assess their receptive and productive language skills. Ask questions. You may want to take notes on their responses.
- Review the Big question: *What can we see of ancient civilisations in our culture today?* Ask learners what new things they have learned about ancient civilisations.

Answers
Learners' own answers.

Look what I can do!

- **Aim:** to check that learners can do all the things from **Unit 7**.
- Review the *I can …* statements.
- Learners reflect on what aspects of the unit they have found most difficult and why.
- Do they have any ideas about how to overcome these difficulties? Encourage learners to think of strategies that may help them improve.

- Have they noticed an improvement in any aspect of their learning?
- Elicit what learners liked most about this unit and encourage them to explain why.

> **Answers**
> Learners' own answers.

Activity Book

Unit 7: Revision

- Learners do the multiple-choice activity that revises the language covered in **Unit 7**.

> **Answers**
> 1 c 2 b 3 b 4 b 5 b 6 c 7 a 8 b 9 c 10 b 11 b 12 c

My global progress

- Tell learners to read the questions and think about what they have studied in this unit.
- Ask them to answer the questions. Encourage them to take time to reflect on their learning and give honest answers.
- **Portfolio opportunity:** If you have been filing learners' work all through this unit, you may find it useful to put all the work of this unit together. You may ask learners to make a cover for their work, decorating it with an image that represents what they have learned.

Photocopiable activity 13

> **Answers**
> was built; was completed; is considered; are called; were destroyed; damaged; were taken; were used; was dedicated; was converted; was turned.

8 Weather and climate

Big question How can we protect our planet?

Unit overview

In this unit learners will:

- talk about the weather and temperatures around the world
- listen and present a newscast about extreme weather
- read a text about rainforests
- read and learn about rainforest animals
- research and write a description of a rainforest animal
- understand and talk about a poem.

Learners will build communication and literacy skills as they read and listen to texts about the weather and temperatures around the world, extreme weather conditions and how to survive them; speak about rainforests, rainforest animals and how to protect the environment; make presentations, complete notes, read and write reports; develop vocabulary study skills; learn to use *should* for advice, adverbs of degree, adjectives in the correct order; and identify stress in sentences.

At the end of the unit, they will apply and personalise what they have learned by working in small groups to complete a project of their choice: making a chart of weather conditions or raising money to help the rainforests.

Language focus

Should/Shouldn't for advice

Adverbs of degree

Adjective order

Vocabulary topics: extreme weather, weather collocations, rainforests, animals, adjectives

Critical thinking

- Analysing information
- Giving opinions
- Predicting
- Comparing and contrasting.

Self-assessment

- I can talk about weather and temperatures.
- I can present a newscast about extreme weather conditions.
- I can read and give my opinion on the subject of the text.
- I can understand a text about rainforest animals and discuss their behaviour.
- I can research and write about a rainforest animal.
- I can read and talk about a poem.

Teaching tip

It is inevitable that learners will sometimes use information in their own language to do some of the activities. Explain that this is all right as long as they read the information in their mother tongue but then explain it or write about it in English.

Review the learners' work, noting areas where they demonstrate strength and areas where they need additional instruction and practice. Use this information to customise your teaching as you continue to **Unit 9**.

Lesson 1: Weather and climate

Learner's Book pages: 110–111
Activity Book pages: 88–89

Lesson objectives

Listening: Listen for information, listen and classify

Speaking: Practise theme vocabulary, speak about extreme weather conditions.

Reading: Read about extreme weather conditions.

Writing: Write about extreme weather conditions.

Language focus: *should/shouldn't* for advice

Vocabulary: *flood, tornado, blizzard, drought, typhoon, sandstorm, heavy, high, severe, torrential, strong, violent;* weather collocations

Materials: Dictionaries, map of your country, map of the world.

Learner's Book

 Warm up

- Ask learners what the weather is like today. Review weather vocabulary.
- What's the weather like in their city or region in the different seasons?
- Do they think the weather is changing? If so, why? Are we humans responsible in some way? Ask learners if they think they can do anything about it.

1 💬 Talk about it

- Ask learners to discuss if they have ever experienced extreme weather conditions. Tell them to talk about what happened and how they protected themselves.

Answers
Learners' own answers.

2 Word study

- Ask learners to look at the photos. Do they know the words to describe these weather conditions?
- Ask them to match the pictures to the words in the box. Tell them to use their dictionaries if necessary.
- Check the answers as a class.

Answers
a drought
b tornado
c typhoon
d flood
e sandstorm
f blizzard

 For further practice, see Activity 1 in the Activity Book.

3 Listen 44 [CD2 Track 13]

- Tell learners to listen to four people speaking about the weather.
- Play the audio a few times. Learners match the speakers to the weather.
- Check the answers as a class.
- **Study skills:** Discuss as a class how many answers they got right and what words in the audio helped them decide.

Audioscript: Track 44

Speaker 1: I live in Qatar – it's dry and warm here but sometimes it's extremely windy as well. We call these sandstorm *shaboobs*. Once, I was in the car with my dad travelling home from school when I saw a wall of sand through the back window of our car. Dad thought it was travelling at about 80 kilometres per hour so we quickly found somewhere to stop indoors before the storm hit. It lasted for three hours and covered everything with sand!

Speaker 2: I live in Canada and during the winter months we have lots of heavy snow and strong winds called blizzards. Last year it snowed for a whole week without stopping which is quite normal where I live. Our car was completely covered in snow and we had to use a shovel to make a path through the snow out of our front door! We had no electricity for two days either so we had to light candles in the evening so we could see.

Speaker 3: I'm from Taiwan. In Taiwan we have violent storms called typhoons. In other parts of the world they are called hurricanes or cyclones. We are used to these storms and we can get three to four typhoons a year. The high winds and heavy rain cause a lot of damage to buildings and sometimes cause flash flooding, so it's best to stay indoors until the storm has finished.

Speaker 4: I'm from Bangladesh. Severe flooding in my country is very common especially in the monsoon season. This happens in the summer when we get most of our rainfall. The problem is we get torrential rain and then we get flooding. Last month a nearby village was flooded. A lot of people lost their homes and animals. The roads were flooded with water so cars couldn't get to the village and schools and shops were closed.

Answers
Speaker 1 – sandstorm
Speaker 2 – blizzards
Speaker 3 – typhoons
Speaker 4 – floods

4 🖾 Listen 44 [CD2 Track 13]

- Ask learners to read the weather fact box and decide if the sentences are true or false.
- When they have finished, ask them to correct the sentences which are false.
- Remind them to use the clauses *I think that/I don't think that ..., I know ..., I believe ...* to give their opinions.
- Play the audio again and ask learners to check their answers.

Answers
1 true **2** false **3** true **4** true **5** true **6** false

5 Word study

- You could ask learners to work in pairs for this activity. They read the adjectives and discuss the meaning of unfamiliar words. They use their dictionaries if necessary.
- Then they complete the weather sentences.

Answers
1 severe
2 heavy/torrential, high/strong
3 severe
4 heavy/torrential
5 violent/severe

 For further practice, see Activities 2 and 3 in the Activity Book.

6 Listen 45 [CD2 Track 14]

- Ask learners what they should do and shouldn't do when there is a thunderstorm and they are outside, e.g. should they stand under a tree or speak on their mobile phone?
- Tell the class that they are going to listen to Habib talking about what you should and shouldn't do when there is a thunderstorm.
- Learners copy the *Should/Shouldn't* table in their notebooks and write each action in the correct column.
- Play the audio a few times.
- Check the answers as a class.

Audioscript: Track 45

Habib: During a severe sandstorm it's best to close all the windows and doors in your house and to stay inside. If you are outside during a sandstorm then you should make sure your body is covered in clothing otherwise the sand and other flying objects could hurt you. You should also wear a mask and goggles to protect your eyes. You shouldn't drive during a sandstorm as you won't be able to see the road very well. Finally if you are with a camel in the desert during a sandstorm then sit it down and lie against its side. Camels are used to sandstorms, so don't worry!

Answers
Should: stay indoors, use your camel to protect you, wear a mask, put a coat on, protect your body, shut all the windows
Shouldn't: drive your car.

7 Talk

- Tell learners to use weather collocations to talk about the type of weather there is in their own country.
- Ask them to discuss what they should and shouldn't do in extreme weather conditions.

Answers
Learners' own answers.

 For further practice, see Activity 4 in the Activity Book.

Wrap up

- When they have finished, learners locate areas in their country where there are sometimes extreme weather conditions.
- Learners share their writing in **Activity 5** in the Activity Book with the class.

Activity Book

1 Vocabulary

- Ask learners to unjumble the letters in the pictures and label the types of weather.
- Check the answers as a class.

Answers
1 flood
2 tornado
3 drought
4 typhoon
5 sandstorm
6 blizzard

2 Vocabulary

- Learners read the sentences and choose the correct answers.
- Check the answers as a class.

Answers
1 b   2 c   3 b   4 b

3 Read

- Ask learners to read the text and match the questions to the correct part of the text.
- They compare their answers in pairs or small groups. Check the answers as a class.

Answers
1 What are tornadoes?
2 What do they look like?
3 How fast do they travel?
4 What should you do?

4 Challenge

- Tell learners to write about an extreme weather situation they have experienced in their own country.
- Then they share it with the class.

Answers
Learners' own answers

Differentiated instruction

Additional support and practice

*   Play Hangman to revise weather vocabulary and collocations.

Extend and challenge

*   Learners search the Internet for information about what to do if they are camping and there is a severe storm. They write some advice for other campers.

Lesson 2: Rainforests

Learner's Book pages: 112–13
Activity Book pages: 90–91

Lesson objectives

Speaking: Talk about rainforests and the environment.

Reading: Read for information, read and answer, read and give opinions.

Write: Complete sentences, answer questions.

Critical thinking: Give opinions.

Vocabulary: *equator, layers, canopy, understory, underneath, bushes, climate, carbon dioxide, greenhouse gas, release, natural resources, cut down.*

Materials: Map of the world, copies of **Photocopiable activity 15.**

Learner's Book

Warm up

*   Display a map of the world and point to the equator. Is their country close to the equator? If not, ask learners if they know what the weather is like in countries near the equator, e.g. in Africa, Asia and America.
*   Elicit vocabulary, e.g *desert, jungle, forest*.

1 Talk about it

*   Ask learners to talk with a partner about rainforests, e.g. where they are and why they are special.
*   What problems are there with rainforests?
*   Ask learners to make some notes of their ideas.

Answers
Learners' own answers.

2 Read

*   Ask learners to read the text and find the answers to the questions from **Activity 1**.
*   Ask learners to re-read the text and identify any new words. Ask them to try to work out the meaning of new words from the context.

*   **Study skills:** Ask learners to look up the new words in the dictionary. Then, they copy the words that they find most difficult in their Vocabulary journal along with a definition.

Answers
Learners' own answers.

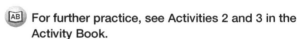 **For further practice, see Activity 1 in the Activity Book.**

3 Talk

*   **Critical thinking:** Ask learners to re-read the text and reflect on what they read before giving an opinion. Tell them that they don't need to agree with something just because it is in a book. They must have their own thoughts and be able to defend them.
*   Ask learners to discuss what is happening in the rainforest. Ask them to give their opinions and justify them.

Answers
Learners' own answers.

For further practice, see Strategy check! in the Activity Book.

4 Read

*   Ask learners to read the questions and match them with the correct paragraph of the rainforest text in **Activity 2**.
*   Check the answers as a class.

Answers
A – 3 What is a rainforest?
B – 2 What are the layers of the rainforest?
C – 5 What lives in the rainforests?
D – 1 Why are rainforests important to us?
E – 4 What is happening to the rainforests?

For further practice, see Activities 2 and 3 in the Activity Book.

5 Word study

*   Tell learners to read the definitions and match them to the words in blue in the text in **Activity 2**.
*   You could ask learners to compare their answers with a partner.
*   Check the answers as a class.

Answers
1 carbon dioxide
2 climate
3 greenhouse gas/carbon dioxide
4 protect
5 natural resources

6 Values

*   Ask learners to think about what they can do to protect the rainforests. The pictures will give them some ideas.

- They discuss with a partner and write down a few ideas.
- Then, they prepare a mini-poster with their ideas and pictures of the animals that live in the rainforests.

Answers
Learners' own answers.

Wrap up
- When they have finished, learners share their ideas about saving the rainforest with the class.
- **Portfolio opportunity:** Collect the mini-posters and file them in learners' portfolios.

Activity Book

1 Vocabulary
- Tell learners to read about and label the different parts of the rainforests and the animals which live there.
- Tell them to use their dictionary to check the words they don't know.
- Check the answers as a class.

Answers
1 canopy   2 emergent layer   3 forest floor   4 understory
5 sloth   6 harpy eagle   7 leafcutter ants   8 red-eyed tree frog
9 spider monkey   10 boa constrictor   11 caterpillar
12 pygmy glider   13 toucan

Strategy check!
- Learners tick the strategies which will help them form an opinion about a text.

  Answers
  Think carefully about the information given in the text.
  Do you agree or disagree with it. ✓
  Evaluate the text carefully as you read. ✓

2 Read
- Learners think about what their furniture, their toys, the food they eat and the medicines that we use all have in common.
- Ask learners to read the text to find out.

Answers
Learners' own answers.

3 Read
- Learners write opinions about the information they have discovered in the text.
- Discuss their answers as a class.

Answers
Learners' own answers.

Differentiated instruction
Additional support and practice
- Ask learners to choose five words from this unit that they find difficult to remember. They copy them in their Vocabulary journal and write a definition and an example sentence.

Extend and challenge
- Learners do **Photocopiable activity 15**. Learners do the rainforest quiz. You could ask them to write two more questions and make a class quiz.

Lesson 3: Extreme weather

Learner's Book pages: 114–115
Activity Book pages: 92–93

Lesson objectives
Listening: Listen to weather reports, listen for information.

Speaking: Speak about a weather report, discuss the weather.

Writing: Make notes for a presentation.

Language focus: Adverbs of degree: *quite, a little, very, extremely*

Vocabulary: *humid, warning, typhoon*

Review: *flood, tornado, blizzard, drought, typhoon, sandstorm*

Materials: Map of the world, Internet access, pictures of extreme weather, drawing supplies, **Photocopiable activity 16**.

Learner's Book

Warm up
- Review weather vocabulary. Show some pictures of extreme weather conditions. Elicit the vocabulary and a description.
- Write on the board: °C, °F and ask the class what this means.
- Explain that temperature can be measured in degrees Celsius (°C) or degrees Fahrenheit (°F). What measurement is used in their country?

1 💬 Talk about it

- Ask learners to discuss what the weather is normally like for each season in their country.
- Ask them to talk about how good weather reports are. Can they be trusted? Do they think it's easy or difficult to make a weather forecast? What do the weather people need to know to make a forecast?

Answers
Learners' own answers.

2 Listen 46 [CD2 Track 15]

- Tell learners they are going to listen to weather reports for two different parts of the world.
- Focus on the pictures and ask learners to describe what they see. Can they identify the symbols?
- Learners listen and match the weather reports with the correct country.
- Play the audio at least twice.
- Check the answers as a class.

Audioscript: Track 46

1

Male weather reporter: … and here's a quick weather update. Today was a beautiful day so let's see what it will be like tomorrow. Tomorrow will be quite warm with temperatures of about 21°C. In the afternoon, it might be a little wet, with some rain in mountain areas. Make sure you have a jumper or a coat if you're going out in the evening because it will be very cold with temperatures of 5°C. I'll be back at 8 o'clock with a full report …

2

Female weather reporter: Good evening and welcome to Global News, today, Friday 9th August. We start with a warning about a typhoon which is coming in across the south of the island. The typhoon will be the worst at 4pm tomorrow when there will be extremely heavy rain and high winds. The storm should pass by 8pm so, please stay indoors during the storm. Temperatures during the day tomorrow will be about 28°C and it will be extremely humid. The temperature will drop to about 23°C at night. Good night and don't forget …

Answers
1 Colombia (Bogota)   2 Taiwan (Taipei)

Listening strategy

- Look at the listening strategy with the class. They need to listen carefully for key words that will help them answer the questions in **Activity 3**.

3 Listen 46 [CD2 Track 15]

- Ask learners to read the questions. Ask them to predict what key words will help them find the answers. Elicit ideas.
- Play the audio at least twice more. Learners take notes and answer the questions.
- Check the answers as a class. Ask learners what key words helped them.

Answers
1 Colombia: day – 21°C, night – 5°C
  Taiwan: day – 28°C, night – 23°C
2 Make sure you have a jumper or a coat if you are going out in the evening.
3 They should stay indoors.

(AB) **For further practice, see Activity 1 in the Activity Book.**

4 📝 Use of English 46 [CD2 Track 15]

- Read the **Use of English** box as a class and discuss the adverbs of degree.
- Give some example sentences using the adverbs.
- Tell learners to complete the questions.
- Then play the audio and ask learners to check their answers.
- As a class, think of some more examples using the adverbs of degree.
- Tell learners to write the examples in their notebooks.

Answers
1 quite   2 a little   3 very cold   4 extremely   5 extremely

(AB) **For further practice, see Activities 2 and 3 in the Activity Book.**

5 💬 Talk

- Ask learners to discuss what they like most and least about the climate in their country.
- Tell them to explain their answers using adverbs of degree.
- **Informal assessment opportunity:** Circulate, listening to learners' interaction. Take notes of common mistakes for remedial work.

Answers
Learners' own answers.

6 📝 Pronunciation 47 [CD2 Track 16]

- Ask learners to read the sentences and think about which the stressed words might be.
- Tell them to listen to the audio recording and identify the stressed words.
- Play the audio at least twice.
- Check the answers as a class. Were the learners' ideas correct?
- Then, in pairs, learners practise saying the sentences using the appropriate pronunciation.
- Circulate, checking for correct pronunciation and intonation.

Answers (and audioscript)
Female weather reporter: Good evening and <u>welcome</u> to Global News, today, Friday 9th August. We start with a <u>warning</u> about a typhoon which is coming in across <u>the south</u> of the island. The typhoon will be <u>the worst</u> at 4 pm tomorrow when there will be <u>extremely</u> heavy rain and high winds. The storm should pass by 8 pm so, <u>please</u> stay indoors during the storm. Temperatures during the day tomorrow will be about 28°C and it will be <u>extremely</u> humid. The temperature will <u>drop</u> to about 23°C at night. Good night and don't forget …

 For further practice, see Activity 4 in the Activity Book.

Speaking tip

- Focus on the speaking tip and tell learners that they will have to rehearse the newscast they are going to prepare before giving the presentation.
- Remind them of the proverb they learnt in **Unit 7** – 'Practice makes perfect'.

Present it!

- Tell the class they are going to prepare a presentation on one of two topics. They can choose either **A** or **B**.

A Write a weather report.
- Learners prepare a weather report for a country they know.
- Focus on the steps outlined in the box and tell learners to use them to organise their work.
- First they choose a country and draw a map of their chosen country or print one out from the Internet.
- They decide what the weather will be and write the weather report.
- Then, they rehearse the presentation, including displaying the pictures. Remind them to practise stressing the important words.

B Research an extreme weather event.
- Learners find out how a particular type of extreme weather happens and what the effects are.
- They find pictures and write advice about what to do in these weather conditions.
- Then they rehearse their newscast using correct stress.
- **Informal assessment opportunity:** Circulate, asking questions while learners are preparing the presentations. Make notes of their performance while they are making their presentation. You may wish to set up some remedial work on the most common mistakes you have observed.

Answers
Learners' own answers.

 For further practice, see Activity 5 in the Activity Book.

Wrap up

- When learners have finished, they present their report to the class.
- **Portfolio opportunity:** Collect the script of the presentation along with the pictures. Write the learner's name and the date and file it in their portfolio.

Activity Book

1 Read

- Ask learners to read the online weather report for Brazil.
- They draw appropriate weather symbols on the map and write the temperature for each city.
- Check the answers as a class.

Answers
Manaus – sunny, cloudy, thunderstorm – 20°C
Recife – cloudy, light rain – 21°C
Porto Alegre – sunny – 26°C
Porto Velho – stormy – 25°C

2 Read

- Ask learners to work in pairs or small groups and read Habib's blog about his trip along the Amazon River in Brazil (near Manaus).
- They decide how accurate the weather report in **Activity 1** was and circle any differences in the blog text.
- Check the answers as a class.

Answers
bright, sunny day (not humid, light cloud)
25°C (not 20°C)

3 Read

- Tell learners to look at the weather and temperatures in the table.
- They complete the sentences using adverbs of degree. They compare their answers with a partner.
- Check the answers as a class.

Answers
1 quite cold **2** very stormy **3** very sunny **4** extremely windy
5 very wet **6** cloudy and quite cold

4 Pronunciation 68 [CD2 Track 37]

- Tell learners they are going to listen and underline the stressed words.
- Then, in pairs, they practise saying the sentence with the correct pronunciation.
- Check the answers as a class.

Audioscript: Track 68 (and answers)
Tomorrow there will be <u>*very*</u> high winds, so be <u>extremely</u> careful if you are <u>driving</u> or out <u>walking</u>.

5 Challenge

- Learners write a weather report for their own town or city for the following day.
- Then they present it to the class.
- Remind learners to stress the important information.

> **Answers**
> Learners' own answers.

Differentiated instruction

Additional support and practice

- Do **Photocopiable activity 16**. Learners work out equivalent temperatures in Celsius and Fahrenheit scales.

Extend and challenge

- Ask learners to work in small groups. They choose a place they have found out about in this unit (e.g. the river Amazon and the Amazon rainforest, Colombia or Taiwan) and search the Internet to find more information about it. They prepare a short presentation on their chosen place.

Lesson 4: Rainforest animals

Learner's Book pages: 116–117
Activity Book pages: 94–95

Lesson objectives

Speaking: Speak about rainforest animals.
Reading: Read about an animal.
Writing: Write a description of an animal.

Language focus: Adjective order
Vocabulary: *endangered, tail, limbs, diurnal, swing, scream, shake, sloth, furry, claws*

Materials: Dictionaries, map of the world, Internet access.

Learner's Book

Warm up

- Review with the class what they have read and learned about the weather in Brazil, the Amazon and rainforests.

1 Talk about it

- Ask learners to talk about the animals that live in rainforests and which part of the rainforests they think these animals live in.

> **Answers**
> Learner's own answers.

2 Read

- Focus on the photo and ask learners why they think this animal is called a 'spider' monkey. Elicit ideas.
- Ask learners to read Mina's description of the spider monkey.
- Ask them to read the text again and identify the adjectives used to describe the spider monkey.
- Encourage learners to guess the meaning of unfamiliar words from the context. If necessary, tell them to use their dictionaries.

> **Answers**
> endangered, thick, black, brown, red, long, diurnal, sociable

3 Read

- Ask learners to re-read the text and choose a heading for each paragraph.
- They compare their answers with a partner.
- Check the answers as a class. Ask learners to justify their answers.

> **Answers**
> **1 – c** Location
> **2 – b** Appearance
> **3 – a** Diet
> **4 – d** Behaviour
> **5 – e** Curious fact

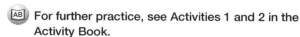 For further practice, see Activities 1 and 2 in the Activity Book.

4 Read

- Focus on the photo of the sloth. Ask learners if they know the name of this animal. Do they like it?
- Ask learners to describe the sloth using adjectives, e.g. *cute, ugly.*
- Ask learners to read the fact file about sloths and match the adjectives in red to the numbers in the **Use of English** box.
- Encourage learners to guess the meaning of unfamiliar words from the context. If necessary, tell them to use their dictionaries.
- Check the answers as a class.

> **Answers**
> **3 Size:** long, tiny, small, short
> **5 Shape:** flat, sharp, thick
> **6 Colour:** grey
> **8 Material:** furry

 For further practice, see Activity 3 in the Activity Book.

Writing tip

> Remind learners to use plenty of adjectives to make their descriptions more interesting.

Write

- Tell learners that they are going to write a description of a rainforest animal using the fact file in **Activity 4** as a model.
- Ask them to search the Internet for information and pictures of some rainforest animals and to choose one that interests them.
- Tell them to follow the steps in the Learner's Book to organise their work.
- They write the description and display it with the pictures the classroom.

Answers
Learners' own answers.

 For further practice, see Activity 4 in the Activity Book.

 Wrap up

- Ask learners to say which animal they find the most interesting and why.
- **Portfolio opportunity:** Collect the animal descriptions and file them in the learners' portfolios.
- **Home–school opportunity:** Learners take their work home and share it with the family.

Activity Book

1 Read

- Learners read the descriptions of the rainforest animals and match them to the correct picture.
- Check the answers as a class.

Answers
1 d   2 c   3 b   4 a

2 Read

- Learners re-read the text. They read the sentences and decide whether each one is true or false.
- Check the answers as a class.

Answers
1 true
2 false
3 true
4 true
5 false

3 Use of English

- Learners reorder the words to make sentences about the animals from the text.
- They should refer to the **Use of English** box to check the order of adjectives.
- Check the answers as a class.

Answers
1 An amazing, long, thin, feathery tail.
2 A small, green Brazilian tree frog.
3 A beautiful, large, grey, African parrot.
4 Two frightening, brown, long-bodied, Australian crocodiles.
5 Three enormous, long-haired orangutans.

4 Challenge

- Ask learners to write a description about the animal in the picture (a jaguar).
- They use the information in the box.

Answers
Learners' own answers.

Differentiated instruction

Additional support and practice

- In pairs or small groups, learners play a game to revise the vocabulary they have learned in this unit so far.
- Each group member thinks of an animal. The rest of the group takes turns to ask questions to find out what animal it is. They can only answer *yes* or *no*.

Extend and challenge

- Learners work in pairs. They write descriptive sentences using a variety of adjectives. Tell them to write about animals, places, monuments, etc. They write the adjectives in each sentence in jumbled order. They exchange their sentences with another pair and rearrange the adjectives correctly.

Lesson 5: Poems: *A Visit with Mr Tree Frog* and *If I Were a Sloth*

Learner's Book pages: 118–121
Activity Book pages: 96–97

Lesson objectives

Listening: Listen to two poems, listen and answer questions, listen and find rhyming words.

Speaking: Speak about the animals in a poem.

Reading: Read two poems, read and match, read and order.

Writing: Answer questions, write similes.

Critical thinking: Predict, compare information.

Language focus: Rhyming words; action verbs: *hang, move, play, whistle, stare*; similes: *like*

Vocabulary: *rattle, bright, wiggle, mellow, dine, crickets, moth, treat, warm, earthly, cure, poisonous, pop up, blink, nap, wonder, cutest, upside down, coconut, fierce, nocturnal, grab, bite, whistle, thrive, jive*

Materials: Dictionaries, Internet access.

Learner's Book

Warm up

- Play a guessing game about animals. Give a definition and ask the class to guess the animal, e.g. *It's a grey and white bird. It likes to eat monkeys. It lives in the rainforest.* (a harpy eagle)

1 🗨 Talk about it

- Ask learners to talk about their favourite animals.
- Talk about the four categories of animals in the box.
- Ask learners which group of animals frogs belong to (amphibian).
- Ask learners if they think a sloth is a mammal (yes).
- Ask learners for more examples of animals in each category.

> **Answers**
> Learners' own answers.

2 Read and listen 48 [CD2 Track 17]

- **Critical thinking:** Focus on the illustrations. Ask learners to predict what this poem is going to be about.
- Tell learners they are going to listen to a poem. Play the audio once through for learners to get an idea of what the poem is about.
- Then play it at least twice and ask learners to read and listen.
- Then learners match the pictures to the relevant lines in the poem.
- Tell them to look at the **Glossary** box for the meaning of unfamiliar words.
- Discuss the answers as a class.

> **Audioscript:** Track 48
> See Learner's Book pages 118–119.

> **Answers**
> a line 13   b line 4   c line 7   d line 9   e line 18   f line 25
> g line 21   h line 31

[AB] **For further practice, see Activities 1 and 2 in the Activity Book.**

3 Pronunciation 48 [CD2 Track 17]

- Tell learners to listen to the poem again and find words that rhyme or partly rhyme with the words in the box.
- Play the audio a few times and allow time for learners to write.
- Then ask them to compare their answers with a partner.
- Check the answers as a class. Ask learners to say the rhyming pairs.

> **Answers**
> class – grass, streets – treat, fame – rain, fight – night,
> plane – name, poisonous – laziness, seen – green, naps – snaps

[AB] **For further practice, see Activity 3 in the Activity Book.**

4 Word study

- Ask learners to match the words highlighted in blue in the poem with the definitions.
- Tell them to use their dictionary and the illustrations to help them.
- Check the answers as a class.

> **Answers**
> 1 bright   2 blinks   3 warm   4 cure   5 wiggle   6 wonder

5 🗨 Talk

- Ask learners what the author of the poem thinks about the tree frog. Ask them to justify their opinions using words from the poem.
- Ask them what they think about the tree frog. Ask them if they like frogs in general.
- Encourage them to explain why.

> **Answers**
> Learners' own answers.

6 Read and listen 49 [CD2 Track 18]

- **Critical thinking:** Focus on the illustrations. Ask learners to predict what the poem is going to be about.
- Tell learners they are going to listen to another poem. They listen and put the illustrations in the correct order.
- Play the audio once through for learners to get an idea of what the poem is about.
- Then play it at least twice more.
- Discuss the answers as a class.

> **Audioscript:** Track 49
> See Learner's Book page 120.

> **Answers**
> 1 c   2 b   3 a   4 e   5 d

[AB] **For further practice, see Activity 4 in the Activity Book.**

7 Word study

- Ask learners to use the action verbs from the poem to complete the sentences.
- Tell them to use their dictionary and the illustrations in the poem to help them.
- Check the answers as a class.

Answers

1 move **2** staring **3** hang **4** play **5** whistles

 For further practice, see Activity 5 in the Activity Book.

8 Read

- Ask learners to re-read the poems and compare the animals.
- Discuss what is similar and different about them.
- Then, ask learners to read the sentences and decide if they are true or false.
- Check as a class and ask learners to justify their choices.

Answers

1 true **2** false **3** true **4** true

9 📝 Word study

- Ask learners what they think a *simile* is. Elicit some ideas.
- Then read the explanation and the examples.
- Ask learners to complete the similes in any logical way.
- Check the answers as a class.

Answers

Learners' own answers.

 For further practice, see Activity 6 in the Activity Book.

10 📝 Write

- Ask the class to write more similes about the sloth and the tree frog.
- Circulate, giving help with additional vocabulary as necessary.
- When they have finished, ask learners to share their similes with the class.

Answers

Learners' own answers.

11 💬 Talk

- In pairs, learners talk about the rainforest animals they have read about. They choose the ones they like best.
- Ask them to explain their answers.

Answers

Learners' own answers.

Wrap up

- Learners share their opinions with the class and vote for the most popular rainforest animal.

Activity Book

1 Read

- Tell learners to read the poem *A Visit with Mr Tree Frog* again.
- They find the words that match the definitions.
- Check the answers as a class.

Answers

1 tiny **2** buddy **3** rattles **4** wiggle **5** crickets and flies
6 moths **7** magic slime **8** blinks **9** naps **10** cutest

2 📝 Read

- Learners read the sentences about the poem and decide whether they are true or false.
- Then, they correct the false sentences.
- Check the answers as a class.

Answers

1 true
2 false. He's a mellow fellow that does not like to fight.
3 true
4 false. He blinks.
5 false. During the day he naps.

3 Listen 69 [CD2 Track 38]

- Ask learners to match the rhyming words.
- Then play the audio at least twice. They listen and check their answers.

Audioscript: Track 69 (and answers)

grass – class

plane – name

fight – night

street – treat

naps – snaps

seen – green

4 Read

- Learners read the poem *If I Were a Sloth* again.
- They read the sentences and circle the correct answer.
- Check the answers as a class.

Answers

1 hangs upside down **2** in the canopy **3** goes down
4 at night **5** makes a similar noise to a bird **6** an endangered
7 extremely long **8** look at it with interest

5 Action verbs

- Learners make sentences about the sloth using the action verbs in the box.
- Check the answers as a class.

6 Word study

- Learners write similes about the animals in the pictures.

Answers
1 The frog is green like the grass.
2 She's as busy as a bee.
3 He eats like a horse.

Differentiated instruction

Additional support and practice

- 💬 In pairs, learners look for poems about the rainforest.
- They choose a poem they like, copy and illustrate it and recite it to the class.
- They could visit http://www.poetrylibrary.edu.au/poems-book/the-great-forest-0528000

Extend and challenge

- 💬 Ask learners to work in pairs or small groups. They search the Internet or visit the local library and find information about amphibians and make a 'curious facts' file about them.
- Then they use this information to make a short presentation.
- They could visit http://animals.nationalgeographic.com/animals/amphibians/
- 💬 Alternatively, learners work in pairs or small groups and write a poem about the rainforest or rainforest animals.

Lesson 6: Choose a project

Learner's Book pages: 122–123
Activity Book pages: 98–99

Lesson objectives

Listening: Listen to class presentations.
Speaking: Present your project to the class.
Reading: Read questions and instructions.
Writing: Write a fundraising plan.

Language focus: Unit 8 Review

Materials:
1 **Chart weather conditions:** Drawing supplies, large sheet of paper.
2 **Raise money to help the rainforests:** Writing supplies.

Learner's Book

☞ Warm up

- Ask learners what they have enjoyed most in this unit. What new information have they learned?
- What words did they find the most interesting/useful/difficult?
- Which rainforest animal do they like best?

Choose a project

- Learners choose an end-of-unit project to work on. Help them choose. Provide materials.

1 Chart weather conditions

- Learners work in groups to make a chart of local weather conditions.
- Tell learners to read and follow the steps of the project.
- They keep a record of the weather conditions over the period of time they have decided to study.
- They could search the Internet to look at weather forecasts for the region and then check how accurate these have been.
- When they have finished collecting their information, they check how similar or different the weather has been compared to previous years.

2 Raise money to help protect the rainforests

- In groups, learners look at the pictures and name the activities that are shown.
- They discuss other ways in which they can raise money.
- They vote on the activity they like best and make notes to organise the activity.
- They prepare posters and a slogan for the campaign.
- Help them organise and carry out the activity.
- Then they donate the money they have raised to the conservation group they have chosen.

☞ Wrap up

- Learners present their work to the class or publish an article about it in the school magazine.
- **Portfolio opportunity:** If possible, leave the learner projects on display for a short while, then consider filing the projects, photos or scans of the work, in learners' portfolios. Write the date on the work.

Reflect on your learning

- Learners think about what they have studied in the unit and answer the questions.
- **Informal assessment opportunity:** Circulate as learners work. Informally assess their receptive and productive language skills. Ask questions. You may want to take notes on their responses.
- Review the Big question: *How can we protect our planet?* Ask what new ideas learners found during their work on this unit.
- Ask learners what new things they have learned about the weather, rainforests and animals. Elicit what they found most interesting about this unit and encourage them to explain why.

Look what I can do!

- **Aim:** To check that learners can do all the things from **Unit 8**.
- Review the *I can …* statements. Learners reflect on what aspects of the unit they have found most difficult and why.
- Do they have any ideas about how to overcome these difficulties? Encourage learners to think of strategies that may help them improve.

Activity Book

Unit 8 Revision

1 Vocabulary

- Learners complete the sentences with words from the box. (Not all words are used and some are used twice.)

Answers
1 heavy 2 tornado 3 violent/high, heavy 4 blizzard
5 high, drought

2 Use of English

- Learners read the text and circle the correct answer.

Answers
1 very 2 extremely 3 big, sharp 4 pale, grey, feathery
5 old, fat, brown 6 tiny, green

3 Over to you

- Learners write about what the weather is like today where they live.
- Tell them to use adverbs of degree.

Answers
Learners' own answers.

My global progress

- Tell learners to read the questions and think about what they have studied in this unit.
- Ask them to answer the questions. Encourage them to take time to reflect on their learning and give honest answers.

- **Portfolio opportunity:** If you have been filing learners' work all through this unit, you may find it useful to put all the work of this unit together. You may ask learners to make a cover for their work, decorating it with an image that represents what they have learned.

Review 4

Learner's Book pages: 124–125

1 Listen 50 [CD2 Track 19]

- Learners look at the pictures. They listen and match the words in the box with the pictures.
- Then, they decide which items are Egyptian and which are Roman.
- Play the recording at least twice.

Audioscript: Track 50

1 **Museum curator:** This is the Ancient Civilisation part of the museum we are walking into now. On the left you can see a working model of a Roman aqueduct which shows how fresh water was transported into the big cities – an incredible piece of engineering!

2 Here is a full-size replica of a Roman chariot! I believe that this one was used in the film *Gladiator*. Romans loved chariot races which were held on special race tracks called circuses.

3 This is a tunic which all Roman men wore. It could be worn on its own or with a belt around the waist. It was also worn under a toga which was a longer piece of material worn around the body and over one arm.

4 Moving on we come to ancient Egypt. Here we have an authentic canopic jar which was used to put the organs of the king's body in, such as the liver and the stomach.

5 Next to this we have examples of hieroglyphics. Egyptians used these pictures to represent objects, actions and sounds.

6 I'm sure you already know what this is! It's a sphinx which archaeologists believed were built to guard the tomb and to frighten away tomb raiders!

Answers
1 aqueduct (Roman)   2 chariot (Roman)
3 tunic and toga (Roman)   4 canopic jar (Egyptian)
5 hieroglyphics (Egyptian) 6 sphinx (Egyptian)

2 Listen 50 [CD2 Track 19]

- Learners listen again and decide if the sentences are true or false.

Answers
1 true 2 false 3 false 4 true 5 false

3 Talk

- Ask learners to talk about what they can remember about everyday life in ancient Rome.
- They use expressions of opinion.

Answers
Learners' own answers.

4 Vocabulary

- Tell learners to read the definitions and try to guess the word.

Answers
1 floods **2** Roman numerals **3** blizzard **4** strong
5 carbon dioxide **6** Learners' own answer **7** emergent layer
8 sharp, long

5 Use of English

- Ask learners to read the text and choose the correct word to complete the sentences.

Answers
1 was told **2** very **3** should **4** extremely **5** tiny
6 poisonous **7** was advised **8** too **9** quite **10** should

6 ☻ Talk

- Ask learners to read the text in **Activity 5** again and talk about things that they should and shouldn't do in the rainforest.

Answers
Learners' own answers.

7 Use of English

- Learners put the words in order to make correct sentences.

Answers
1 A tiny, pink, poisonous frog.
2 It has got long, sharp claws.
3 Three furry, brown sloths.
4 Spider monkeys have got thick, brown fur.

8 ☻ Write

- Learners choose one of the places and write a paragraph giving advice to people who are going to visit.
- Tell them to use *should* and *shouldn't*.

Answers
Learners' own answers.

Photocopiable activity 15

Answers
1 The Democratic Republic of Congo
2 Because of its climate and its canopy.
3 Madagascar
4 It is an animal related to Giraffe that lives in Africa.
5 Because it is hunted for its fur.
6 True
7 Plant more trees, teach others about the importance of the environment and establish parks to protect rainforests
8 Recycle, don't waste water and turn off electrical devices when you finish using them.

Photocopiable activity 16

Answers

PLACE	°C	°F
Helsinki	17	62.6
Taipei	34	93.2
Ushuaia	5	41
Dubai	38	100.4

9 Planet Earth

What lessons can we learn from the animal kingdom?

Unit overview

In this unit learners will:
- talk about animal habitats
- learn about food chains
- read a text about animal camouflage
- talk about caring for a pet
- write a leaflet about a children's farm
- read a poem about pets.

Learners will build communication and literacy skills as they read and listen to texts about the weather and temperatures around the world, and extreme weather conditions and how to survive them; speak about rainforests, rainforest animals and how to protect the environment; make presentations, complete notes, read and write reports; develop vocabulary study skills; learn to use *should* for advice, adverbs of degree, adjectives in the correct order; and identify stress in sentences.

At the end of the unit, they will apply and personalise what they have learned by working in small groups to complete a project of their choice: designing a poster for a wildlife park or animal centre or carrying out a nature study.

Language focus
Personal pronouns: *it, its*

Obligation and necessity: *must, should, have to, need to*

Advice: *It's best to …, It's a good idea to …, It's important that …*

Review of imperatives

I'd like/I wouldn't like

Vocabulary topics: animal habitats, animal characteristics, food chains, slogans

Critical thinking
- Analysing information
- Solving problems.

Self-assessment
- I can talk about animal habitats and the animals that live there.
- I can understand diagrams about food chains.
- I can read and understand a text about animal camouflage.
- I can talk about how to care for a pet.
- I can write a leaflet advertising a children's farm.
- I can read and understand a poem about pets.

Teaching tip
- After the class has finished the last lesson of this unit, write the following question on the board: *What lessons have we learned …?*
- Have an open class discussion and encourage learners to give reasons for their answers.
- Ask learners to reflect on the things they have learned during the year, e.g. to eat healthily, to appreciate different cultures, to become aware of environmental problems.
- Do they think this has changed them in any way? How?
- Ask them to write at least one sentence about what they have learned.
- File this work in learners' portfolios.

Lesson 1: Planet Earth

Learner's Book pages: 126–127

Activity Book pages: 100–101

Lesson objectives

Listening: Listen for information, listen and take notes.

Speaking: Practise theme vocabulary, speak about animals and their habitats.

Reading: Read about food chains, interpret diagrams and flowcharts.

Critical thinking: Analyse, classify, take notes, interpret diagrams and flowcharts.

Vocabulary: *forest, Antarctic, savannah, freshwater, ocean, desert, habitat, horned, viper, seal, antelope, eagle, dwarf, clownfish*

Materials: Dictionaries, map of the learners' country, map of the world.

Learner's Book

⇨ Warm up

- Ask learners what their region is like. Encourage them to describe it in as much detail as possible, e.g. weather, vegetation, animals.
- What animals do they like? What are these animals like?
- Ask the class if they think we can learn anything from animals. Elicit some ideas.

1 ⌕ Talk about it

- Ask learners to look at the photographs of different habitats. Do they live near any of these habitats?
- What do they think the weather might be like in these places?
- What helped them decide?
- Remind learners to use expressions of opinion and modals, i.e. *might, could, must, can't, I think/believe/know …*

> **Answers**
> Learners' own answers.

2 Word study

- Ask learners to look at the photos and the names for each habitat. Display a map of the world and ask learners to identify places where these habitats can be found.
- Then ask them to try to match the animals to their habitats. This is a challenging activity which should provoke some discussion. Reassure learners that they will have a chance to check their answers by listening to the audio in the next activity.
- Discuss the answers as a class. Remind learners to use *I think/don't think that …, I know …, I believe …* to give their opinions.

- **Critical thinking:** Ask learners to look at the names of the animals. Why do they think they have those names? Ask them to use a dictionary to help them.

> **Answers**
> See **Activity 3**.

3 Listen 51 [CD2 Track 20]

- Tell learners to listen to the audio about the animals and their habitats and check their answers to **Activity 2**.
- Play the audio a few times.
- Check the answers as a class.

Audioscript: Track 51

1 This is a reptile called a horned viper snake. It lives in the Sahara Desert in Africa where it's very dry and hot. It likes to bury itself in the sand where it waits for its prey. Lizards and birds are its favourites!

2 The stick insect looks like the twigs and branches of the trees it lives on. It lives in forests all over the world and likes to eat the leaves of the trees. It's nocturnal so it spends most of the day keeping very still, hidden in plants and trees so birds don't see it and eat it. It eats leaves and other small bugs.

3 The elephant seal is an aquatic mammal that lives in the Antarctic. It is extremely cold but the elephant seal has a lot of fat on its body to help to keep it warm. It spends most of its time hunting fish, octopus and squid under the water.

4 A clownfish lives in the Indian and Pacific oceans where the sea is warm. It's called a clownfish because it's very colourful and active. It eats algae (which are small plants) and small fish and it lives around anemones which help protect it from predators.

5 This amphibian is called an African dwarf frog. It lives in freshwater rivers and ponds in Africa where it is cool. It's called a dwarf frog because it's so tiny. It eats blood worms and water fleas and spends most of its time under water.

6 This bird lives in the Swiss mountain ranges. It's a golden eagle – one of the largest birds of prey. It's used to living in cold conditions and it makes its nest high up in the mountain rocks. It eats hares, foxes and birds which live on the ground.

7 This animal lives in the African savannah where it is hot all year round. It's a medium-sized mammal called an antelope and it likes to eat a lot of grass. It has horns to protect itself from predators such as lions and hyenas.

> **Answers**
> a stick insect – forest
> b elephant seal – Antarctic
> c African dwarf frog – freshwater
> d antelope – savannah
> e golden eagle – mountain
> f clownfish – ocean
> g horned viper snake – desert

4 Listen 51 [CD2 Track 20]

- Ask learners to listen to the audio recording again and take notes to complete the table.
- Play the audio a few times more.
- Copy the table on the board and ask learners to come up and complete it.

- When they have finished, ask the class to add more animals to the different habitats.
- **Critical thinking:** Learners take notes, analyse and classify the information into categories. This requires identifying key information and looking for patterns.

Answers

Type of animal	Name of animal	Habitat	Eats
1 amphibian	African dwarf frog	freshwater rivers	blood worms/ water fleas
2 fish	clownfish	Indian/Pacific ocean	algae
3 mammal	antelope	savannah	grass
4 aquatic mammal	elephant seal	Antarctic	fish, octopus, squid
5 insect	stick insect	forests	leaves, bugs
6 bird	golden eagle	mountain	hares, foxes, birds
7 reptile	horned viper	desert	lizards, birds

5 Talk

- In pairs, learners look at the food chain and discuss how to explain the information.
- **Crtitical thinking:** Learners have used some diagrams to interpret information, e.g. Venn diagrams. These tools require them to find and analyse key information in order to be able to classify it.

Answers
Learners' own answers.

> **[AB]** For further practice, see Strategy check! in the Activity Book.

6 Read

- Tell learners that reading a text can help them understand a flowchart or a diagram.
- Ask them to read the text about food chains. Were the ideas they discussed in **Activity 5** correct?
- Discuss the answers as a class.

Answers
Learners' own answers.

7 Read

- Tell learners to look at the illustrations and put the items in the food chains in the right order.
- Learners can re-read the text in **Activity 6** if necessary.
- Check the answers as a class.

Answers
1 grass – mouse – snake
2 algae – clown fish – shark
3 grass – antelope – lion

> **[AB]** For further practice, see Activities 1 and 2 in the Activity Book.

8 Read

- Tell learners to choose one of the habitats in **Activity 3**. They draw a diagram of a food chain which might exist in that habitat.
- They label the part of the food chain as *producer, primary/secondary or tertiary consumer.*
- They present their food chain to the class.
- **Portfolio opportunity:** Collect learners' work and file it in their portfolios.

Answers
Learners' own answers.

> **[AB]** For further practice, see Activities 3, 4 and 5 in the Activity Book.

9 Talking game

- Learners play a game in pairs. They think of an animal and then take turns to ask and answer questions about it. They can only ask *yes/no* questions.
- **Informal assessment opportunity:** Circulate listening to the learners' interactions and taking notes on their performance.

Wrap up

- When they have finished, learners tell the class about their choice of animal for the guessing game. Which animal has been the most popular choice?

Activity Book

1 Vocabulary

- Ask learners to look at the picture. Then they write herbivores, carnivores or omnivores next to the correct animal.
- Check the answers as a class. Ask learners to explain their answers.

Answers
a bird – omnivore
b squirrel – herbivore
c owl – carnivore
d snail – herbivore
e fox – carnivore
f rabbit – herbivore
g mouse – herbivore

2 Vocabulary

- Learners look at the picture and again and match the words.
- Check the answers as a class.

Answers
1 c 2 d 3 b 4 a

3 Vocabulary

- Ask learners to draw a food chain using the animals from the picture in **Activity 1**. They could do this activity in pairs or small groups.
- When they have finished, have an open class discussion about the food chains.

Answers
Learners' own answers.

Strategy check!

- Learners tick the strategies which will help them to interpret diagrams.

Answers
Use your previous knowledge to help you. ✓
Use reading texts to help you understand the diagrams. ✓

4 Read

- Ask learners to label the ocean food chain with the words in bold from the text.

Answers
a plankton – producers
b jellyfish and starfish – primary consumers
c minnows – secondary consumers
d tuna or sharks – tertiary consumers

5 Challenge

- Tell learners to draw a food chain in their notebook for one of the habitats in the box. Ask them to choose a different habitat from the one they chose for **Activity 8** in the Learner's Book.
- They can do this activity in pairs or small groups.
- Then they share it with the class.

Answers
Learners' own answers.

Differentiated instruction

Additional support and practice

- Play Hangman to revise new vocabulary.

Extend and challenge

- Learners search the Internet for information about their region and the animals that live in it. Then they make a poster about this habitat and a diagram of a food chain which exists within it.

Lesson 2: Animal camouflage

Learner's Book pages: 128–129
Activity Book pages: 102–103

Lesson objectives

Speaking: Talk about animal adaptation and characteristics.
Reading: Read for information, read and answer.
Writing: Complete sentences, answer questions.
Critical thinking: Giving opinions.

Language focus: Personal pronoun: *it, its*
Vocabulary: *chameleon, background, predator, venomous, fangs, chase, shoot, inkcoat, tail, stripes, scales, hump*

Learner's Book

⮫ Warm up

- Ask learners if they know what *camouflage* is. What is it used for? (It's used to hide, so that people can't see you.)
- Ask the class who uses camouflage. They may say that it is soldiers who use camouflage. Point out that camouflage is very important for animals.

1 Talk about it

- Ask learners to look at the photos and discuss what they can see.
- Ask them to write down words they associate with the photos.

Answers
Learners' own answers.

2 🖾 Read

- Tell learners that they are going to read the text related to the photos. What information do they expect to find in it? Elicit some ideas.
- Ask learners to read the text and decide which adaptation is being described. Have they found the information they expected?
- Ask learners to re-read the text and identify any new words. Ask them to work out the meaning of new words from the context.
- **Study skills:** Ask learners to look up the new words in the dictionary. Then, they copy the words that they find most difficult in their Vocabulary journal along with a definition.

Answer
camouflage

3 Read

- Ask learners to work in pairs or small groups. They re-read the text and find the information.
- Check the answers as a class.

For further practice, see Activities 1 and 2 in the Activity Book.

4 Use of English

- Focus on the **Use of English** box and the examples. Ask learners to find more examples in the text. You may wish to ask them to copy these examples in their notebooks.

> **Answers**
> Learners' own answers.

 For further practice, see Activities 3 and 4 in the Activity Book.

5 Word study

- Tell learners to work in pairs or small groups.
- They look at the animals in the picture and use the words in the box to describe how the animals' characteristics help them.
- Tell them to use *it/its* whenever possible.
- Ask learners to use their dictionary for help if necessary.
- Then, check the answers as a class.

> **Answers**
> Learners' own answers.

6 Over to you

- Ask learners to search the Internet or visit the library to find out how other animals have adapted to their environments.
- Tell them to research one of the animals shown or choose another one. They prepare a fact file about the animal.
- Learners present their findings to the class.

> **Answers**
> Learners' own answers.

Wrap up

- When they have finished, learners vote for the animal that shows the most original adaptation.
- **Portfolio opportunity:** Collect the fact files and file them in learners' portfolios.

Activity Book

1 Read

- Learners read and answer the questions about the animals.
- You could do this as a pairwork or group activity, or as a class competition.
- Check the answers as a class.

> **Answers**
> 1 zebra 2 chameleon 3 rabbit 4 camel 5 clownfish
> 6 penguin 7 African dwarf frog 8 elephant 9 monkey
> 10 cuttlefish 11 snake 12 antelope

2 Read

- Ask learners to read four short texts on different animals.
- Then, they match the questions to the correct text.
- Check the answers as a class.

> **Answers**
> 1 Why has an ostrich got long legs?
> 2 Why has a zebra got stripes?
> 3 Why has a giraffe got a long neck?
> 4 Why has an elephant got big ears?

3 Use of English

- Learners complete the sentences with *it* or *its*.
- Check the answers as a class.

> **Answers**
> 1 **It** has got black and white stripes. **Its** stripes protect **it** from predators.
> 2 **It** uses **its** powerful legs to kick predators.
> 3 **Its** long neck helps **it** to reach the high leaves on the trees.
> 4 **It** flaps **its** large ears to help **it** cool down.
> 5 **It** uses **its** horns to protect itself from predators.

4 Challenge

- Ask learners to make sentences about animals using the personal pronoun (*it*) and the possessive pronoun (*its*).
- They use the prompts to help them.
- Check the answers as a class.

> **Answers**
> 1 Its ink protects it from predators.
> 2 Its two humps store fat to give it energy.
> 3 It changes its skin colour to protect it from predators.

> **Differentiated instruction**
>
> **Additional support and practice**
>
> Play *I Spy*. For example, say: *I spy with my little eye something that changes colours.* Learners try to guess the word (e.g. *chameleon*).
>
> **Extend and challenge**
>
> Ask a learner to come up to the front and show him/her a photo or whisper the name of an animal. That learner should draw it on the board. The first learner to guess the picture gets a point. This game can also be played in teams.

Lesson 3: Looking after pets

Learner's Book pages: 130–131
Activity Book pages: 104–105

Lesson objectives

Listening: Listen and match, listen for information.

Speaking: Speak about pets and how to look after them.

Writing: Make notes for a presentation.

Language focus: Expressing obligation and necessity: *must/should/have to/need to*; giving advice: *It's best to ..., It's a good idea to ..., It's important that ...*

Vocabulary: *feed, groom, clean, exercise, visit, vet, look after*

Materials: Copies of **Photocopiable activity 17**.

Learner's Book

Warm up

- Review animal vocabulary. Write three headings on the board: *Wild animals, Farm animals, Pets.*
- Ask learners to think of animal words for each category.

1 Talk about it

- Ask learners to talk about pets. Do they have a pet? What is it? Would they like to have a pet?
- Ask them to discuss what animals make good pets and why. Ask them to explain their answers.

> **Answers**
> Learners' own answers.

2 Listen 52 [CD2 Track 21]

- Tell learners they are going to listen to Tilly talking about her family's pets.
- Focus on the pictures and ask learners to describe the animals they see. Do they like these animals? Have they got a pet like these?
- Tell the class they are going to listen to the audio recording. They listen and match the children with the pets.
- Play the audio at least twice.
- Check the answers as a class.

> **Audioscript:** Track 52
>
> **Tilly:** Today, I'd like to talk to you about my pet. We live on a farm and there are lots of animals. My younger brother, David has a rabbit and my older sister, Hannah has a guinea pig but my pet is much bigger than this! I've got a horse and his name is Heathcliff. I love horses. My mum said a horse was too expensive, but we saw Heathcliff at a sanctuary where they help horses to get better. He wasn't well looked after and he was poorly. So, he is a special horse because we rescued him.

Heathcliff and I are the best friends and he needs a lot of looking after. He needs feeding twice a day – once in the morning and once in the evening. I give him hay and sometimes apples and carrots for a treat. You must give your horse food and fresh water every day.

Here are some more tips for horse care:

- You should groom your horse regularly. It's best to use a brush or a special comb.
- A horse needs lots of exercise so I try to ride him twice a day. When I can't ride him, he spends some of the day in the field where he has lots of room to run around.
- It's important that a horse goes for regular check-ups at the vets.
- It's a good idea to check your horse's teeth on a regular basis too.

> **Answers**
> David – rabbit
> Hannah – guinea pig
> Tilly – horse

3 Word study 52 [CD2 Track 21]

- Ask learners to match the correct word with each picture.
- Then, they listen to the audio again to check their answers.
- Check the answers as a class. Ask learners what words helped them.

> **Answers**
> **a** groom **b** feed **c** exercise **d** clean **e** look after (teeth)
> **f** visit (the vet)

[AB] For further practice, see Activities 1, 2 and 3 in the Activity Book.

4 Use of English

- Ask learners to read the **Use of English** box and the **Speaking tip** box. Look at the examples as a class.
- Explain the difference between necessity (things we *must* do) and obligation (things we *should* do).
- Supply more examples and ask learners to give their own.
- Now focus on the activity and ask learners to put the words in order to make sentences.

> **Answers**
> **Suggested answers:**
> 1 You must feed your hamster every day.
> 2 You need to put clean water at the side of his cage.
> 3 You should clean out his cage once a week.
> 4 You don't need to groom the hamster – he will clean himself.
> 5 You should put something in his cage for him to play with, so he gets exercise.

[AB] For further practice, see Activity 4 in the Activity Book.

Present it!

- Focus on the steps outlined in the box and tell learners to use them to organise their work.
- First they decide what pet they are going to talk about – either their own pet, or a pet that they would like to own.
- They decide what the needs of this pet are and the type of attention it requires.
- Learners prepare their notes using expressions of necessity, advice and obligation.
- They draw a picture or take a photo of the pet and give their presentation.
- **Informal assessment opportunity:** Circulate, asking questions while learners are preparing the presentation. Make notes of their performance while they are making their presentation. You may wish to set up some remedial work on the most common mistakes you have observed.

> **Answers**
> Learners' own answers.

 For further practice, see Activity 5 in the Activity Book.

Wrap up

- When learners have finished their presentations, they discuss which the most popular pet is.
- **Portfolio opportunity:** Collect script of the presentation along with any pictures, write the learner's name and the date and file it in their portfolio.

Activity Book

1 Listen 70 [CD2 Track 39]

- Ask learners to listen to Paolo talking about his pet hamster.
- They listen and put the pictures in order. They compare their answers with a partner.
- Check the answers as a class.

> **Audioscript:** Track 70
>
> **Paolo:** Hi! My name's Paolo and I'm going to talk to you about my pet hamster, Cheeks. I decided on this name because he loves to fill his cheeks with his favourite food – seeds and grains. I fill his bowl with food twice a day and it's important that he always has fresh water in his water bottle too.
>
> Hamsters are very active so it's a good idea to buy an exercise wheel for their cage. Cheeks loves it! He's got a ladder too as he's a great climber.
>
> I clean out Cheek's cage once a week. I clean the bottom with soap and water and I put down fresh bedding. Hamsters are clean animals. They organise an area in their cage for sleeping and another for their toilet area. They clean and groom themselves regularly too by licking their fur.
>
> Believe it or not, a hamster's teeth never stop growing, so it's a good idea to give it wood chews or a hard dog biscuit to keep your hamster's teeth short.

> **Answers**
> 1 feeding   2 exercise   3 cleaning   4 teeth

2 Listen 70 [CD2 Track 39]

- Ask learners to complete the sentences with the correct form of the words in the box.
- Then they listen again and check their answers.

> **Answers**
> 1 feeds   2 exercises   3 cleans   4 grooms   5 looks after

3 Write

- Tell learners to write sentences giving advice about looking after a hamster.
- They can work in pairs or small groups.
- Then they share their ideas with the class.

> **Answers**
> Learners' own answers.

4 Use of English

- Tell learners to read the information about having a parrot as a pet and complete the sentences with a word from the **Use of English** box.
- You could do this as a pairwork activity.
- Check the answers as a class.

> **Answers**
> Suggested answers:
> 1 have to
> 2 should
> 3 must
> 4 should
> 5 need to

5 Challenge

- Learners write their own blog about looking after a pet.
- They choose a pet and draw a picture of it.
- Then they write advice about how to look after it.

> **Answers**
> Learners' own answers.

Differentiated instruction

Additional support and practice

- Do **Photocopiable activity 17**. Learners complete tips for looking after cats. Then they add some ideas of their own.

Extend and challenge

- Ask learners to work in groups. They think of an imaginary pet and prepare a presentation about it – its characteristics, its habits and how to look after it.

Photocopiable activity 17

> **Answers**
> 1 You mustn't give your cat too much food.
> 2 Kittens should eat three times a day.
> 3 Your cat must always have a bowl of fresh water.
> 4 You have to clean the water bowl every day.
> 5 You need to ask your parents to help you bathe the cat.

Lesson 4: Writing a leaflet

Learner's Book pages: 132–133
Activity Book pages: 106–107

Lesson objectives

Speaking: Speak about visits.

Reading: Find information, read slogans.

Writing: Design and write a leaflet, write a slogan.

Language focus: Review of imperatives

Vocabulary: *goats, lambs, tractor, trailer, ride, stroke, chicks, llama, raccoon, meerkat, boa constrictor, python, bird of prey, pensioner, budget*

Materials: Dictionaries, writing and drawing supplies, leaflets of visitor attractions.

Learner's Book

Warm up

- Show the class some leaflets of different visitor attractions. Ask them where they would like to go and why.

1 Talk about it

- Ask learners if they have ever visited a place where they could see animals, e.g. a farm, a zoo or a safari park.
- Learners talk about what they saw, the kind of trip it was and what they did there.

> **Answers**
> Learner's own answers.

2 Read

- Ask learners to read the leaflet about the opening of a new safari park. What information have they found in the leaflet, e.g type of activity, opening times, prices.
- Ask them if they would like to go there and why.
- Encourage learners to guess the meaning of unfamiliar words from the context. If necessary, tell them to use their dictionaries.

> **Answers**
> Learners' own answers.

3 Read

- Ask learners to re-read the leaflet and answer true or false.
- They compare their answers with a partner.
- Check the answers as a class. Ask them to justify their answers.

> **Answers**
> 1 false   2 true   3 false   4 true   5 false

[AB] For further practice, see Activity 1 in the Activity Book.

4 Problem solving

- Read the problems as a class. Discuss any unfamiliar vocabulary.
- Ask learners to work in pairs and solve the problems.
- Check the answers as a class.
- **Informal assessment opportunity:** Circulate, asking questions while learners are working. You may wish to set up some remedial work on the most common mistakes you have observed.

> **Answers**
> 1 £5.50   2 £37

[AB] For further practice, see Activity 2 in the Activity Book.

5 [AB] Write

- As a class, read the explanation of what slogans are. Can learners think of popular slogans on TV or in magazines?
- Discuss what makes slogans attractive, e.g. rhythm, choice of words, the sound of the words, play on words.
- Ask learners to find more examples of slogans in the text about the wildlife park.
- Check the answers as a class.

> **Answers**
> Don't miss the tractor and trailer ride!
> Be the first to collect the fresh eggs!
> Stroke the baby chicks!
> There's lots to see at Durdle Moor ...
> Come and see our ...
> Ride our shire horse and don't leave without ...

[AB] For further practice, see Activity 3 in the Activity Book.

Writing tip

- Point out the use of affirmative and negative imperatives for slogans.
- Elicit some more examples from learners.

Write

- Focus on the steps outlined in the box and tell learners to use them to organise their work.
- Ask learners to work in pairs or small groups.
- They decide what place they are going to write about.
- Then they work together to come up with ideas for activities and write slogans.
- They choose photos for the leaflets or draw their own pictures.
- They should include information about prices and opening and closing times.

> **Answers**
> Learners' own answers.

[AB] For further practice, see Activity 4 in the Activity Book.

Wrap up

- Ask learners to present their leaflet and attraction to the class.
- **Portfolio opportunity:** Collect the leaflets and file them in the learners' portfolios.
- **Home–school opportunity:** Learners take their work home and share it with the family.

Activity Book

1 Read

- Learners read and complete the dialogue with information from the leaflet.
- Check the answers as a class.
- Then you could ask learners to act out the dialogue.

> **Answers**
> **1** lions **2** tigers **3** lynxes **4** opens from Sunday to Saturday **5** from 9 am to 8 pm **6** $17 **7** Summer concert **8** Friday 18th July

2 Read

- Learners work in pairs or small groups.
- They re-read the details in the leaflet and work out how much it will cost the families to visit the Wild Animal Sanctuary.
- Check the answers as a class.

> **Answers**
> **1** $44.50   **2** $45.00   **3** $27.00

3 Write

- Learners work in small groups and write slogans for the Wild Animal Sanctuary using the imperative.
- When they have finished, they share their slogans as a class.

> **Answers**
> Learners' own answers.

4 Challenge

- Tell learners to work in small groups and think of another special activity for the Wild Animal Sanctuary's summer plan.
- Ask learners to imagine what it could be and write about the activity.
- They draw a picture and write a slogan for it.
- Then they share it with the class.

> **Answers**
> Learners' own answers.

Differentiated instruction

Additional support and practice

- In pairs or small groups, learners look for popular slogans. What products or attractions do they advertise? What interesting vocabulary is used?
- Ask learners to write some slogans for things they like, e.g. food, a film, a restaurant.

Extend and challenge

- Learners work in pairs. They write a dialogue for their leaflet using the dialogue in **Activity 1** in the Activity Book as a model.

Lesson 5: Poem: *Mum Won't Let Me Keep a Rabbit*

Learner's Book pages: 134–137
Activity Book pages: 108–109

Lesson objectives

Listening: Listen to a poem, listen and match, identify rhyming words, identify alliteration.

Speaking: Discuss a poem.

Reading: Read a poem.

Writing: Complete sentences.

Critical thinking: Predict.

Value: Taking care of animals.

Language focus: Rhyming words; alliteration; *I'd like …/I wouldn't like …*

Vocabulary: *keep, porcupine, water-rat, pigeons, snail, kangaroo, wallabies, nails, rattlesnake, mamba, mouse, wombat, iguana, jellyfish, deer, cockroach, bumblebee, earwig, maggot, flea, wildebeest, mallard, dabchick, piranha, octopus, water-hog*

Materials: Dictionaries, Internet access, copies of **Photocopiable activity 18**.

Learner's Book

 Warm up

- Ask learners what poems they remember from previous units.
- Encourage them to recite the poems.

1 Talk about it

- Ask learners if they ever wanted to have a pet and were not allowed to. They speak about why they couldn't have a pet and how they felt.
- Are there sometimes reasons why it's not possible or responsible to have a pet? Elicit some ideas, e.g. living in a flat as opposed to living in a house with garden, the pet is too big or potentially dangerous, responsibility for looking after it.

2 Read and listen 53 [CD2 Track 22]

- **Critical thinking:** Focus on the illustrations. Ask learners to describe what they see and predict what the poem is going to be about.
- Tell learners they are going to listen to the poem. They listen and match the pictures with an animal in the poem.
- Play the audio once through for learners to get an idea of what the poem is about.
- Then play it at least twice again.
- Discuss as a class.

Audioscript: Track 53.
See Learner's Book pages 134–135.

Answers
bat
porcupine
pigeon
snail
rattlesnake/vipor/mambo
mouse
wombat
iguana
deer
cockroach
duck
toad/frog
octopus
water-hog
earwig (?)

3 Read

- Ask learners to guess what the secret animal in the attic is. Elicit ideas.
- They reorder the letters to find out. Were they right?

Answer
a secret elephant

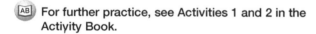 For further practice, see Activities 1 and 2 in the Actiyity Book.

4 Pronunciation 54 [CD2 Track 23]

- Tell learners to read the poem again and find words that rhyme with the animals.
- Then they listen to the audio again and check their answers.
- Ask learners to say the rhyming pairs of words aloud.

Answers
1 bat – water-rat
2 snails – nails
3 deer – clear
4 bumble bee – flea
5 duck – luck
6 water-hogs – frogs

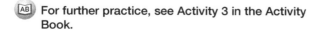 For further practice, see Activity 3 in the Activity Book.

5 Read

- Ask learners to work in pairs or small groups.
- They re-read the poem and find all the animals. Then they classify the animals into groups.
- Tell learners to use their dictionary and the Internet to help them.
- When they have finished, ask them to compare their work with another pair.
- Check the answers as a class.

Answers

Mammals	Insects	Birds	Amphibians	Reptiles
rabbit	flea	pigeons	toads	snake
bat	cockroach	duck	iguana	rattlesnake
porcupine	earwig	dabchick	frogs	mamba
water-rat	bumblebee	mallard		
kangaroo	ant			
mouse	maggot			
wombat				
deer				
wildebeest				
water-hog				
elephant				

Other: snails, jellyfish, piranha, octopus

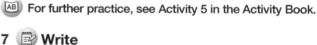 For further practice, see Activity 4 in the Activity Book.

6 Write

- Ask learners to write three sentences about the animals in the poem that they would like to keep as pets, and three about those they wouldn't like to keep.
- Ask them to explain why.
- Share as a class.

Answers
Learners' own answers.

For further practice, see Activity 5 in the Activity Book.

7 Write

- Ask the class to write a verse about the animals they are sure they can't keep in their house.
- Tell learners to try to make the words in line two and line four rhyme.
- Circulate giving help with additional vocabulary as necessary.
- When they have finished, learners read their rhymes to the class.

Answers
Learners' own answers.

8 📝 Over to you

- In the poem there are some animals that are likely to be new to leaners.
- Tell learners to find out information about one of the animals they haven't heard of before.
- They write a paragraph about this animal and find a picture to go with their writing.
- When they have finished, display their work in the classroom.

> **Answers**
> Learners' own answers.

9 Read and listen 55 [CD2 Track 24]

- Tell learners to read and listen to the animal alliteration sentences.
- Then, they match each sentence with the correct illustration.
- Ask learners what they notice about the words in the sentences. Encourage them to work out the meaning of *alliteration*.

Audioscript: Track 55

1 Larry the lucky lion laughed loudly as he leaped over Lucy the lazy lizard while she lovingly licked a lemon lollipop.

2 Charlie the cheerful cheetah chose to chew cheese and cherries as he chomped his chops.

> **Answers**
> 1 b   2 a

10 Read

- Ask learners to read the two definitions and choose the correct one for *alliteration*.

> **Answer**
> b The main words all start with the same sound.

📖 For further practice, see Activity 6 in the Activity Book.

11 Write

- Tell learners to copy and complete the table. Explain that they don't need to think of a word for every column.
- When they have finished, they share their answers with a partner.
- Then, they share their ideas as a class.
- You could make a table on the board with learners' contributions.

> **Answers**
> Learners' own answers.

12 📝 Write

- Using the completed table from **Activity 11**, learners write their own animal alliteration sentence.
- Then they draw a picture to illustrate it.
- Ask learners to share their work with the class by reading out their sentences.

> **Answers**
> Learners' own answers.

13 💬 Values

- In groups, ask learners to discuss the questions.
- Ask them to make notes of their ideas.
- When they have finished, each group appoints a spokesperson and reports their ideas back to the class.

> **Answers**
> Learners' own answers.

📖 For further practice, see Activity 7 in the Activity Book.

➡️ Wrap up

- Learners read the new verse they wrote in **Activity 7** to the class.
- **Portfolio opportunity:** Collect the poems and the files learners wrote in **Activity 8** and file them in their portfolios.
- **Home–school opportunity:** Learners recite the poem to their family and teach them the new animal names.

Activity Book

1 Read

- Tell learners to read the poem again and label the pictures with the correct names.
- They can do this activity with a partner.
- Check the answers as a class.

> **Answers**
> 1 bat   2 snail   3 iguana   4 jelly fish   5 octopus
> 6 cockroach   7 bumblebee   8 piranha   9 frog

2 Vocabulary

- Learners find and circle the animals which the boy in the poem can't keep.
- Check the answers as a class.

> **Answers**
> rabbit, porcupine, pigeon, ant, wombat, mamba, elephant, kangaroo, earwig, wildebeest

3 Pronunciation

- Ask learners to complete the sentences with a rhyming word from the poem.
- Then ask them to read the poem aloud.

> **Answers**
> **1** bat **2** snail **3** luck **4** flea **5** wildebeest

4 Read

- Learners circle the odd one out in each category.
- Then, they add a correct subsitute of their own for each category.
- They share their answers with the class.

> **Answers**
> **1** ant **2** duck **3** toad **4** snake **5** octopus
> Substitutes: Learners' own answers.

5 Write

- Learners choose their favourite animal from the poem.
- They draw a picture of it.
- Then they find out about it and complete the information.
- They share their work as a class.
- They could make a mini poster using their information and display it in the classroom.

> **Answers**
> Learners' own answers.

6 Write

- Learners unjumble the words to make an animal alliteration sentences.
- Then they match each sentence to the correct picture.
- Ask learners to read the sentences aloud a few times, getting quicker each time.

> **Answers**
> **1** Larry the lazy leopard lies lazily on the log. – picture d
> **2** Betty the busy bumblebee buzzes busily. – picture a
> **3** Felicity the fat flea flies fabulously. – picture b
> **4** Sid the slimy snail slides slowly. – picture c

7 Values

- Learners write a list of things they have learned about looking after animals.

> **Answers**
> Learners' own answers.

Differentiated instruction

Additional support and practice

- Do **Photocopiable activity 18**. Learners solve the crossword. Then they make their own crossword or wordsearch using vocabulary from the unit.

Extend and challenge

- Ask learners to work in pairs or small groups. They search the Internet or visit the local library and find information about Brian Patten.
- They prepare a short biography and choose some poems to read to the class.
- Learners may find these sites useful: http://www.brianpatten.co.uk http://www.poemhunter.com/brian-patten/

Photocopiable activity 17

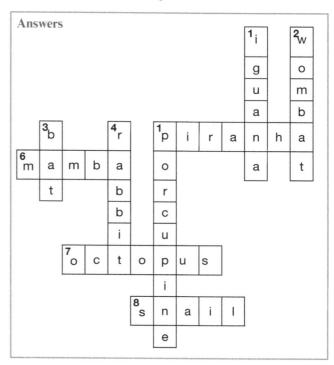

Answers

Lesson 6: Choose a project

Learner's Book pages: 138–139
Activity Book pages 110–111

Lesson objectives

Listening: Listen to class presentations.
Speaking: Present a project to the class.
Reading: Read questions and instructions.
Writing: Write slogans, take notes.

Language focus: Unit 9 Review

Materials:

1 Design a poster: Drawing supplies, large sheet of paper, pictures or photos.

2 A nature study: Writing and drawing supplies, access to school grounds.

Learner's Book

Warm up

- Ask learners what they have enjoyed most in the unit. What new information have they learned?
- What words did they find the most interesting/useful/difficult?
- Which pet do they like best?

Choose a project

- Learners choose an end-of-unit project to work on. Help them choose. Provide materials.

1 Design a poster

- Learners work in groups to make a poster for the opening of a new animal centre or wildlife park.
- Tell learners to read and follow the steps of the project.
- They print out or draw pictures and stick them to the poster.

2 A nature study

- This project has two parts to it.
- First, learners find a habitat to study.
- They study the habitat over a number of days.
- Working in small groups, learners take notes of their observations.
- Then, learners write a report of their findings.
- They draw the picture of one of the insects or animals they observed and label its parts.

Wrap up

- Learners present their work to the class.
- **Portfolio opportunity:** If possible, leave the learner projects on display for a short while, then consider filing the projects, photos or scans of the work, in learners' portfolios. Write the date on the work.

Reflect on your learning

- Learners think about what they have studied in the unit and answer the revision questions 1–7. Learners consider the Big question for the unit: *What lessons can we learn from the animal kingdom?* Elicit opinions and ask learners to justify them.
- **Informal assessment opportunity:** Circulate as learners work. Informally assess their receptive and productive language skills. Ask questions. You may want to take notes on their responses.

Look what I can do!

- **Aim:** To check that learners can do all the things from **Unit 9**.
- Review the *I can …* statements.
- Learners reflect on what aspects of the unit they have found most difficult and why.
- Do they have any ideas about how to overcome these difficulties? Encourage learners to think of strategies that may help them improve.
- Elicit what they liked most about this unit and encourage them to explain why.

> **Answers**
> Learners' own answers.

Activity Book

Unit 9 Revision

- Learners read the clues and complete the crossword using words from **Unit 9**.

> **Answers**
> **Across**
> **2** ant **3** must **5** groom **7** elephant **10** producer
> **Down**
> **1** bat **4** stripes **6** clean **8** tertiary **9** humps

My global progress

- Tell learners to read the questions and think about what they have studied in this unit.
- Ask them to answer the questions. Encourage them to take time to reflect on their learning and give honest answers.
- **Portfolio opportunity:** If you have been filing learners' work all the way through this unit, you may find it useful to put all the work of this unit together. You may ask learners to make a cover for their unit work, decorating it with an image that represents what they have learned.

Review 5

Learner's Book pages: 140–141

Photocopiable activity 19

Quiz

- Learners work in pairs to do the quiz tasks.
- Then they work out their scores.

1

- Learners write down four adjectives we use to describe personality.
- They act out four of the adjectives they have on their list.
- Their partner has to guess what they are.

2

- Tell learners to write down the names of three illnesses.
- They do a dialogue with their partner. One learner asks: *What's the matter?* The other acts out the illness for them to guess.

3

- Learners give two adjectives to describe a city and two to describe the country.
- They take turns to compare the city and the country using the adjectives they have thought of.

4

- Learners write down four things they either wear, eat or do during a celebration.
- They define each word using *who, that* or *which*.

5

- Learners name as many jobs they can think of in a minute.
- Then they discuss which ones are their favourite jobs.
- Ask learners to give reasons for their answers.

6

- Learners tell their partner about their last holiday or school trip.
- They should use three verbs in the past simple and two in the past continuous.

7

- Learners tell their partner what they can see in the pictures and what each thing was used for.
- They use expressions of opinion: *I think, I know, I believe.*

8

- Learners prepare a weather report for tomorrow's weather.
- They describe the weather in the morning, the afternoon and the evening.
- They use *will* and adverbs of degree.

9

- Learners give each other advice on how to look after a pet of their choice.
- They use *should*.

10

- Learners write five quiz questions for their partner to answer about types of animals, their characteristics, their habitats and what they eat.
- Make up a certificate for each learner using **Photocopiable activity 19.** Don't forget to celebrate their achievements!

Photocopiable activities

Photocopiable activity 1: This is me!

Use *Wh-* words to complete the questions.
Then answer the questions about Evie.

Hi! My name's Evie. I'm 12 years old and I'm from Liverpool. I live in the suburbs with my family. We don't live near the city centre so there isn't much to do, but we live in a house with a nice garden and that's great because we can have pets. I have a dog called Night – he's a black collie. We live near school so we don't get up too early. We go walking and we meet our friends on the way. It's fun. On Saturdays, I attend Drama School with Ryan. I love acting and reading theatre plays. Ryan is my best friend. When we finish school we are going to start taking classes at the Liverpool School of Performing Arts.

1 _____ is her name? _____

2 _____ is she from? _____

3 _____ does she live? _____

4 _____ her pet's name? _____

5 _____ is it? _____

6 _____ does she go to school? _____

7 _____ is her best friend? _____

8 _____ do they like doing? _____

9 _____ is she planning to go when she finishes school? _____

_____

Now write about you. Include a photo or draw a picture.

Photocopiable activity 2: This is my friend Ryan!

Underline the correct adjective to complete the sentences. Then talk about what is true for you. Write a few sentences about you in your notebook.

Ryan is *interested / interesting* in drama. He wants to be an actor. He thinks football is *excited / exciting*. He supports Liverpool FC and he sometimes goes to Anfield when they play at home. He never watches TV. He finds TV programmes really *bored / boring*. He prefers reading or watching films on DVD.

Ryan thinks that the weather in Liverpool isn't very good. He feels *depressed / depressing* when it rains. He prefers hot and sunny weather.

Ryan says: 'I'm not *frightened / frightening* of insects or animals except bats. I find bats extremely *disgusted / disgusting*.'

Now write about a friend. Use the text about Ryan as a model. Add a photo of your friend or draw a picture.

Photocopiable activity 3: Wordsearch

Find the words and phrases for illnesses and symptoms. Write them in your notebook.

S	T	O	M	A	C	H	A	C	H	E
O	C	O	L	D	F	E	E	Y	E	S
R	L	V	O	I	T	C	H	Y	A	W
E	O	I	C	Z	N	O	S	E	D	E
T	A	S	C	Y	X	I	L	L	A	A
H	F	E	E	L	V	S	S	I	C	K
R	U	N	N	Y	C	O	U	G	H	S
O	E	Y	E	A	C	F	E	V	E	R
A	S	H	I	V	E	R	I	N	G	S
T	U	M	M	Y	H	U	R	T	S	A

Now make a wordsearch for your friend.

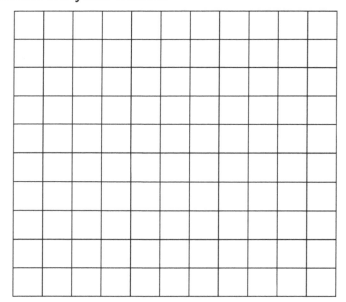

Photocopiable activity 4: A healthy lunch

Look and match the foods to the correct food group. Then write a healthy lunch menu. Compare it with a partner. Are they similar?

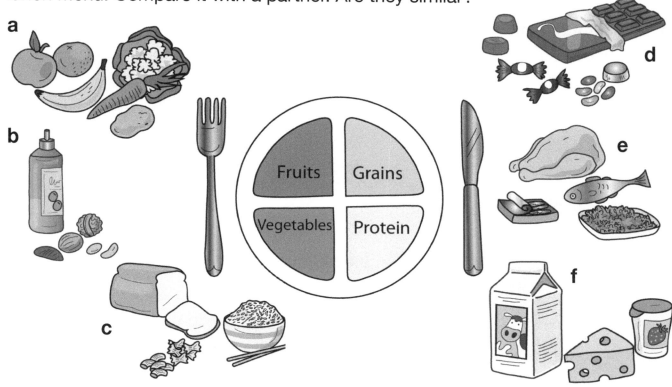

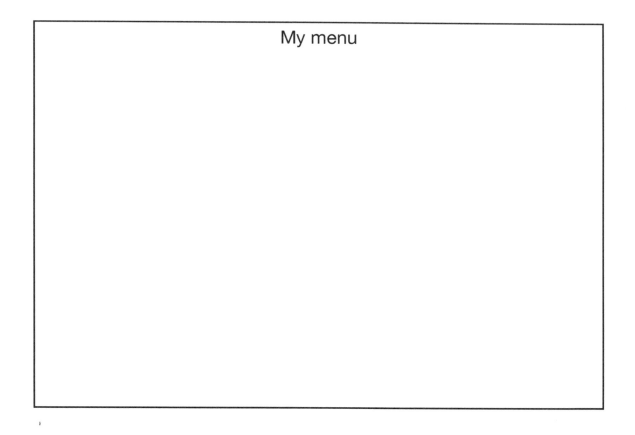

My menu

Unit 3

Photocopiable activity 5: Three cities

Compare the information and write sentences using the comparative and superlative forms of the adjectives.

1 Look at the number of people who live in these places and write about the places using **crowded**, **noisy** and **peaceful** in your notebook.

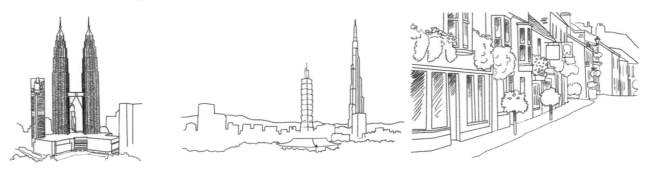

Kuala Lumpur 1,630,000   **Taipei 2,620,000**   **Glastonbury 8,800**

2 Apparently, Glastonbury is 6,000 years old. Kuala Lumpur is around 210 years old. Write about Kuala Lumpur using **modern** and **spectacular**.

3 Think about cities and places in your country and write about them in your notebook. Use beautiful, clean, popular, pretty and noisy.

Compare your sentences with your partner. How similar or different are your opinions? Make a few notes in your notebook.

What do you know about Kuala Lumpur, Taipei and Glastonbury? Search the Internet and find out more information about them. Then make a fact file.

Name of city: _____

Country: _____

Population: _____

Language: _____

Attractions: _____

Two adjectives to describe the city: _____

Look for pictures to go with your fact files.

Photocopiable activity 6: Trees

Read about why trees are important and complete the sentences.

Trees are an important part of our lives. They absorb carbon dioxide and give us oxygen to breathe. Trees make our environment beautiful with their different colours, flowers and shapes and they give us shade and relief from the sun's heat. Trees help absorb the rain and give us medicines. Trees are very important to us, but some people are cutting them down and burning them to make more farm land to feed the human population and farm animals.

What do you think about this?
Can you and your friends do something to help?

I think _____ .

I believe _____ .

I hope _____ .

I know _____ .

Can you start a project similar to the one in El Trapiche in Argentina? What can you do with your class? Write some ideas.

What do you need? _____

_____

Who can help? _____

_____

Can you think of a slogan? _____

_____

Photocopiable activity 7: Quiz time!

Complete the sentences with the correct relative pronoun and then solve the riddles. Write three more riddles for the class.

1 A dance _____ people like in Brazil. _____

2 A festival _____ takes place in February. _____

3 A strong person _____ can carry an elephant. _____

4 A gas _____ can be a problem. _____

5 A part of the earth _____ has melting ice. _____

6 A boy _____ has no friends. _____

7 A festival _____ is celebrated in India. _____

My new riddles

1 _____ _____

2 _____ _____

3 _____ _____

Photocopiable activity 8: Wordsearch – opposites

Read the clues and find the words. Find the opposite of:

anxious _____   clever _____

moody _____   hard-working _____

rude _____   weak _____

miserable _____   dry-eyed _____

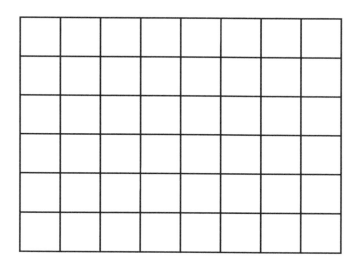

C	H	E	E	R	F	U	L
I	T	C	A	L	M	A	A
J	O	L	L	Y	B	O	Z
T	U	E	W	E	E	P	Y
A	G	P	O	L	I	T	E
I	H	S	T	U	P	I	D

Make a wordsearch for the class. Use words you have learned in this unit.

Unit 5

Photocopiable activity 9: What do you think?

Complete these sentences using **must**, **can't**, **might** or **could**.

1 I don't know where Sammy lives but he _____ live near here because he comes to school on foot.

2 Did you hear that noise? I think there _____ be a thief downstairs. Call the police!

3 It _____ be a thief. All the doors and windows are locked. I think it _____ be the cat.

4 Look! There's ice on the grass. It _____ be really cold outside.

5 Dad has to go to the office and it's Saturday! He _____ be very happy about that.

What do you think about these people? Use **must**, **can't**, **might** or **could** and the words in the box to write sentences.

> president   teacher   doctor   vet   doctor   writer
> musician   tennis player   swimmer

1 _____

2 _____

3 _____

4 _____

Photocopiable activity 10: Special superstars

Match the headings to correct paragraphs of the biography of Lionel 'Leo' Messi. Underline the words or phrases that helped you decide.

☐ Quick facts ☐ Humanitarian work ☐ Career ☐ Personal life

1 Lionel Andrés 'Leo' Messi is an Argentine footballer.
He was born in the city of Rosario in 1987. He plays as a forward for FC Barcelona and the Argentina national team. He is also the captain of his country's national football team.

2 At the age of five, Messi started playing football for a local club coached by his father. At the age of 11, Messi was diagnosed with an illness. Because of this illness, he was much shorter than other children of his age. FC Barcelona wanted him to play in the junior divisions of the club because they knew he was very good. They offered to pay for Messi's medical treatment, if he went to Spain. Messi and his father moved to Barcelona. In 2004, when he was 17 years old, he played his first match with the first division team of the club. He has won four Balon d'Or, FIFA World Player Awards and many others.

3 In 2007, Messi established the Leo Messi Foundation, a charity supporting access to education and health care for vulnerable children. He is also a goodwill ambassador for UNICEF, supporting children's rights. He has also donated a lot of money to the children's hospital of his hometown, Rosario.

4 In November 2012, his first son was born. His name is Thiago.

What is your opinion of Leo Messi? Write a few sentences saying what you think about him. Remember to use adjectives to make your description more interesting and modals to show how sure you are of what you say.

_____

_____

_____

Photocopiable activity 11: Storytime

Write a story beginning: *One evening, I was walking down the street when …*

1 Make notes and plan your story. Use correct tenses – the past simple and the past continuous.

How many characters are there? _____

Adjectives that describe the characters: _____

Setting: _____

Problem: _____

What happens in order to resolve the problem: _____

_____

Resolution: _____

2 Now organise your story. Think about what happens first, what next.

My Story
What happens first
What happens next
What happens after
How it ends

3 Use correct punctuation.

4 Write your story.

5 Give your story to a partner to read.

6 Read your partner's story. Think about these questions: Are the characters well described? Is the story exciting? Is the resolution interesting? Would you recommend the story to a friend?

7 Illustrate your story.

Photocopiable activity 12: It's punctuation time!

Read the sentences and put in the correct punctuation.
Then read the sentences aloud with the correct intonation.

1 What is your name asked the teacher

_____

2 Paul said you must be Dave's sister hello

_____

3 Jill asked is lunch ready mum

_____

4 I am so hungry said Paul I could eat a horse

_____

5 Do you know where the post office is the lady asked the policeman

_____

6 The teacher asked has anyone seen Dianne and Yasmine

_____

Now write three more sentences. Don't use any punctuation.
Exchange your sentences with a partner and punctuate them correctly.

_____

_____

_____

Photocopiable activity 13: The Parthenon

Read about The Parthenon and put the verbs in brackets into the past passive.

The Parthenon is a temple in Athens, Greece. It _____ (*build*) by Pericles. The construction of The Parthenon began in 447 BCE and it _____ (*complete*) in 438 BCE. It _____ (*considered*) one of the most important buildings of ancient Greece.

It had many statues. These statues _____ (*call*) metopes. Many of the metopes _____ (*destroy*) or _____ (*damage*). Some others are still there or they _____ (*take*) different museums around the world.

The Parthenon _____ (*use*) for different religions. First, it _____ (*dedicated*) to the goddess Athena. In the 5th century CE, it _____ (*convert*) into a Christian church and in the early 1460s it _____ (*turn*) into a mosque.

Look for information about another famous monument and write a description in your notebook. Use the description of The Parthenon as a model.

Photocopiable activity 14: Be an archaeologist!

Imagine you are an archaeologist on Professor Jelly's expedition.
Make an album with pictures of the objects and paintings you found in
the tomb in your notebook using ideas from the unit and your imagination.
Write sentences explaining what they are.

In the tomb, you found a mysterious message written in hieroglyphics.
Write the message using the hieroglyphics on page 108 of the Learner's Book.
Then ask the class to break the code.

Make a model of the pyramid where you found the objects.

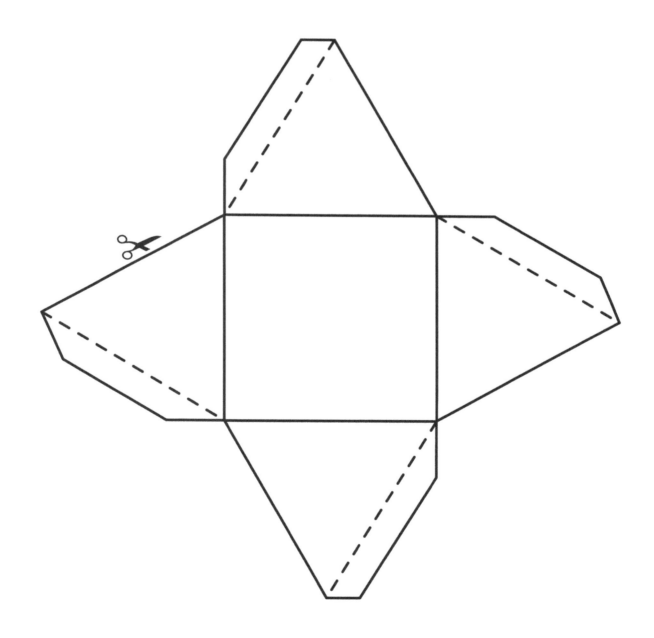

Photocopiable activity 15: Who wants to be a rainforest expert?

Search the Internet and find the answers to the rainforest quiz.

1 What is the country with the second largest amount of rainforests? Mark it on the map. _____

2 Why are there a lot of plants and animals in a rainforest? _____

3 Lemurs are found in only one place. Where? _____

4 What is an okapi? _____

5 Why are jaguars endangered? _____

6 Rainforests absorb carbon dioxide. True or false? _____

7 Name three things that can help save rainforests. _____

_____

_____

8 What can we do at home to protect the environment? _____

_____

_____

Write two more questions for a class quiz.

_____

_____

Unit 8

Photocopiable activity 16: Fahrenheit and Celsius

To convert a temperature of degrees Fahrenheit into a temperature on the Celsius scale you do this simple calculation:

temperature in degrees Celsius = (temperature in degrees Fahrenheit – 32) then divide by 1.8

A calculater may be used.

To find the temperature in degrees Celsius:

- take the temperature in Fahrenheit.
- subtract 32
- divide by 1.8.

To find the temperature in degrees Fahrenheit:

- take the temperature in Celsius.
- multiply by 1.8
- add 32.

Now solve these problems. Look at today's temperatures and complete the table.

Then add two places and the temperature and ask a partner to complete it.

PLACE	°C	°F
Helsinki		62.6
Taipei	34	
Ushuaia		41
Dubai	38	

Photocopiable activity 17: Caring for cats

Put the words in order to make sentences about looking after a cat.

1 food / too / cat / You / your / give / much / mustn't

_____

2 three / Kittens / times / day / eat / should / a

_____

3 water / cat / have / must / a / Your / always / bowl / fresh / of

_____

4 water / to / You / day / have / bowl / every / clean / the

_____

5 cat / You / your / parents / need / the / ask / help / bathe / to / to / you

_____

Have you got a cat? Do you do these things?
Write some more things about looking after cats.

It's best to _____ .

It's a good idea to _____ .

It's important to _____ .

Photocopiable activity 18: Crossword

1 Do the crossword puzzle, using the picture clues to help you.

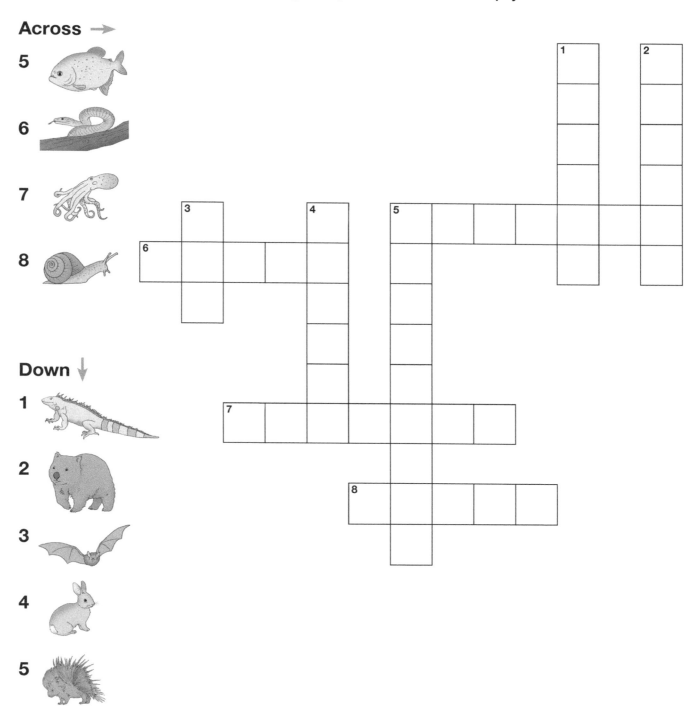

Across →

5

6

7

8

Down ↓

1

2

3

4

5

2 Now read the poem *Mum Won't Let me Keep a Rabbit* again (Learner's Book pages 134–135). Find 11 animals. Then make a crossword or a wordsearch for the class using vocabulary you have learnt in this unit. Draw pictures to use as clues!

Photocopiable activity 19: Congratulations certificate for completing Stage 5 of *Cambridge Global English*

Congratulations!

You have completed Stage 5 of *Cambridge Global English.*

Name: _____

Class: _____

Teacher: _____

Word lists

generous	cheerful	bad-tempered
selfish	nervous	untidy
hardworking	outgoing	surfer
tiger shark	attack	blood
board	hiking	rollerblading
download	exhilarating	superlatively
dozen	hoist	enormous
bulge	ripple	juggle
airborne	somersault	champion
masterful	wrestle	

sore throat	cough	headache
stomach ache	energy	itchy
shivering	tummy	hurt
sweating	blocked nose	dizzy
fever	temperature	infection
disease	infect	tropical
mosquito	parasite	vaccine
vaccination	appointment	prescription
homemade	intolerance	sensitive

village	vehicle	crowded
peaceful	spectacular	footprint
emissions	underground	horse-drawn
carriage	microwave	magical
enchanting	mysterious	exciting
wondrous	ancient	bamboo
starving	roar	sparkle
jade	ivory	gold
silver	rubies	chirp
reward	precious	riches

costumes	fireworks	feast
lantern	symbol	amazing
fabulous	rhythmic	blessing
candles	mixture	pancake
frying pan	syrup	shamrock
clover	mythical	zodiac
cornucopia	harvest	moody
jolly	tough	anxious
weepy	weak	cheerful
hardworking	miserable	

explorer	scientist	entrepreneur
caring	creative	songwriter
extremely	remarkable	amazing
exotic	awards	successful
nutritious	capsule	skydiver
helicopter	stratosphere	brave
rigging	anchor	mast
sails	deck	crew
ropes	prow	caring
positive	foolish	determined

myth	abominable	snowman
Cyclops	unicorn	creature
slither	gallop	grasshopper
starving	advice	hungry
camping	forest	bear
mountain	noise	scared
gossip	cushion	throw
feathers	characters	setting
resolution	worm	knight
tough	awful	browse

Colosseum	sphinx	pyramid
aqueduct	mummy	stomach
heart	preserved	pharaoh
archaeologist	treasures	magnificent
jewellery	mummified	sandals
chariot	gladiator	merchant
engineer	mystery	infection
amazed	winged	hooded
hawk	tubby	pudgy
excited	worried	

flood	tornado	blizzard
drought	typhoon	sandstorm
canopy	understory	underneath
bushes	greenhouse	humid
warning	endangered	swing
scream	shake	sloth
furry	claws	rattle
bright	wiggle	mellow
crickets	moth	earthly
poisonous	thrive	jive

forest	savannah	dwarf
clownfish	chameleon	predator
venomous	chase	shoot
feed	groom	stroke
raccoon	meerkat	pensioner
budget	porcupine	water-rat
pigeons	wallabies	rattlesnake
wombat	jellyfish	cockroach
bumblebee	maggot	wildebeest
mallard	dabchick	piranha